Lloyd George and the Lost Peace

Lloyd George at the Paris Peace Conference, 1919 (*William Orpen*):
'Mr Lloyd George . . . sat, his face lit with that smile, so quick and sunny, yet so obscure . . .
his whole air, at once so alert and self-poised, full of a baffling fascination and disquiet.'
— A. G. Gardiner

Lloyd George and the Lost Peace

From Versailles to Hitler, 1919–1940

Antony Lentin
Professor of History
The Open University

First published 2001 by
PALGRAVE
Houndmills, Basingstoke, Hampshire RG21 6XS and
175 Fifth Avenue, New York, N. Y. 10010
Companies and representatives throughout the world

PALGRAVE is the new global academic imprint of
St. Martin's Press LLC Scholarly and Reference Division and
Palgrave Publishers Ltd (formerly Macmillan Press Ltd).

ISBN 0–333–91961–0

This book is printed on paper suitable for recycling and made from fully managed and sustained forest sources.

A catalogue record for this book is available from the British Library.

Library of Congress Cataloging-in-Publication Data
Lentin, A. (Antony)
    Lloyd George and the lost peace : from Versailles to Hitler, 1919–1940 / Antony Lentin.
        p. cm.
    Includes bibliographical references and index.
    ISBN 0–333–91961–0 (cloth)
    1. Lloyd George, David, 1863–1945—Views on foreign relations.
    2. Great Britain—Foreign relations—1910–1936. 3. Great Britain–
    –Foreign relations—1936–1945. 4. World War, 1939–1945–
    –Causes. 5. Treaty of Versailles (1919) I. Title.

    DA566.9.L5 L45 2001
    941.083'092—dc21
                                                    2001021260

10   9   8   7   6   5   4   3   2   1
10   09 08 07 06 05 04 03 02 01

Printed and bound in Great Britain by
Antony Rowe Ltd, Chippenham, Wiltshire

To Michael Duffy, Barrister-at-Law
Vir bonus, peritus dicendi

Contents

List of Illustrations

Lloyd George at the Paris Peace Conference, 1919 (William
Orpen; courtesy National Museums and Galleries of Wales)

frontispiece

Every effort has been made to contact the copyright holders for the
illustrations. If anyone has been overlooked, the publishers will be
pleased to make the necessary arrangements at the first opportunity.

Acknowledgements

For permission to consult and quote from unpublished material, my thanks are due to: the British Library (Balfour Papers); the Clerk of the Records, the House of Lords Record Office, on behalf of the Beaverbrook Foundation Trust (Bonar Law and Lloyd George Papers); (the British Library and Professor A.K.S. Lambton (Robert Cecil Papers); the Bank of England Archives (Cunliffe and Montagu Norman Papers); Lord Cunliffe (the first Lord Cunliffe's letters to his wife); the Clerk of the Records, the House of Lords Record Office (J.C. Davidson Papers); Lambeth Palace Library (Randall Davidson Papers and George Bell Papers); Lord Derby and the British Library (letter from 17th Earl of Derby to A.J. Balfour); the Bodleian Library, Oxford (H.A.L. Fisher Papers); the Churchill Archives Centre, Churchill College, Cambridge (Hankey Papers); the Syndics of Cambridge University Library (Hardinge Papers); the Provost and Scholars of King's College, Cambridge (Keynes Papers); the Scottish Record Office, Edinburgh, and the Marquess of Lothian (Lothian Papers); the Bodleian Library and the Warden and Fellows of New College, Oxford (Milner Papers); Trinity College, Cambridge (Edwin Montagu Papers); the National Library of Wales, Aberystwyth (A.J. Sylvester Papers); the Public Record Office, Kew, Archives du Ministère des Affaires Etrangères, Paris, and Service historique de l'Armée de Terre, Vincennes. I also wish to thank Mr Magnus John; Dr Barbara Slater; the Open University for grants in aid; and the President and Fellows of Wolfson College, Cambridge, for a further agreeable year as a Visiting Fellow.

Preface

In Mr Lloyd George there are so many facets that a new study at a
fresh angle inevitably and always suggests a new conclusion.

The Earl of Birkenhead, *Contemporary Personalities* (1924)

Well, said Merlin, I know whom thou seekest, for thou seekest
Merlin; therefore seek no farther, for I am he.

Mallory, *Le Morte d'Arthur*, chapter 1

This is an account, drawn from six different perspectives, of David Lloyd
George in relation to the lost peace of Versailles, from its creation in
1919 to its overthrow in 1940 with the fall of France. It takes the form of
an enquiry, or sequence of enquiries, into six salient episodes; and it falls
broadly into two parts. The first four chapters take a fresh look at Lloyd
George at the Paris Peace Conference, 1919. Chapter 1 reviews his
activities there and attempts to define the nature of his contribution
overall. Chapter 2 re-examines his reparations strategy and the place in
it of Lord Cunliffe, the ex-Governor of the Bank of England, traditionally cast as an ogre in the historiography of the Peace Conference.
Chapter 3 probes the mystery of 'the treaty that never was', the Anglo-
French alliance negotiated by Lloyd George, on which French acceptance of the Versailles Treaty was premised. Chapter 4 analyses the
emergence among the British delegates at the Conference, and Lloyd
George's part in that emergence, of the phenomenon of 'Appeasement'
or 'guilt at Versailles', which, it seems to me, goes far to explain the lost
peace. Each of these four chapters in its different way, while indicating
Lloyd George's policy and tactics, also suggests some of the elements
which counteracted the treaty from the outset.

The two decades of Lloyd George's career after he left Downing Street
in 1922 are often considered an anticlimax or 'twilight'.[1] That is not
how it seemed at the time, nor does it provide an accurate image either
of his amazing vigour in his sixties and seventies or of his coruscating
interventions in British public life, the flashing thunderbolts that
periodically illuminated and shook the political and parliamentary
scene up to and including the cataclysms of 1940. Throughout these
years, he expected and was expected to return to office, to the constant

alarm of what Andrew Roberts calls 'the Respectable Tendency of British politics':[2] of Baldwin, who had done most to turn him out in 1922, but who contemplated inviting him to join the National Government in 1935; and of Neville Chamberlain, who with a tenacity born of years of enmity, kept the door to Downing Street tightly shut against him, even when war broke out in 1939. Lloyd George was thought of as a possible successor to Chamberlain, and was instrumental in forcing his resignation in 1940. He was asked by Churchill to join his Government of National Unity. Had things gone badly for Britain after the fall of France, he might well have replaced Churchill as Prime Minister.

That is some measure of Lloyd George's abiding influence in the second period to which this book relates, when the peace of Versailles slithered towards its decline and fall. Chapters 5 and 6 examine the two episodes commonly felt to be the most damaging to his reputation: his meeting with Hitler in 1936 and his bid to bring the war to an end, in October 1939 and June 1940.

My first attempt to come to grips with Lloyd George and the lost peace produced *Guilt at Versailles: Lloyd George and the Pre-History of Appeasement,* first published in 1984.[3] With the exception of Chapter 5, all the chapters which form the present book originated as papers presented at national and international conferences since 1990.[4] All six studies have undergone considerable modification. I have recast them to meet the demands of a coherent whole. I have returned to them obsessively, to reconsider the facts and to test my conclusions. More than once I have changed my mind. It is at once the attraction and the despair of the chronicler of Lloyd George that in grappling with the evidence, fragmentary and inadequate or superabundant and contradictory, he can seldom let bygones be bygones or achieve a satisfactory finality. Always there is 'the "And yet" factor'.[5] If time lends perspective, in Lloyd George's case, as Lord Birkenhead perceived, it leads to a variety of perspectives.

Of the evidence left by Lloyd George himself in *The Truth about the Peace Treaties* I have made only occasional use. The historian does well to sip sparingly of that fiery cordial, and never to take it neat. Like his *War Memoirs,* compelling in its scale, sweep and flow, it comprises, to a significantly greater degree than most political memoirs, a striking example of what may be called self-hero-worship. Lloyd George, no matter what his tergiversations, always mounted a determined, indeed defiant air of consistency and infallibility. Frances Stevenson, his secretary, companion and second wife, noted his ability 'always to make out such a completely good case for everything – the instinct of the clever lawyer at all times'.[6] I have rather relied on other primary sources, including the accounts of those who observed him closely and critically over many years, notably such incomparable diarists as his friend, George Riddell and his secretaries, A.J. Sylvester, Thomas Jones and Frances Stevenson herself.

I have also tried to resist the temptation to be wise after the event in relation to Lloyd George's varying attitudes to Germany. From 1919 until 1939 the notion of 'Appeasement' had a positive resonance and formed one aspect of British foreign policy, including Lloyd George's, long before becoming, under Neville Chamberlain, 'an abysmal failure'.[7] To all but a few in 1936, war with Germany did not seem inevitable – indeed in this writer's view it was not inevitable; nor was victory over Germany more than a remote prospect in 1939, or, in 1940, more than a magnificent act of faith and defiance. Lloyd George was not a traitor or a Nazi sympathiser for talking peace with Hitler in September 1936 or for seeking to do so in October 1939. In 1936 he spoke for most right-thinking people, certainly for the government, in seeking an accommodation with Germany. In 1939 he spoke for more people than is commonly supposed, in seeking to stop the war before it became a world war. The legend of a united people, stalwart in its rejection of Hitler's peace offer in October 1939, does not represent the whole picture. In May and June 1940, Churchill himself accepted that in a matter of weeks or even days his administration might be swept away and a successor called upon to treat with Hitler.

Every historian is to some extent the prisoner of his own time and his own beliefs. I share with most students of Lloyd George a tempered but heartfelt admiration for one who 'managed to leave his mark upon the fortunes of his country, both at home and abroad, to a degree which has been equalled by no other modern statesman'.[8] Lloyd George was still vociferously alive when I was born; at 78 years of age still qualified and still anxious to serve his country again in its time of greatest danger, though ambiguous whether he should best do so by defying Hitler or coming to terms with him. The key to Lloyd George's foreign policy, it seems to me, is that, in contrast to his radicalism in domestic affairs, he believed firmly in Britain and its empire as a force for order and civilisation in the world, at all times placed its interests first, and fought, without stint and sometimes without scruple, to make those interests prevail. I venture the personal opinion that if anyone was capable of reaching agreement with Hitler in 1936 – admittedly a big if – Lloyd George stood a better chance than anyone. In 1939 he was among the first to insist on the now obvious truth that the only step likely to deter Hitler from war was alliance with Russia. In May 1940, he wrote to

Churchill, 'Had you and I been brought into consultation even as late as twelve months ago, the country would not have been brought into the terrible situation into which it has been muddled.'[9] That part of the letter was never sent, but I believe it to be true. I believe, in other words, that Lloyd George could have saved the peace. This is perhaps not saying much, since no one in my judgement could have done worse than Neville Chamberlain.

These, however, are might-have-beens. The historian is concerned to elucidate what was. This in itself is difficult enough when confronting a statesman still within living memory,[10] of whose character and intentions both contemporaries and historians agree only that there is seldom a last word.[11] Like them, I find him full of surprises. The Merlin whom we all seek to pin down remains elusive and continues to mock our best efforts, his laughter still echoing down the receding corridor of time.

A. L.

Introduction

The first impression that Lloyd George made on you was of keen delight in your acquaintance and rapt attention to your every word. An excellent listener, he had the knack of putting you instantly at your ease, drawing you out and bringing out the best in you, leaving you with the pleasing conviction that you were, after all, someone in your own right.[1] Your short, stocky interlocutor gave out an air of radiant good humour, exuberant vitality and an irrepressible interest in people, beginning with yourself. This flattering impression would fade on a subsequent encounter, when it was *his* brilliance rather than yours which struck you. Bustling into a room, he became the immediate centre of attraction, communicating a brisk expectancy into any company and charging it with his own sparkle and tempo. He possessed in the highest degree the human and the humorous touch which lightens and enlivens any situation, and dissipates awkwardness with the saving grace of laughter. 'It is not so much', wrote Lord Birkenhead, 'that he ever says anything extraordinarily witty in company; it is that he creates an atmosphere of easy and pleasant bonhomie'.[2] Austen Chamberlain recalls him whiling away a train journey to the Paris Peace Conference. He 'kept us all lively with his amusing talk, straying from the present to the past and back again, full of fun and good humour and wisdom'.[3] He was, of course, Welsh: 'genial, humorous, tolerant, broadminded and warm-hearted. He has the imagination and suppleness of mind of a purely Celtic race.'[4] These words are his own. He was describing his Breton counterpart, the French Prime Minister, Aristide Briand; but he might have been, and almost certainly was, thinking also of himself.

It was his ready sociability that made him such an engaging negotiator; but his success was grounded in qualities both deeper and sterner, that made him, said Birkenhead, 'the most subtle and persuasive negotiator in the world'.[5] Entranced by his happy flow of intoxicating spontaneity, it was later, if at all, that you began to realise that you were the victim of a master politician, cajoling, manipulative and shot through with the most formidable energy and will-power. What you took for a lithe and playful tom-cat, purring benignly on the hearthrug could suddenly turn into a tiger on the prowl, in his strength, his stealth, his rapidity of concentrated thought and action, the sudden leap which revealed him, in the words of his secretary, Philip Kerr, as 'a ruthless and resourceful fighter'.[6] And afterwards, the smile on the face of the tiger. . . To vary the metaphor from the feline to the nautical, 'it was this combination of qualities', Harold Macmillan recalled, 'that made him, all through his life, at once so attractive and so formidable. He could blow you out of the water with a broadside of vilification; the next moment you were rescued, soothed, captivated into helpless surrender.'[7]

These strengths were informed by a profound grasp of human nature and a penetrating, almost uncanny insight into the individual. He studied his man, addressing not so much his reason as his emotions and what he divined to be his vanity and his motive-force. 'When I speak to a particular man', he told Riddell, 'I consider what words will be best suited to appeal to him.' In the case of a foreigner, 'I want the interpreter to use my very words. I don't want him to convey only the sense of what I say. That is not enough.'[8] 'In this method', Frances Stevenson observed, 'lies nearly the whole of his success in dealing with men.'[9] You did not always know where you were with him. He was often equivocal and sometimes underhand, devious in the literal sense in his preference for 'a way round'[10] an apparently insurmountable obstacle. His words acquired the elusive consistency of quicksilver. An initial crystal-clear impression of a firm undertaking on his part might later become alarmingly indistinct, blurred by a creeping penumbra of ambiguity and doubt. You would follow with your eye the iridescent soap-bubble of a promise as it floated alluringly through the air. Suddenly it shimmered and burst as if it had never been. 'I don't like being lied to', Clemenceau complained of Lloyd George at the Peace Conference.[11] He had yet to learn the full depths of his duplicity.

As a speaker, on the floor of the House of Commons or addressing an audience of thousands, Lloyd George had few rivals in an age rich in forceful persuaders. 'No-one living has such platform arts', was the judgement of A.J. Sylvester.[12] Hitler himself in *Mein Kampf* held out Lloyd George's speeches in the Great War as 'psychological masterpieces in the art of influencing the masses'.[13] His speeches, never merely ornamental, were charged with purpose, designed not merely to impress but irresistibly to impel his listeners to a desired end; and he had crafted his oratory to the finest of fine arts. Beginning slowly and quietly, he gradually worked up to a pitch of emotion, enlivened with telling gestures and flourishes, the pawing foot, the whirling arms, inspired departures from his notes and sparkling and crushing repartee. He had learned his trade from the Welsh preachers of his youth, of whose oratory he never tired though he might privately have departed from their religion.

To appreciate the full force of his parliamentary invective, you had to see him in action. 'I am like the matador when I get in the ring', he said.[14] In 1936, he flayed the National Government with such devastating vehemence that the House was 'almost hysterical';[15] and Baldwin and Neville Chamberlain quailed before 'the most tremendous Philippic directed against an Administration since the war'.[16] Afterwards, a young Tory member went up to Churchill and said he had never heard anything like it. 'Young man', replied Churchill, 'you have been listening to one of the greatest parliamentary performances of all time.'[17] This was three months before his visit to an admiring Hitler. In 1940 he discharged his last and most deadly parliamentary salvo. Arousing and unleashing the House's pent-up discontent at the conduct of the war, and concentrating its fury and frustration on the Prime Minister, Neville Chamberlain – 'the same terrifying ring of scorn and anger in his voice'[18] – he helped to bring him down.

These, then, were among the main constituents of what Philip Kerr called his 'quality of human forcefulness'.[19] He had a strong sense of history and of his own unfolding part in it, looking at himself obliquely and self-admiringly 'as a performer on a moving stage',[20] and casting himself in a variety of beguiling roles, notably that of Merlin, 'an old Briton, who belongs to the most ancient race in these islands'.[21] As a historian of his own times, he refought the Great War in his *War Memoirs*, completed in 1937. Desiring to vindicate his role at the Peace Conference in the changed circumstances of the 1930s, he completed *The Truth about the Peace Treaties* the following year. In these brilliant, declamatory and outspoken volumes he re-lived and relieved his feelings at the expense of his enemies, past and present, including the now ascendant Neville Chamberlain, in whom he unerringly detected the fatal flaw, 'a vein of self-sufficient obstinacy'.[22]

Shakespeare's reflection on those 'Who, moving others, are themselves as stone' is echoed by Frances Stevenson in her verdict on Lloyd George: 'Influencing others, he was himself impervious to influence.' Such was her 'considered conclusion'. For all his charm and geniality, the flexibility and openness to others operated only up to a point. 'At no time was it possible for anyone to influence Lloyd George', she insisted.[23] At the Peace Conference, virtually his entire delegation pressed him to settle then and there the vexed problem of reparations. Despite the endeavours of a dozen colleagues, who included some of the most able and masterful personalities of the age – Smuts, Milner,

Churchill, Birkenhead – they could not shift him. He had his own purposes, he made up his own mind, and that was that. In 1940, at the age of 77, some thought him fit to lead the country in its supreme crisis. He was, said Garvin, 'still good for six hours a day, and it would be six hours of radium'.[24] But neither Garvin, Thomas Jones, Robert Boothby, Harold Macmillan, A.J. Sylvester, nor Frances Stevenson herself could persuade him to join Churchill. He was 'adamant against going on'.[25]

'His desires and concerns are those of the realist every time.'[26] The verdict, again, is Frances Stevenson's. The year was 1917. One who spoke to him in 1940 made the same observation. 'Of all the political figures I have talked politics with, Lloyd George seemed to me the most realistic. He sums the situation up, as it is, without any trace of wishful thinking.'[27] It was true; and yet there are degrees and varieties of realism. And an infinity of ways in which a man may react to its promptings. He was not as Keynes depicted him, beyond good and evil;[28] like all men, he partook of both, but to a higher degree and operating on a larger stage and with correspondingly greater consequences. Ever a fascinated student of human paradox, he himself reflected, 'It is a mistake to assume that the best are devoid of the worst and that the worst possess no trace of the best.'[29] His interest in the Tudors, in Machiavelli, suggests an aspect of Lloyd George as a throw-back to the amorality of the Renaissance politician, save that for him not only did the ends justify the means, but the means were often a hugely enjoyable end in themselves. The ambiguity of the word 'statecraft' is peculiarly apposite to a study of one adept at outdoing others. During the Great War, Frances Stevenson taxed him to his grinning face with being 'a past master in craft'.[30] To A.J. Sylvester during the Second World War, he was still 'as artful as a cartload of monkeys'.[31] To the last, however, his thoughts were of peace-making: of preserving, promoting and presiding over the destinies of Great Britain and securing her place among the nations.[32]

1
Enigma Variations: Lloyd George at the Paris Peace Conference, 1919

Lloyd George's controversial role at the Peace Conference—his characteristics as a negotiator—reviews the peace terms—his liberal instincts—the Fontaine-bleau Memorandum—his understanding of France and Germany—reparations—parliamentary pressures—the war-guilt clause—policy towards France—his ultimate aims and achievements

αἰὲν ἀριστεύειν καὶ ὑπείροχον ἔμμεναι ἄλλων (always to excel and to be ahead of the others)
Iliad, vi, 208

Now I understand why you are Prime Minister. You are far and away ahead of the whole lot
Bernard Baruch, addressing Lloyd George, 5 April 1919

Eighty years on, Lloyd George's role at the Paris Peace Conference continues to dazzle and bemuse and almost to defy classification. Of the importance of that role there is no doubt: at the height of his authority and prestige, he was engaged in peacemaking on the grandest scale since the Congress of Vienna in 1815. Together with Woodrow Wilson, President of the United States, and the French Prime Minister, Georges Clemenceau, 'he was', as Beaverbrook wrote, 'giving the law to Europe, fixing the boundaries of all the nations, giving out encouragement to some countries and severely reprimanding others. He was the arbiter of all Europe.'[1] 'For good or bad', as Birkenhead pronounced, 'the influence and the ascendancy which he established at Paris were among the most remarkable achievements of a remarkable life.'[2]

What continues sharply to divide opinion is the quality and significance of that role. The historian confronts not only a kaleidoscopic mass of evidence, often complex and often contradictory, but also a politician whose character and intentions remain profoundly enigmatic. The jerky cine-cameras at Paris revive for us the familiar externals of his self-projected persona: active, genial, whimsical, mysterious. The brisk, jaunty stride, the cane poised at a dramatic angle, the swirling cape, the plump, cajoling hands, the hat set aslant the flowing, white, bardic locks; the twinkling blue eyes, the smile – winsome, roguish, enigmatic. And behind the smile? Everyone at the Conference agreed that he was many-sided and mobile, unpredictable and elusive. To Wilson, he was 'a chameleon'.[3] 'Lloyd George', observed Clemenceau, 'travels in every direction, so inconsistent is he from day to day.'[4] Orlando, the Italian Prime Minister, described him as 'a slippery prestidigitator'.[5] 'Our mercurial, tricky Prime Minister', noted General Smuts, who found him 'unstable, without any clear guiding principles... One never knows the orbits of minds like his.'[6] To his bitter enemy, Northcliffe, he was 'oblique, evasive and Welsh... You never know what he is up to.'[7]

What was he up to? There are two basic but opposite schools of thought. Some portray his achievement – he did so himself in *The Truth about the Peace Treaties* – as a consistent pattern of constructive statesmanship and liberal principle. Professor Kenneth Morgan maintains that 'perhaps alone of the three major peacemakers he had long-term objectives in Europe'; that he was 'the most persistent advocate of moderation throughout the entire Conference', or at any rate that he was 'the least guilty of the peacemakers'.[8] Others, sharing Keynes's perceptions in *The Economic Consequences of the Peace*, see in him a fickle opportunist of 'goat-footed' agility, improvising policy on the hoof, with one eye on the main chance, while squinting out of the corner of the other at public opinion; an artful dodger living from hand to mouth, reckless of the true interests of Europe, and, in the words of Professor Alan Sharp, 'not devoted to the truth except in the titles of his books'.[9] On the one hand he is commended as the author of the Fontainebleau Memorandum, that clarion-call for magnanimity in peacemaking, and as a pioneer of Appeasement in its original, positive and hopeful sense. On the other hand he is denounced as an unprincipled demagogue and the co-signatory of a 'Carthaginian peace': the man who for electoral gain promised to 'hang the Kaiser' and to 'make Germany pay', instigator of the notorious 'war-guilt' clause. A wealth of plausible evidence can be adduced on either side of the argument. Can a common thread be disentangled? Which, if any, was the real Lloyd George?

I

His critics cannot deny his indefatigable energy, much as they question the spirit in which he applied it, the ends which he had in mind and the means whereby he advanced towards them. Rather they set him down as politically hyperactive, that 'very terrible thing', in Baldwin's words, 'a dynamic force',[10] overpowering, unrestrained, irresponsible and out of control – 'quite the most dangerous representative it was possible to have', wrote Lord Hardinge, Permanent Under-Secretary of the Foreign Office and nominally Organising Ambassador of the Conference.[11] Certainly Lloyd George revelled in 'the great game of politics'.[12] He threw himself headlong into the hurley-burley of each day's multiple challenges and faced them with zeal, bustle and high good humour, operating, as Thomas Jones noted, like an expert signalman manipulating lever after lever at a busy railway junction.[13] On 31 March 1919, to take a random working day of the Council of Four, he pressed home the war-guilt clause, approved the articles on reparation and the Saar, opposed Clemenceau over the occupation of the Rhineland, cross-questioned Foch about French schemes for an autonomous Left Bank, had a row with the Belgian Prime Minister and heard reports on Bolshevik insurrection in Hungary and Bavaria. Driving home afterwards with Riddell, he was 'full of fun'.[14]

Even after the terrible strains of his war premiership, he worked harder at Paris, he recalled, than ever before in his arduous career. Industrial unrest and parliamentary pressures vied for his attention simultaneously with the awesome demands of peacemaking. Twice he was called back to London to face a crisis. At Paris he worked against a raucous background of noises-off which could not be ignored, of insistent clamour from press and parliament; a background, as he picturesquely told the Commons, of 'stones clattering on the roof and crashing through the windows, and sometimes wild men screaming through the keyholes'.[15] 'His responsibilities', Riddell noted, 'are enough to make the stoutest heart quail.'[16] After the Conference he returned to England 'whitened and lined, looking to his friends as if ten years had been added to his age'.[17] Yet his resilience and zest for life were stimulated as never before. 'It has been a wonderful time', he exclaimed, as his train sped homeward from the Gare du Nord.[18]

Traditionalists queried his credentials to attend the Conference at all. To the Archbishop of Canterbury, an ardent Asquithian, the thought of Lloyd George representing Great Britain was 'intolerable'.[19] 'It is humiliating', echoed George Prothero, of the Foreign Office Political

Intelligence Department, 'to be represented by such a little cad.'[20] It is true that, while conscious of contributing to momentous events and capable of a corresponding dignity, Lloyd George showed little taste for gentlemanly reserve or statesmanlike pomp. Sociable and ebullient, utterly without 'side', his was the antithesis of the bland, patrician style of diplomacy personified by Lord Curzon. He disconcerted French diplomats by *'sa désinvolture ordinaire'*[21] – his easy and unaffected informality, verging, as they saw it, on offhandedness and even reckless-ness. In the flat allocated to him in the rue Nitot he gave free rein to a love of merry, even boisterous entertainment, leading the company in postprandial sing-songs around the piano. He seems to have invented that amalgam of business and pleasure, the 'working breakfast'; and amid the most exacting crises he retained his unfailing good temper, 'apparently as free from care as a schoolboy on holiday', Austen Cham-berlain reported.[22] His life of cheerful adultery with Frances Stevenson, who ministered to his creature comforts, was part and parcel of this breezy indifference to convention. In the evenings, off to boulevard restaurants and cafés. There he sat, blithely listening to the band, beat-ing time, watching the passers-by with real, if transient, curiosity and a running commentary on people and affairs, often astute and always lively. 'He is so easy in manner', noted Beatrice Webb, 'so amusing, so direct and apparently spontaneous in his observations and retorts.'[23] The man or woman in the street he found no less absorbing for the moment than his fellow peacemakers, whose characters and concerns he watched attentively in his working hours, and whose strengths and foibles he penetrated and turned to his own ends.

Much was made of his amateurism, his performance as a one-man band, his frequent seizure of the initiative from the Foreign Office, his reliance on his own intuition, his preference for his own advisers. He often avoided the 'usual channels'. Practised diplomatists like Lords Hardinge and Curzon, whom he kept in the dark, deplored what they saw, with some exaggeration, as the 'complete absence of any system on the part of the Prime Minister, who declines to utilize the services of experts'.[24] It was easy to deride, as they did, his avowed ignorance of geography. He had never heard – few had – of the duchy of Teschen, did not know that Luxembourg was a duchy, confused Silesia with Cilicia, was vague about the whereabouts of Transylvania and even of New Zealand.[25] Such objections were essentially trivial, snobbish even. He made up amply for lack of detailed knowledge by his wonderful powers of assimilation, his rapid mastery of memoranda, his instant flair for the essence of a problem, his openness to imaginative solutions from gifted

juniors. He argued his case with infectious energy and pushed it vigorously home at the all-important sessions of the Council of Four, 'the
four men', as he put it, 'who are endeavouring to make the world spin
round the way it ought to spin'.[26] These meetings of the 'Big Four',
convened at his instigation at the end of March to speed up the Conference's flagging progress, took place twice daily for a hundred days and
produced the main provisions of the peace. It was here, behind
closed doors, in the panelled fireside privacy of Wilson's apartment,
face-to-face with the President, Clemenceau and Orlando, that Lloyd
George – striding about the room in voluble flow, engaged in earnest
tête-à-tête, or perched attentively on the edge of his armchair, his hands
clasped around his knees – exercised his very personal direction of
British policy.

His determination to dictate that policy stemmed partly from his
mistrust, as a Welsh outsider, of a traditional diplomacy and a compla-
çent social caste which he believed had muddled Britain into catastrophe in 1914. It also derived from a boundless and on the whole
justified confidence in his own unique ability to dominate events.
While relying therefore on the Foreign Office for information on particular cases, he usually looked for broader ideas elsewhere than to the
Whitehall mandarins or to his somewhat passive and lackadaisical Foreign Secretary, Arthur Balfour. A careful listener, he welcomed contribu-
tions from his Cabinet secretaries, Maurice Hankey and Philip Kerr, and
from such independent-minded advisers as General Smuts and Sir Henry
Wilson. It was Hankey, Kerr and Wilson whom he called suddenly into
weekend conclave at Fontainebleau towards the end of March, when he
felt that the Conference was getting bogged down. There he invited
their free-ranging advice, took careful note, and pondered. He dictated
the outcome in a blueprint, wise and far-sighted, of what he called 'the
kind of treaty of peace to which alone we were prepared to append our
signature'[27] – the Fontainebleau Memorandum – which he at once
adopted as his policy and sprang resolutely upon President Wilson and
Clemenceau. 'He means business this week', Frances Stevenson noted,
'and will sweep all before him. He will stand no more nonsense either
from French or Americans.'[28]

II

He was an unrivalled negotiator: on top of his brief, full of bounce, sure
of himself, forceful, engaging, compelling, endlessly patient. Deftly he
exploited the balance of human forces in the Council of Four to his own

advantage, supporting Wilson against Clemenceau on the Saar and Left Bank, and Clemenceau against Wilson on reparations and the war-guilt clause. Acutely sensitive to what he divined as the motive force in his listeners, he was adept at finding the right tone and turn of phrase to divert that force in the desired direction. His assurances of a Channel tunnel to speed British troops to France were particularly effective in persuading Clemenceau, 'very moved'[29] by these blandishments, to accept his offer of a military guarantee, on the strength of which Clemenceau gave up the Rhine frontier. He induced Wilson, or so he boasted, to accept his scheme for a 'free city' of Danzig, in part by the flattering hint that the idea was the President's own.[30] A nostalgic appeal for Allied solidarity moved Orlando to prolonged and uncontrollable tears.[31] Lloyd George was amazingly quick on the uptake. Arguing one complex case with all his strenuous amiability, he was, in the full flow of his eloquence, passed a note by Keynes to the effect that British interests would be better served if the opposite case prevailed. Glancing rapidly at the note, he continued, unperturbed and without interruption, in the same drift, then deftly and gently changed tack, until, imperceptibly, he coaxed his listeners into the preferred haven, adding for good measure a telling point of his own, thought up on the spur of the moment.[32] An electric rapidity of apprehension, a ready and inexhaustible well of inventiveness, an air of assurance, a warm enthusiasm, a hypnotic flow of language, informed and inspired his tactics at all times.

He could switch at will to a dictatorial, aggressive, even a cruel and ruthless side. One signal occasion saw him in heated combat with the French. Fearful of driving a desperate Germany into Bolshevism, he wished to allow her to purchase Allied food supplies. For the French, maintaining the blockade constituted a vital pressure on the enemy. To release that pressure without a quid pro quo was to them folly. Lloyd George would have none of it. He had information that German civilians were starving. He had seen a telegram to this effect; indeed he had arranged for it to be sent by General Plumer, Commander-in-Chief of the British army in the Rhineland. He had the telegram brought into the Conference room at the operative moment, as if it had just arrived. He re-opened it, adjusted his pince-nez, and asked permission to read the telegram, which, he said, 'he had just received'. 'Please inform the Prime Minister', it began, 'that in my opinion food must be sent into this area by the Allies without delay.' Clemenceau's Finance Minister, Lucien Klotz, continued to argue that since Germany possessed the gold to pay for food, reparations for France, not food for Germans, must be the first charge on the Reichsbank's reserves. Now Klotz was a Jew: 'the only Jew he ever met', Clemenceau grumbled, 'who knew nothing of finance'.[33] Lloyd George, let it be made clear, was no vulgar anti-semite. His closest friend, if he can ever be said to have had one, was Rufus Isaacs, Lord Reading; but he made use of the prejudices of others, as he did their vanities, to gain his point. Lloyd George saw his moment and pounced. Rounding on the unfortunate Klotz with gleeful ferocity, he directed at him the paralysing ray of his mimetic gifts. Hunching his shoulders, spreading out his arms, adopting a nasal whine, he treated the company to an electrifying and disturbing evocation of Shylock, crooning and slavering over his money bags. Klotz, he said, to general amusement, would rank with Lenin and Trotsky for bringing Bolshevism into Europe. 'All round the room', Keynes recalled, 'you could see each one grinning and whispering to his neighbour "Klotzky".' Lloyd George won his point. Not that he was without designs of his own on German bullion.[34]

These forensic and histrionic gifts were matched by powerful combative instincts, executive drive and an indomitable determination to win. Back in London in February, he complacently reviewed the first round of the Conference. 'Wilson has gone back home with a bundle of assignats', he chortled. 'I have returned with a pocket full of sovereigns in the shape of the German colonies, Mesopotamia, etc...Everyone to his taste.'[35] 'The truth', as he told Riddell at the end of March, 'is that we have got our way. We have got most of the things we set out to get.'[36] 'We are making headway', he told Frances Stevenson, after securing the inclusion of the war-guilt clause, 'which means that I am getting my own way!' An admiring Bernard Baruch of the American delegation went up to him afterwards: 'Now I understand why you are Prime Minister', he said, 'you are far and away ahead of the whole lot.'[37] If by the art of politics is meant the ability to impose one's will on others by sheer force of personality, Lloyd George was certainly the consummate politician of the Big Three. He succeeded through a combination of charm, psychological insight, resource, forcefulness, daring, pugnacity, and an amazing rapidity in following up every advance, which amounted to shock tactics. 'I am making a good fight for the old country', he boasted to Frances Stevenson, 'and there is no one but me who could do it.' Miss Stevenson commented in her diary: 'It is perfectly true.'[38] It *was* perfectly true, as the Cabinet recognised. That was why they continued to give him, in peace as in war, what Balfour called 'a free hand for the little man'.

III

As he was the most quick-witted of the Big Three, so he was the most volatile and unpredictable: to such an extent that he is regularly portrayed as without fixed principles or aims. 'The snipe', he was called,[39] a creature of impulse and caprice, reacting haphazardly to the pressure of the moment, a soap-bubble at the mercy of the breeze, a bouncing rubber ball in a squash court, or, in an American view, 'a greased marble spinning on a glass table-top'.[40] He was reproached with ever changing his mind, with blowing hot and cold, 'at one moment truculent', Lord Hardinge complained, 'and a few hours later ready to make any concession'.[41] To many he seemed a shooting star or whirling dervish, *'l'instabilité même'*, sighed the exasperated Paul Cambon, French ambassador in London.[42] Wilson and Clemenceau alternated between amusement and indignation at his continual chopping and changing. 'Figaro here, Figaro there', muttered Clemenceau during a performance of *The Barber of Seville*, 'he's a kind of Lloyd George'.[43] Yet weathercock volatility was not necessarily proof only of unreliability. It often meant a commendable readiness to examine complex problems from different angles and in the round, to reconsider, to return to first principles, to indulge second thoughts. So many decisions at Paris were taken in haste, and were based, as Lloyd George pointed out, on *ex parte* evidence from interested applicants, that he was quite prepared to think again, once apprised of the full facts.

Twice during the Conference he took time off with his advisers for a thoroughgoing review of the peace. His first appraisal – 'the hardest forty-eight hours' thinking I have ever done'[44] – produced the Fontainebleau Memorandum. The document's official title itself invited pause for sober reflection – 'Some considerations for the Peace Conference before they finally draft their terms'. Two months later, he called the British Empire delegation, including Smuts, his severest critic, into urgent weekend session for a final intensive discussion. To add yet more weight to its deliberations he summoned from London his coalition colleagues – Birkenhead, Churchill, Austen Chamberlain, Milner, Edwin Montagu, Herbert Fisher and George Barnes – politically varied and staunchly independent-minded. One by one he asked for their comments on the treaty. After almost all in turn had voiced the gravest doubts, Lloyd George took up the cudgels on their behalf in a tremendous struggle with Wilson and Clemenceau to unscramble the terms and to go back on agreed points, including points on which, as Wilson justly complained, he had previously been the most adamant and unyielding.

There was some truth in the jibe that to know Lloyd George's mind, you had to ask the person he had last consulted. On the other hand, the fact is that before putting his signature to the final terms, Lloyd George, unlike Wilson, made certain of acting with the full backing of his Cabinet. In these breathless and belated attempts to revise and to improve, to concede and to conciliate, Lloyd George, who looked with legitimate pride on the Versailles settlement as its principle architect, also emerges as one of its first and most radical critics.

For all his volatility, his instincts were for genuine peace. He was against the hotheads. He had no time for French hopes of an Allied march on Berlin and the imposition of a crushing, Napoleonic peace, still less for a crusade against Bolshevism. 'Military intervention in Russia', he told the Commons, 'would be the greatest act of stupidity that any Government could possibly commit.'[45] He wanted to lift the blockade, he wanted demobilisation and an end to conscription everywhere. He saw German disarmament as a prelude to universal disarmament, and he had a clause to that effect inserted in the treaty.[46] He wanted Europe, including Russia, to return to normality. He asked why a democratic Germany should not be admitted at once to the League of Nations. No hypersensitivity or false pride inhibited Lloyd George, as it inhibited Wilson, from seeking to rectify obvious errors. His ultimate purpose, behind many of his tergiversations, was serious and wise. 'The first thing', he told his delegates, 'was to have an absolutely just peace ... They must have no hesitation in admitting that they were wrong, if they *were* wrong, and in modifying the terms accordingly.'[47]

He was horrified to learn from the German counter-proposals that he, Wilson and Clemenceau were assigning swathes of German-populated territory to Poland. 'If the facts alleged were accurate', he warned, 'then the Peace Treaty would be setting up something that would end in a great catastrophe for Europe.'[48] Once convinced that this was indeed so, he threw himself might and main – 'like a Welsh terrier', Nicolson observed[49] – into an eleventh-hour struggle to put things right. It was thanks to his intervention, his dogged insistence in the teeth of resistance from Wilson and Clemenceau, that Danzig became a free city and that plebiscites were held which restored to Germany parts of East Prussia and Upper Silesia previously earmarked for Poland. As he justifiably retorted to a tight-lipped President Wilson, 'I am doing nothing other than abiding by your Fourteen Points.'[50] If Versailles remained a bad settlement, Lloyd George recognised at least some of its faults and saw to it that they were mitigated.

'With all his faults', observed Colonel House, the President's right-hand man, who negotiated with Lloyd George in Wilson's absence, 'he is by birth, instinct and upbringing, a liberal.'[51] His liberalism found classic expression in the Fontainebleau Memorandum. In calling for a 'just peace', he meant above all a peace which, while meeting legitimate Allied expectations of redress, should not sow seeds of fresh discord by leaving behind palpable grievances. With his soaring imagination, he saw beyond the passions of the moment, beyond the fear and hatred of Germany that prevailed at Paris. He warned prophetically against terms that went beyond what was absolutely necessary: 'You may strip Germany of her colonies, reduce her armaments to a mere police force and her navy to that of a fifth-rate power; all the same, in the end, if she feels that she has been unjustly treated in the peace of 1919, she will find means of exacting retribution from her conquerors.'[52]

IV

The test he applied was simple: were the Allies certain that any given provision of the treaty was such that they would in after years unhesitatingly enforce it? If not, it should be revised. Alsace-Lorraine and Danzig were cases in point. Should Germany ever attack Alsace-Lorraine, he declared, Britain would rush to France's aid without a second thought. Would the same hold good if Germany sought to recover Danzig? Let them prune the treaty of anything that failed that simple standard. This was liberalism, and it was realism, too; and in pursuit of it Lloyd George stood out boldly against Wilson and Clemenceau. No one at Paris spoke more tellingly against over-harsh, humiliating terms that would drive Germany to extremes, or more clearly foretold the consequences of 'injustice, arrogance, displayed in the hour of triumph'.[53] No one protested more presciently against creating, as he said repeatedly, 'new Alsace-Lorraines' at Germany's expense or peppering Eastern Europe and the Balkans with fresh trouble spots. National self-determination, the 'guiding principle of the peace', he interpreted in a sage and purist spirit: 'that as far as is humanly possible the different races should be allocated to their motherlands, and that this human criterion should have precedence over considerations of strategy or economics or communications'.[54] Wilson himself did not improve on this statement of principle; and Lloyd George did more than Wilson to see that the new boundaries, and above all the boundaries of Germany, were drawn without undue violence to ethnicity.

The French, unimpressed by the Fontainebleau Memorandum, accused Lloyd George of seeking to appease Germany at their expense, once he had secured his own main objectives. They were right, in the sense that in pursuit of a settlement 'which will contain in itself no provocations for future wars',[55] he opposed much of what Clemenceau fought for. Repeatedly he pointed out that for the treaty to endure, 'it must be a settlement which a responsible German government can sign in the belief that it can fulfil the obligations it incurs'.[56] It was one of the wisest things said by anyone at the Conference; and its validity is not lessened by the fact that Lloyd George tended to lose sight of it himself whenever he felt British interests were at stake. As for the French, he agreed that they were entitled, thoroughly entitled, to security and restitution; but to no more. This meant a peace which Germany might find severe, but to which she would assent because she recognised its essential justice; hence a peace as far as possible self-enforcing, which reconciled France's need for security with Germany's sense of fairness, and which required no prolonged military presence to ensure its fulfilment.

To Clemenceau, this was trying to square the circle: to him, Germany would always kick against the traces, would never be reconciled to defeat. That was why France sought 'physical' guarantees of security through the detachment of German territory. This too was realism of a kind; and yet, as events soon showed, without British support, postwar France lacked the means to restrain a restless and resentful Germany. Lloyd George's judgement was sound, therefore, when he opposed in the Fontainebleau Memorandum the incorporation within a Greater Poland of 'large masses of Germans, clamouring for reunion with their native land'.[57] 'We must not', he warned Clemenceau, 'create a Poland separated from her birth by an ineradicable quarrel from her most highly civilised neighbour.'[58]

In seeing Lloyd George as the author of a peace at their expense, 'an opponent and almost an enemy',[59] the French were right, if it is true that every concession to Germany struck at vital French interests. Yet no one showed better understanding of France's sense of vulnerability as a state twice in 50 years the victim of German aggression. It was Lloyd George who, while setting his face against annexation, engineeered the compromise settlement over the Saar and made France the crucial offer of a military guarantee. He drew on a well of imaginative insight into his colleagues' preoccupations: for Orlando in his dilemma over Fiume as for Clemenceau in his obsession with security. He laboured tirelessly 'to patch up an arrangement with Italy'[60] and with France, to reconcile acute inter-Allied differences and to save the Conference from collapse. It is one of the tragic ironies of Versailles that this 'brilliant conciliator of apparently irreconcilable positions'[61] was so much more zealous in devising compromises between the victors than in working for that genuine settlement with Germany which he rightly identified in the Fontainebleau Memorandum as the essence of lasting peace. 'Agree with thine adversary whilst thou art in the way with him', Churchill reminded him.[62] So tightly, however, were the Allies bound together by the chain of interconnecting deals, largely brokered by Lloyd George, that there remained little room for concession to Germany, even when Lloyd George himself battled for it singlehanded against Clemenceau and Wilson.

For just as he sympathised with the French in their anguish, so Lloyd George was instantly responsive to the German counter-proposals. He accepted the force of some of their objections to the often one-sided application of the Fourteen Points. He urged his delegates to be astute to any instances of 'real injustice to Germany'.[63] It was not that he was 'pro-Boche', much as the Northcliffe press strove to tar him with that brush. Throughout the Conference he nursed a visceral sense of outrage at the war, looking back on it with passionate revulsion as a 'crime against humanity', whose ringleaders should be brought to book. He was among the first – and the last – to call for the Kaiser to be put on trial and 'ruthlessly punished' as 'the person supremely responsible for this war'.[64] 'Lloyd George wants to shoot the Kaiser', noted Henry Wilson.[65] There was nothing factitious about these vehement reactions: the Prime Minister fully shared the public emotion which he represented. 'We want a stern peace', he told the Commons, 'because the occasion demands it. The crime demands it.'[66] He accepted that the provisions of Versailles were 'in many respects terrible terms to impose upon a country. Terrible were the deeds which it requites.'[67]

Yet few gatherings of statesmen can have shown such sympathetic detachment as the special meetings of the Empire delegation which Lloyd George chaired for a final revision of the treaty. 'The whole discussion', he said, 'had taken the form of an earnest and sometimes a passionate plea for justice for the fallen enemy.'[68] It was only momentarily, when angered at the foolish ill manners, the histrionic attitudinising, of Count Brockdorff-Rantzau, Germany's chief representative at Versailles – the Count refused to stand, on receiving the draft treaty, and delivered an outspoken speech of protest from his seat – it was only then that Lloyd George admitted to feeling against the Germans 'the same hatred for them that the French feel'.[69] It was not a lasting sentiment:

Lloyd George seldom bore grudges. In any case, as he recognised, Europe had to live with Germany; and British interests, economic and political, favoured the rapid restoration of normal relations. Lloyd George was to be among the first to point out these truths. At the time, however, facing the united opposition of Clemenceau and Wilson, he failed in his attempts at radical revision; and in the matter of reparations he was himself, as Robert Cecil noted, 'curiously reluctant to make any changes'.[70]

V

To understand Lloyd George's reparations policy is to appreciate that what took place at Paris was in part a tale of two cities. In the thick of things in the Council of Four, Westminster too was continually at the back of his mind. In the newly elected parliament of 1919 he faced an abnormally febrile House of Commons. His authority came into question at the end of March, when a long pent-up storm of backbench unrest blew up over reparations. The crisis arose from press rumours, assiduously spread by Northcliffe, that Lloyd George was attempting to back away from his electioneering pledges of December 1918 to 'make Germany pay'. The rumours were correct. Sceptical as to what Germany could really pay, Lloyd George sought to damp down the expectations which he had aroused at the hustings. In the Fontainebleau Memorandum he argued that payment of reparations 'ought to disappear, if possible, with the generation which made the war'.[71] In an interview for the *Westminster Gazette* he called for a 'sane peace', in which 'there must be no *casus belli* left to Germany',[72] and deprecated the idea which he had encouraged only four months earlier of a £25 billion indemnity. What became known as the 'moderation article', however, unleashed pandemonium at Westminster, with a backbenchers' round robin, calls for a full-scale debate, and a message, practically an ultimatum, cabled *en clair* to Lloyd George in Paris. Signed by some 200 backbenchers and published in the *Times*, it pointedly reminded him of his electoral promises and called on him to fulfil them.

   Such a challenge could not go unanswered. Lloyd George responded with vigour and dash. Returning to London, he addressed the Commons on 16 April in pugnacious, swashbuckling mood. Of his many displays of parliamentary oratory, this was among the most dazzlingly effective. From his moving invocation of the high seriousness of the issues to the withering scorn and intoxicating banter with which he sidetracked his critics in a diversionary attack on Northcliffe and the *Times* – 'merely a threepenny edition of the *Daily Mail*[73] – the speech was a climactic succession of 'knock-out blows'. 'Every sentence', an observer noted, 'he uttered with appropriate expression, and his gestures were free and dramatic. Again the pointed finger, the clenched fist, the outstretched arms, the shrug, the thump on the box, the gleam of the eye, the twitch of the mouth, set off the accusing, the appealing or the mocking word.'[74] The House roared its approval. 'Lloyd George's oratorical Austerlitz' was Garvin's verdict in the *Observer*. 'A wonderful performance', echoed Thomas Jones.[75] Austen Chamberlain concluded: 'He never did anything better if he ever did as well.'[76] He gained, as Frances Stevenson significantly noted, 'complete mastery of the House, while telling them absolutely nothing about the Peace Conference.'[77] Having quelled the backbenchers and vindicated his authority, he was subsequently able, as Wilson conspicuously was not, to secure triumphant ratification of the Treaty of Versailles.

Lloyd George's reparations policy has traditionally provoked much indignation. In themselves, however, reparations were a valid objective, not a mere vulgar response to popular clamour. From the first, Lloyd George was alive to their crucial geopolitical dimension. The war, as he informed the public, had cost Britain far more than it had cost Germany. Britain was encumbered, as Germany was not, by colossal war debts to America, constituting 'a heavy handicap in commercial competition with the United States and other nations'.[78] In seeking to exact 'as large an indemnity out of Germany as possible',[79] therefore, Lloyd George was actuated not solely by electoral calculations, large though these loomed in his thinking, as in that of any Prime Minister, but also by an overriding concern to recover from Germany something to offset those crippling debts. 'Otherwise', as he pointed out, 'Germany will be in a more favourable position for commercial competition than Great Britain.'[80] Legitimate misgivings arise rather from the lengths to which he went in his efforts to satisfy public expectations. These, certainly, he had raised at the general election, saddling himself with the awkward pledges to 'make Germany pay'. The impingement on foreign policy of domestic politics, the constant distraction of home thoughts from abroad, made reparations, as he many times admitted, 'the most baffling problem of the Peace Treaty'.[81]

Lloyd George had taken particular pains in the drafting of the Pre-Armistice Agreement with Germany of 5 November 1918, which made Wilson's Fourteen Points the contractual basis of the peace. A reservation, inserted at his insistence, stipulated that 'compensation will be paid by Germany for all damage done to the civilian population of the

Allies and their property by the aggression of Germany by land, by sea and from the air.'[82] As he conceded, then and later, his emphasis on civilian losses implicitly ruled out an indemnity for war costs in the sense of expenditure incurred in waging war.[83] At the Conference, however, he took a very different line. For unless war costs in some form were recoverable, then Britain and the Dominions, having suffered no territorial invasion and negligible civilian losses, could expect next to nothing, in contrast with the enormous claims of war-ravaged France and Belgium, or indeed 'nothing at all', if those claims were given priority.[84] His anxiety to secure a substantial share of reparations for Britain – he put this at roughly one-third of the total, as against one-half for France – is wholly understandable, since British war costs exceeded those of any other belligerent. Whatever the limitations of the Pre-Armistice agreement, no Prime Minister could have faced parliament without the promise of a respectable share of compensation.

President Wilson, who maintained that Britain had foregone her right to war costs, had earlier proclaimed to the world in his Fourteen Points speech of January 1918 that the peace should be based on 'the principle of justice to all peoples'. Where was the justice, Lloyd George now asked him, in crediting France for the loss of a chimney-pot on a house destroyed by enemy action, while making no demands for the widow and orphans of a British soldier killed defending it? He insisted on Germany's liability for the costs of pensions for Allied wounded and for dependants of the dead and injured. He wanted pensions included in the reparations bill in order to offset French claims and because he did not wish to be seen to fall short of his public promises. But pensions, as Wilson objected, were manifestly in breach of the Pre-Armistice Agreement. 'Let this be well understood', Lloyd George replied bluntly, 'we cannot leave the interpretation of such a clause to the lawyers.'[85] Without pensions, he told Bonar Law, 'I might as well go home'.[86] Thus, after casting about vainly for compromise solutions, he threw his authority not behind Keynes and the Treasury, who from the start had advised a reparations bill of around £2 billion, but behind his notoriously extremist delegates, Lords Cunliffe and Sumner and Prime Minister Hughes of Australia, whose minimum demands of four, five or six times that amount he later described as 'a wild and fantastic chimera'.[87] With characteristic intuition, he also prevailed on Smuts, whose influence on Wilson he knew to be considerable, to exert his powers of persuasion on the President, and thus secured the latter's reluctant consent to the inclusion of pensions.[88]

Though at one point he professed indifference to popular clamour and appeared ready 'to face the situation boldly and go under if necessary',[89] this was the last thing he had in mind. Whilst almost the entire Empire delegation and his Cabinet colleagues were urging him to settle the reparations issue once for all by fixing a sum for immediate insertion in the treaty, he rejected every figure mentioned. Rejecting out of hand the Treasury proposal of £2 billion, he dismissed not only George Barnes's suggestion of £3 billion, but even the £6 billion recommended by a special inter-Allied commission set up with his blessing, while admitting privately to being 'perfectly certain', so he said, 'that the utmost Germany could pay was one third of the amount'.[90] He ignored the £5 billion urged on him by most of his delegates, and even Bonar Law's £6 billion figure. This, because the trio whom he had sent to Paris in order to appease backbench opinion would not go below £10 or £11 billion, and because he feared, he said, that he would be 'crucified at home if his original experts were not also brought down to reasonable figures'.[91] The nub of the problem, as he explained, was political: whatever figure was named, public opinion would inevitably complain: 'It's too little.'[92] So often dismissed as hasty and impulsive, Lloyd George opted for a policy of 'wait and see': a postponement until 1921 of the final account. By then, he calculated, the dust would have settled.

It was easy for Wilson and high-minded colleagues like Smuts to urge Lloyd George to follow the inner light, to do the right thing, 'to go back to England and address the House of Commons as he alone could, pointing out boldly that his pre-election estimates as to Germany's capacity to pay were wrong'.[93] Lloyd George, as a twentieth-century democratic politician, could hardly disdain, like some grandee in the era of pocket boroughs, the clamour of a new parliament, a legislature now elected by universal male suffrage and swept into power with an unprecedented majority, above all on the strength of his promises to make Germany pay. As he admitted to Colonel House, 'he did not want to let the Conservatives "throw him" on a question of such popular concern'.[94] As the ostensibly Liberal Prime Minister of a predominantly Tory coalition in an overwhelmingly Conservative House of Commons, Lloyd George was a political maverick, a leader without a party. His authority, inherently precarious, required a constant personal ascendancy and a continual show of success. Far from disengaging from his electioneering pledges, a task well within his oratorical capacity, he reaffirmed them in full in his tremendous speech of 16 April. 'There are some', he told the House, 'who suggest that at the last election, I and my colleagues were rushed into declarations of which we are now rather ashamed, and wish to get out of. I do not wish to get out of them in the least.'[95] If it was a bluff, it would not be called, if at all, for another two years, since no one would know until then how much Germany would be asked to pay. Whatever happened, as far as he personally was concerned, to use one of his favourite expressions, it was a case of 'heads I win, tails you lose'.

'We were sinning against the light.' Thus George Barnes, like Smuts, a sober critic of the peace settlement.[96] Lloyd George's refusal to consider a German counter-offer of £5 billion and his abandonment of a time limit for payment of reparations were demonstrably among the worst legacies of the Conference, combining, as Robert Cecil warned, 'the maximum of financial disturbance with the minimum of actual result'.[97] They gave rise to intractable problems of enforcement and to a dozen years of strife, as much between the Allies themselves as with Germany. They served to perpetuate German bitterness at the treaty generally. Contrary to what was once supposed, it is clear that Lloyd George, rather than Clemenceau, was the obstacle to an immediate, agreed and workable solution to reparations.[98]

Another dark irony of Lloyd George at the Conference is that the voice of moderation was largely responsible for the war-guilt clause. Lloyd George was not vengeful. He was thinking, not of German opinion but of British opinion, when he insisted on the inclusion in the treaty of article 231, a general statement of German liability for the totality of losses to the Allies incurred 'as a consequence of the war imposed upon them by the aggression of Germany and her allies'. That this liability was purely academic was clear from article 232, which confined actual liability to reparations. But Lloyd George felt it necessary for domestic reasons to proclaim the principle of total liability. 'From the political point of view', he told Wilson, 'it is very important to mention that our right is unlimited.'[99] The war-guilt clause was an exercise in public relations, a cosmetic touch designed, in Nicolson's words, 'solely to please the House of Commons'.[100] In Germany, however, it was at once and predictably understood as an odious imputation on the German people. By his own definition of a good treaty as one broadly acceptable to 'a responsible German government', Lloyd George, of all men, with his keen imaginative insight and his fiery Welsh pride of race and culture, should have been the first to grasp the supreme unwisdom of article 231. In a treaty which exalted the principle of nationality above all else, its inclusion could not fail to provoke, to alienate and to enrage. So preoccupied was he, however, with public sensibilities at home, that he remained blind to the inevitable effects in Germany. For some years, indeed, he continued to maintain, quite unnecessarily and imprudently, that the Treaty of Versailles as a whole was based on German war-guilt, and that if that premise were abandoned, 'the treaty is destroyed'.[101] This was precisely the German argument. Unwittingly, Lloyd George became in this respect the agent of German revisionism.

VI

What of his policy towards France? Heading a delegation many of whom believed France to be excessively grasping in victory, Lloyd George stands out as an understanding observer of her continuing fear of Germany.[102] He also seemed a loyal and protective ally. In extending to Clemenceau the unprecedented offer of an alliance that promised instant British intervention in the event of a future German aggression, he may be seen as demonstrating statesmanship and vision of a high order. Even though the alliance came to nothing, Professor Northedge has hailed it as 'the greatest achievement of the personal diplomacy of the Prime Minister'.[103] Yet the evidence points to a very different conclusion if one considers the circumstances of Lloyd George's offer. When, half a year later, the proffered treaty vanished into thin air, the French were left helplessly in the lurch.

This outcome was the culmination of his increasingly ambiguous attitude. For all his bubbling good humour and his affectionate regard for Clemenceau, there was nothing sentimental about Lloyd George. He was in Paris to pursue British, not French interests. When these clashed, as over Middle East mandates, he opposed Clemenceau tooth and nail: the two almost came to blows when Clemenceau challenged his good faith over Syria. The Fontainebleau Memorandum itself, considered in context, was more than a statement of British peace aims and an appeal to liberal idealism: it was a deliberate attack on French policy, and it was understood as such. It resisted that policy at almost every turn. It opposed the creation of a Greater Poland, the keystone of France's eastern barrier against Germany. It denounced French hopes of a military frontier on the Rhine, without which, Foch insisted, there was no security. From the first, Lloyd George was alert to a new postwar balance of power. He had no intention of helping to replace a German hegemony in Europe with a French one or of underwriting France's imperial ambitions. While maintaining solidarity with Clemenceau on such common interests as reparations, therefore, he pursued an underlying policy of gradual disengagement from the Entente. His vanishing trick in the matter of the treaty of alliance – now you see it, now you don't –

left him liberty of action for the future. Henceforth he could exert British influence as he chose, whether on the side of France or of Germany. A chastened Clemenceau later taxed him to his face with turning against France the moment the war was over. Lloyd George did not deny it. 'Well', he said demurely, 'was it not always our traditional policy?'[104]

VII

Lloyd George was in his element at the Peace Conference. His manifest enjoyment of the experience disposed him to repeat it and to resume at frequent intervals his appearance as star performer on the European stage – 'the doyen of Prime Ministers'.[105] Not the League of Nations nor the conference of ambassadors, but his own brand of 'shuttle diplomacy' in a hectic round of two dozen 'summit conferences' at home and abroad, characterised his conduct of foreign policy for the rest of his premiership. An ebullient creativity, an openness to possibilities, a plentiful supply of ploys and devices remained his stock-in-trade. Resort to spectacular triumphs was, it seems, as much a psychological addiction as a political stratagem. The actor in him, playing up to his role as the 'Welsh Wizard', revelled in self-generating agility and cunning. Simultaneously enraptured and detached, he was often moved by his own performance, though he knew it was a performance. He craved an audience and a good press: when he was alone, it was said, there was no one there. The 'little Welsh conjuror', as Beatrice Webb called him,[106] relished the limelight and could not resist playing to the gallery. He was, Robert Cecil noted, 'always scoring'.[107] At Paris, he carried off every advantage to Britain and the Empire that circumstances could suggest and his own dexterity engineer. He fought to win, he was out for every trick, he wanted to be top dog, to enjoy the last word, at the bar of the House of Commons and at the bar of history: and in his *War Memoirs* and *The Truth about the Peace Treaties* he was to write that history, at epic length and with the same defiant panache as he had made it, himself cast in the role of hero.

It cannot be said that he was always constrained by the maxim which he often enjoined on others: to 'play the game'. 'If you want to succeed in politics', he chuckled to Riddell, 'you must keep your conscience well under control.'[108] 'He does not', Colonel House agreed, 'seem to have any ingrown sense of right or wrong, but only looks at things from the standpoint of expediency.'[109] Some instances of his craft at Paris are explored elsewhere in this account. The failure of the

Anglo-French alliance may now be understood, not as an unlucky mis-carriage of his plans, but rather as the very outcome he anticipated. And why did he plainly imply in the Pre-Armistice Agreement that compensation for injury and loss to civilians was the utmost that would be demanded of Germany, when what he really had in mind was a massive war indemnity? This was no error in drafting, but a premeditated *ruse de guerre*, an inducement to Germany to lay down her arms on the understanding that her liability would be limited, but with the mental reservation that, as he confided to the Allies at the time, 'once you get the armistice and the bridgeheads on the Rhine, you can interpret this as you like'.[110]

By such wiles and equivocations he turned obstacles into stepping-stones, over which he scrambled, flustered but impish and jubilant, from success to success. He reckoned himself 'a bonny fighter'.[111] 'I like fighting', he declared, 'and love to flatten out my assailants';[112] but he fought by no known rules. 'There were moments', in the words of Thomas Jones, 'when he stooped to low artifice.' [113] He did not scruple, when advantage beckoned, to unleash from his capacious bag of tricks the *suppressio veri* and the *suggestio falsi*: to hoodwink the Germans in the Pre-Armistice Agreement, President Wilson in the matter of pensions, Clemenceau with the guarantee to France and the British public on reparations.

'I wish Mr Lloyd George could tell us just what he finally wants', a weary American delegate complained.[114] He spoke for many at the Conference. He speaks for many now. Is the historian in any better vantage point four-score years on to determine the ends, if ends there were, which define and explain Lloyd George's strategy? To this spry and subtle practitioner, the game of politics, endlessly enthralling, was an end in itself. Yet it was more. His tactics on reparations and the guarantee to France exemplify, to be sure, a passion for dramatic improvisation; but it was improvisation aimed at the resolution of real problems. Harold Nicolson, a student and observer of that policy, expressed his conviction in strong terms. 'The volatility of Mr Lloyd George's methods', he wrote, 'has concealed from the eyes of many a critic the rock-like immobility of his aims.'[115] One broad conclusion may be advanced with confidence. Resolute in the pursuit and retention of power, Lloyd George kept a firm grasp on its various levers. He maintained his personal ascendancy over his delegation at Paris and his coalition colleagues in London. He consolidated his mastery over the House of Commons. In modern parlance, he secured his power base. His specific mandate as newly elected Prime Minister concerned the Kaiser and the cost of the war. That mandate he followed to the letter: indeed, as it turned out, he fulfilled it only in the letter. The Kaiser, he announced, would be tried by an Allied tribunal in London, forgetting the adage about first catching your hare. On reparations, he could claim that 'every pledge we have given with regard to what we pressed for insertion in the peace treaty is incorporated in the demands which have been put forward by the Allies'. This was true as far as it went, which was not very far; but it sounded plausible and it evoked the loudest ovations from the back benches.[116]

Meanwhile, as visible and immediate trophies, there were the spoils of Empire: the coveted Middle Eastern mandates, protecting the route to India and rich in oil. There were the confiscated German colonies in Africa and the South Pacific, making a reality of British rule from Cairo to the Cape and setting the far-flung bounds of Empire at their widest ever. In gathering in these glittering prizes, Lloyd George pursued a policy both national and popular, and peculiarly appropriate to himself as head of a coalition dominated by the Unionists. Imperial expansion recalled the traditions of Disraeli; those of Salisbury were reflected in the option of isolation from continental entanglements. The idealism of the Fontainebleau Memorandum, calling for reconciliation in a Europe of sovereign nation states, attracted liberals; at the same time it was wholly in accord with British interest in a balance of power.

VIII

Returning to London after the signing, Lloyd George was met by the King-Emperor at Victoria Station, and rode with him in an open landau to Buckingham Palace. Someone in the cheering crowds tossed a wreath of bay leaves into the carriage. 'This is for you', said the King.[117] Lloyd George kept the laurels, but he spurned the peerage that would have exiled him from the Commons and belied his radical antecedents and that scorn for aristocracy for which he had made himself notorious in the pre-war struggle against the Upper House – and which he continued to show by his amused and lucrative connivance in the sale of honours. The Order of Merit he deservedly accepted. This was no venal gewgaw, but the sovereign's personal gift – not that Lloyd George held George V or monarchs generally in any greater esteem than he did the nobility. It was with difficulty that he was persuaded in the Hall of Mirrors to write a few ink-spotted lines to the King, 'with his humble duty to Your Majesty', offering congratulations on the conclusion of peace. He really did not see what it had to do with the King.[118]

Besides, he was bent on a state trial in Westminster Hall for the King's cousin, the ex-Kaiser, with all the paraphernalia of justice, though he had given little thought to the practicalities. The King, with his nautical passion for detail, reduced the baroque vision to farce, asking in some vexation 'where the Kaiser was to be lodged. Lloyd George did not know; he thought perhaps in the Tower. The King asked "Are you going to take him backwards and forwards in a black maria, or what do you mean to do?"...Lloyd George had no idea.'[119] There was one royal trophy, however, which he liked to sport. It belonged to the Kaiser's son, Crown Prince Wilhelm, also originally designated to stand trial in London: his field-glasses, abandoned at the German army headquarters at Spa in the haste and confusion of the Hohenzollern skedaddle, and thereafter put to peaceful and picturesque use by Lloyd George on mountain climbs and picnics in North Wales.

2
Reparations and Reputations: Lloyd George and Lord Cunliffe

Lords Cunliffe and Sumner—traditionally cast as villains of the peace—Cunliffe and Lloyd George—the Hughes Committee—Cunliffe's 'shot in the dark'—negotiations with Americans and French—influence of Lord Sumner—the crisis—Lloyd George's solution—the traditional interpretation—Lloyd George and the Americans—his strategy and tactics—rejects a lump sum—solution by postponement—Cunliffe's true role

> He did not say that the Germans could pay a particular sum or could not pay it.
>
> Lloyd George at meeting of British Empire delegation, Paris, 1 June 1919

> The Prime Minister refuses absolutely to let me go, although I seem to be worse than useless here.
>
> Lord Cunliffe, Paris, 2 April 1919

The Lords Cunliffe and Sumner, Lloyd George's delegates on reparations at the Paris Peace Conference, have gone down to posterity, irredeemably, it would seem, as what James Headlam-Morley called 'the two bad men of the Conference'.[1] 'They always go about together', he noted, 'and are always summoned when some particularly nefarious act has to be committed'.[2] Those lumbering Titans – the Gog and Magog of the Conference – have cast a long shadow across its historiography: the misanthropic, beetle-browed Sumner, 'that grim old judge',[3] and Cunliffe, ex-Governor of the Bank of England, at once sprightly and sinister, 'a forbidding, purposeful figure' to his own family;[4] to his critics a moustachio'd bully, half-ogre, half-clown.[5]

23

Cunliffe boasted the opposition of every liberal-minded member of the British delegation. 'I'm thankful', he wrote afterwards to Sumner, 'that Herr Von K[eynes], Barnes, Smuts and many more of our number advertised their views and that it can never *truthfully* be said that we (say *you*) let the Hun down gently for all his squealing.'[6] To General Smuts, George Barnes, Edwin Montagu and Robert Cecil, to James Headlam-Morley and Harold Nicolson, above all to John Maynard Keynes – Cunliffe and Sumner were 'the Twins', whose abrasive personalities and flint-like obduracy made them obvious culprits for the perceived unwisdom of the treaty's reparation clauses, foremost among the men who fashioned a treaty of ill-repute. Nicolson pronounced the general verdict from Paris. 'The fault', he wrote, 'is that there is an old man called Lord Sumner and an old man called Lord Cunliffe, and they have worked away without consulting anyone, with the result that the Treaty is only worth the *Daily Mail* which it will be printed in.'[7]

It was Keynes, it seems, who dubbed them 'the Twins', or 'the Heavenly Twins':[8] because they shared a study at the Hotel Majestic[9] where they 'worked away' with such fearful assiduity, Cunliffe esteeming work 'the best of all hobbies';[10] because, both large, heavy, imposing men, with a certain loud self-assertiveness, they were invariably in each other's company, purposefully striding the boulevards together; and because of the astronomical sums, plucked by Cunliffe from the skies, which they insisted could and should be extorted from the enemy. For it was Cunliffe's peculiar distinction, as Lloyd George himself recalled afterwards in finger-wagging reproof, to have produced, even before the Conference began, 'the highest estimate given by anyone of Germany's capacity to pay',[11] and to have held out to the last for legendary figures.

In Keynes's case, there were powerful reasons, personal and emotional as much as intellectual, for his particular antipathy to the Twins. As chief Treasury representative at the Conference, the reparation clauses were for him the worst of what he was to denounce as 'the Carthaginian peace'; and the two old men personified his own impotence to moderate those clauses in any way. Acknowledging defeat, he resigned from the British delegation and left Paris in despair. 'The battle is lost', he wrote to Lloyd George. 'I leave the Twins to gloat over the devastation of Europe.'[12]

He took his revenge in *The Economic Consequences of the Peace*, though neither Sumner nor Cunliffe appears directly in the book. Having drafted a sentence of barbed malignity, describing Cunliffe as literally pig-headed, and Sumner as a vulture, he decided to leave them out,

'Like a giant cherub with a moustache and a sense of humour.' – Frances Stevenson

Figure 2.1   Lord Cunliffe as Governor of the Bank of England (Francis Dodd, 1932)

contenting himself with an oblique reference to Cunliffe as 'a high City authority'.[13] But their influence on the treaty, and Keynes's embittered reaction to that influence, are all-pervasive.[14] The Twins became the unnamed villains of the peace. Add to this the common though questionable association of reparations with the decline and fall of the

Weimar Republic, the rise of Hitler and the coming of the Second World War, and the Twins still stand out in the demonology of Versailles. No one, Alan Sharp observes, has yet ventured to rehabilitate Sumner;[15] and the same is true of Cunliffe.[16] Eighty years on, how well deserved is his dire reputation?

I

In 1919 Walter Cunliffe was sixty-three years old. A burly, pipe-smoking giant of a man, well over six feet tall, with an odd, rolling gait, his stocky frame topped by a big, round, chubby face, with a straggly walrus moustache, he appeared roguish and even comic. But he was also gruff, dictatorial and short-tempered, tenacious in his likes and dislikes, the latter including most politicians, with the notable exception of Lloyd George. A surly and thunderous irascibility alternated in Cunliffe with a droll, self-deprecating, schoolboy jollity. 'A curious character', Bonar Law's secretary, J.C. Davidson, recalled: 'He looked like a farmer, was definitely a bully and had withall a certain cunning.'[17] Frances Stevenson struck a friendlier note. 'Jovial and conservative and typically British', she wrote: 'Like a giant cherub with a moustache and a sense of humour.'[18] While the Conference awaited the German decision on the treaty – to sign or not to sign – and the Allied armies made ready to march on Berlin, Cunliffe joked: 'They are all laughing at me because I have offered to be the first man over the top at the advance next Monday if they will only order it.'[19]

There were those who liked him, more or less: Asquith, Lord Reading, William McAdoo, Secretary to the United States Treasury, above all Lloyd George. What did the subtle, mercurial Welshman see in this ponderous, bucolic and by all accounts profoundly uncerebral Anglo-Saxon? The attraction of opposites, perhaps. Perhaps on the other hand certain marginal affinities. In a remarkable portrait by Francis Dodd (Figure 2.1), Cunliffe struts and saunters in the garden of the Bank of England: four-square, frock-coated, wing-collared and top-hatted. There radiates from the canvas a jaunty flamboyance in this postwar pastiche of an Edwardian banker. Yet Dodd has only slighty parodied his subject; for Cunliffe parodied himself. Though no intellectual, and notoriously inarticulate,[20] his common reaction a disapproving grunt or growl, he was also, like Lloyd George, something of a showman, who courted – yet at the same time strangely shunned – publicity.[21] Behind a curt or breezy exterior, he could, again like Lloyd George, be both shy and sly. To Keynes and to Montagu Norman, that other controversial

Governor of the Bank, he was 'a bluffer – and enjoyed playing the part'.[22] Little known before August 1914 and then raised to unexpected celebrity, his pluck and decisiveness on the outbreak of war made him in some respects the man of the moment. Add to this a 'bull-dog tenacity', testified to, respectfully or otherwise, by general consent,[23] and Cunliffe was what Lloyd George liked to call himself – 'a bonnie fighter' – a combative, controversial character of 'massive strength',[24] used to having his way and 'who minded not whether he pleased or displeased'.[25] 'He was not', as his daughter recalled, 'a man to be trifled with.'[26]

In the last days before war became inevitable, Cunliffe begged Lloyd George, then Chancellor of the Exchequer, 'with tears in his eyes', to 'keep us out of it';[27] but he acted swiftly to prevent the removal of securities from London, by posting guards on the German banks; and war once declared, his bold announcement that the Bank of England would meet all outstanding bills of exchange – these totalled hundreds of millions of pounds – prevented a run on sterling likely to have proved catastrophic, and stiffened international confidence in the Government. This timely resolve won him the approval of Lloyd George, who shared the credit for averting financial disaster;[28] and of the Prime Minister, Asquith, who rewarded Cunliffe with the first peerage of the war. Cunliffe was asked to remain in office until March 1918, three years beyond the normal term.

During the war he accompanied Lloyd George and other members of the government abroad to advise on loans to Allies and to negotiate loans from America.[29] At home, for three years, he was virtually 'the financial dictator of Great Britain',[30] assuming supreme authority on credit, exchange rates and gold reserves. In all but name he was a member of the government, but he behaved like a sovereign potentate and treated the Treasury as if it were merely the West End branch of the Bank of England. He insisted that meetings between himself and McKenna as Chancellor of the Exchequer should take place only in the presence of the Prime Minister. His brusque high-handedness and peremptory, contentious decisions provoked a mounting succession of clashes. When Lloyd George became Prime Minister, however, and McKenna was replaced as Chancellor by Bonar Law, Cunliffe overreached himself. Finding, on his return from America, that the Treasury had taken direction of exchange controls, he demanded the dismissal of Keynes, who, McKenna had assured him, 'should not meddle again in City matters',[31] and even of the Permanent Secretary himself, Sir Robert Chalmers. Law, a man of sterner stuff than McKenna, charged Cunliffe with taking 'an absolutely unwarrantable liberty'. 'He entirely misunderstands the relations between the Government and the Bank', he told Lloyd George.[32] Cunliffe, however, compounded his offences by countermanding Treasury orders for the transfer of Bank of England bullion, 'an act', as the outraged Law complained to him,[33] 'of extraordinary disrespect towards the British Government'.[34] Law demanded Cunliffe's head. 'The present position is impossible', he informed Lloyd George, 'and must be brought to an end.'[35] After a tremendous struggle to rally support in the City, Cunliffe capitulated when Lloyd George threatened to nationalise the Bank of England; and Law, while permitting Cunliffe to remain as Governor, stipulated that he should not stand for re-election when his extended term of office expired the following spring. These high political secrets were unknown outside government circles; and Cunliffe's return to a simple directorship was plausibly represented to the public as an honourable retirement after years of strenuous service.[36]

Notwithstanding these backstage dramas, or perhaps because of them, Lloyd George continued to hold Cunliffe in a kind of amused but genuine respect. He protected and promoted him, enhancing his authority as the war drew to its close. First he made him chairman of the Committee on Currency and Foreign Exchanges, whose orthodox recommendation in August 1918 of a postwar return to the gold standard was accepted by governments throughout the 1920s.[37] Then, immediately after the armistice, Lloyd George appointed him to the Hughes Committee on indemnities, a Cabinet body set up to advise the Government on the burning issue of reparations.[38] Lloyd George had called a general election. The campaign was in full swing. Nothing captured the public imagination so much as the government's pledge to punish the Kaiser, unless it was its pledge to 'make Germany pay'.

How much Germany should pay was another matter. A Treasury report by Keynes rated Germany's capacity at £3 billion. The Hughes Committee, under the deaf, difficult, and, to the British government, politically tiresome Prime Minister of Australia, William Morris Hughes, was set up partly in order to counter, or at least to query, this modest-seeming figure; and it was Cunliffe, the day after the committee began its work, who produced the notorious estimate which he always admitted was a 'guess' – £20 billion, nearly seven times Keynes's amount. 'It is very rough', he agreed, adding, with reckless aplomb, 'and if anyone went for *forty* billions, I should not disbelieve him'.[39] It was rough indeed: Cunliffe did not conceal that it was 'little more than a shot in the dark'.[40] Ironically, he had taken his cue from Keynes, who, giving evidence to the committee and asked to name the total cost of the war to the Allies, assessed it at £20 billion. Cunliffe at once swooped on this sensational figure and next day named £20 billion as the measure of Germany's capacity.[41] He then topped it up with another £4 billion for good measure. He proposed payment through the issue by the German government of 5 per cent gold bonds on the world markets, so as to yield the Allies an annual tribute, including principal and interest, of £1.2 billion over 50 years. His recommendations were at once adopted by the Hughes Committee – and by Lloyd George.[42]

II

In January 1919, Hughes, Cunliffe and Sumner, a law lord of sharp mind and tongue, and with burgeoning political ambitions,[43] arrived in Paris as the British Empire representatives to the inter-Allied Reparations Commission.[44] Cunliffe was made chairman of the second subcommittee, set up to determine Germany's capacity to pay.[45] His main antagonists were the French and American delegates, Louis Loucheur, Clemenceau's Minister of Reconstruction, and the New York banker, Thomas Lamont.[46] After some preliminary skirmishing as to who should start the bidding, which Cunliffe, according to Lamont, 'seemed disinclined to do',[47] evidently preferring to let the others show their hands first, he eventually named, on the Prime Minister's authority, the figure which he privately called 'my London guess'[48] – £24 billion. Payment by Germany should begin within two years with a down payment of £1 billion, mainly in kind, based on estimates of her liquid assets, including her gold reserves and merchant fleet. These assets being quantifiable, the question of down payment was relatively uncontroversial and quickly agreed. Not so the long-term figures, which throughout the Conference were to remain the single biggest bone of contention. They caused, Lamont recalled, 'more trouble, contention, hard feeling and delay...than any other point of the Treaty of Versailles'.[49]

America was not interested in claiming reparations. Not only were her material losses insignificant: they were massively offset by her enormous profits. Having gained by the war to displace Britain as the world's chief creditor, America sought to make the world, if not safe for plutocracy, then as profitable for her postwar investors as it had proved lucrative for the duration. America accepted that France and Britain would claim damages from Germany; but hoped that these would be of a moderate order and not such as to impede the revival of Germany's economy. France and Britain, on the other hand, were in fierce mutual competition for reparations to offset their colossal war debts to America and to regain as much as they could of their pre-war financial prosperity. They also feared a physically undamaged and economically still highly redoubtable Germany as a trade rival. Both therefore aimed at the highest possible figures.[50] In France's case, the devastation of her industrial north-east meant that her recovery must inevitably lag behind that of Germany. Since few believed that Germany would ever make good French and British losses in full, the governments of both countries were all the more intent on exacting the utmost from Germany, in order not to be outdone by the other.

For these reasons, Loucheur initially raised the bidding by canvassing even higher figures than Cunliffe – £40 billion (a sum which Cunliffe himself, however, had stated a month before would not have surprised him) – while Lamont named a maximum £12.7 billion, just over one-half of Cunliffe's figure. Lamont had no belief in this sum as a measure of German capacity; he named it simply in order to bring his French and British colleagues down to what he considered more rational levels of discourse. As matters stood, however, none of the three could see his way to satisfying the others. 'I have not the least hope of moving either', Cunliffe noted of Loucheur and Lamont: 'My Subcommittee will not be able to make up its mind.'[51] This certainly proved true. Loucheur, who in his own figure had consciously been flying a very high kite, now scathingly observed that while he could 'just about see' how the American figure might be met, as for Cunliffe's £24 billion – 'we leave to the poets of the future the task of finding solutions'.[52]

These were opening moves, made in an atmosphere of shadow boxing. But even when the bidding began in earnest, again, what largely continued to dictate it was Franco–British rivalry rather than any pretence at a serious estimate of German capacity. Loucheur, however, was soon persuaded by the Americans that under the Pre-Armistice Agreement definition of reparations as compensation for physical war damage rather than as indemnity for the costs of the war France stood to gain far more by claiming a larger share of a finite sum by way of war damage than by pressing for war costs in competition with Britain; and that in pursuing this line, France would enjoy American support. Loucheur therefore sided with Lamont against Cunliffe in urging a downward total of £8 billion. Outnumbered, Cunliffe quickly threw in his hand, dropping to the proposed sum, a figure, be it noted, one-third of his original demand. 'The Americans and French are consorting against us, as I feared', he observed, 'and if we get eight billion we shall be fortunate.'[53]

He was irritable but not immovable – realistic, indeed; and agreement seemed briefly within reach. 'While we were quite a distance apart', Lamont recalled, 'the difference did not seem to be irreconcilable.'[54] Forwarding Cunliffe's report to the Prime Minister, Lloyd George's secretary, Philip Kerr, confirmed Cunliffe's readiness to settle. In a covering note he wrote: 'I think Cunliffe is quite willing to take the responsibility of coming to terms if necessary, but he naturally would like to have support.'[55] The moment passed, however. While Loucheur remained willing to endorse the £8 billion figure, Lamont, who, as before, had proposed it only for bargaining purposes and in a further effort to bring Cunliffe down to earth, refused to be bound.[56] Colonel House, deputising in Wilson's absence, told Lamont that the figure was 'perfectly absurd'.[57] As Cunliffe predicted, agreement remained as elusive as ever.

At this point, Cunliffe himself sensed that he had acted out of turn. The £8 billion figure received no hint of endorsement from Lloyd George. Rather, the Cabinet warned its delegates against any relaxing of Britain's demand for full indemnity, though it was soon compelled to abandon this stance by the determined opposition of President Wilson.[58] Cunliffe therefore once more raised the stakes by reverting to his previous figure of £12 billion. He had also fallen increasingly under the influence of Lord Sumner. Cunliffe was much in awe of the iron logic and imperious certainty of his learned colleague, who held Germany liable in law for every penny of Britain's war costs, and was busy elaborating heads of damages to match France's claims in respect of her devastated war zone. Of the two men, Lloyd George declared that Cunliffe was 'more tractable, despite much innate stubbornness – but', as he told President Wilson, 'he is under the influence of Lord Sumner, who never leaves his side'.[59]

It was at this point, in Lamont's well-known phrase, that Cunliffe and Sumner 'put their heads together, went off the deep end, and refused to compromise at all'.[60] Whether or not assisted by Sumner, Cunliffe was soon enlightened as to the reason for Loucheur's volte-face, which would entitle France to the lion's share of reparations if indemnity for war costs were abandoned; for, as he wrote to Lloyd George, 'the result is that we shall be practically left out in the cold'.[61] The problem of the proportions in which reparations should be shared among the Allies being no less controversial than was the issue of German capacity, Cunliffe could not put his name to any figure without the Prime Minister's authority; and he duly turned to Lloyd George for instructions, pending which he deferred completion of the subcommittee's report.[62]

Agreement on a figure being deadlocked, the problem was now taken up by Lloyd George, Clemenceau and Colonel House as a matter of high politics. On 10 March, they appointed an informal subcommittee of three, to examine the problem afresh and see whether it might be possible to arrive at a figure politically acceptable to the plenipotentiaries. Clemenceau retained Loucheur to represent French interests; but Lamont was replaced by Norman Davis, Assistant Secretary to the United States Treasury and President Wilson's principal financial adviser; while Lloyd George appointed Edwin Montagu, formerly Financial Secretary to the Treasury, and now at the Conference as British minister in charge of finance. These three met in secret – '*dans la coulisse*', as Loucheur noted, '*dans le plus grand secret*'[63] – and behind the back of Cunliffe and Sumner, who were wholly unaware of the subcommittee's existence.

The subcommittee recommended a figure of £6 billion. Of this, at least half was intended for cosmetic purposes, it being privately agreed that the utmost that Germany could pay over thirty years was £3 billion, the figure originally named by Keynes in his Treasury report.[64] Loucheur even confided his personal belief that £2 billion was a truer measure of German capacity.[65] Lloyd George, though visibly shocked at these figures, appeared momentarily tempted to strike a deal. 'Well, Lamont', he declared, after the latter had pleaded with him at length, ' "*Almost thou persuadest me!*".'[66] But as his words indicated, the answer was no. He could not, he said, go over the heads of his official delegates in the current state of British opinion; and to refer the matter back to Cunliffe's committee was a waste of time. It was 'useless', he insisted, for it to 'meet yet again'.[67]

This was not an implausible conclusion. If Cunliffe, his zeal reanimated by Sumner, had already refused to split the difference between £8 billion and £6 billion, he was unlikely to compromise between £12 billion and £6 billion. The Americans then suggested disbanding the Reparations Commission and dispensing altogether with Cunliffe, Sumner and Hughes, in order, as Davis put it, to 'get around with some human beings and start quite afresh'.[68] Davis's impatience is understandable; but if his proposal was intended to help Lloyd George out of his difficulties, it was unlikely to find acceptance, since overruling his delegates was just what Lloyd George had said he could not do. Hughes, Cunliffe and Sumner were the last men to go quietly. Even Keynes, who would have liked nothing better, admitted that it might not be so easy to persuade the Twins 'to commit hari-kiri'.[69] Instead the Prime Minister fell in with an alternative proposal, now gaining ground among the

French and Americans – and indeed recommended by Cunliffe himself – who concluded that the time had come for the Allies to 'agree to differ'.[70] The proposal was that the Cunliffe subcommittee report should name no figure at all. A decision on the final sum should be deferred for two years, pending investigation by a permanent Inter-Allied Reparations Commission of experts. This Commission would report on Germany's finances at leisure, free from Conference pressures and parliamentary uproar. Meanwhile Germany would make the agreed down payment of £1 billion, including £160 million in gold.[71] This much criticised solution by postponement, supported by Lloyd George and Clemenceau, and ultimately though reluctantly endorsed by Wilson, was duly incorporated in the Treaty of Versailles.

Any attempt to close down the existing Reparations Commission would certainly have exposed Lloyd George to a political hurricane. As it was, Hughes was loud in protest at the agreed solution; and Lloyd George deployed Cunliffe in an urgent attempt to pacify him. Hughes, a diminutive but cantankerous Welshman, was outraged at what he saw as the craven abandonment of war costs. As chairman of the third sub-committee on the means of exacting reparations, he continued to grumble, as he had since before the armistice, that British – and Australian – claims on Germany had been abandoned under pressure from America. Hughes had demanded full indemnity from the first, and was indignant at Cunliffe's retreat from his original figures. He was even more furious to learn that the Cunliffe report would not recommend any figure at all and that none would appear in the treaty. On 8 April, when Cunliffe's report came up for approval by the full Reparations Commission, of which Hughes was chairman, Hughes voted angrily against acceptance.[72] Cunliffe noted: 'Hughes, as expected, turned nasty over the report of my 2nd Sub-[committee].'[73] Hughes was threatening to break with the Reparations Commission and even with the Empire delegation itself, 'to stand out', wrote Cunliffe, 'from all the arrangements that we have taken all these months to make', and to embarrass Lloyd George by publicising his dissent. He was known to be in league with Lloyd George's enemies in parliament and with the Northcliffe press.[74]

The awkwardness of such a démarche by a senior Dominion Prime Minister in the existing state of public agitation, was obvious. Lloyd George cursed Hughes as a "damned little Welshman" who wouldn't play fair'.[75] The parliamentary crisis was at its height, with much sound and fury. That same day 200 Unionist backbenchers cabled Lloyd George to complain of 'persistent rumours from Paris', and called on him to make good his election pledge 'to present the bill in full'.[76] Cunliffe himself, while observing that Hughes's 'tactics in holding things up at this stage are not defensible', conceded, significantly, that 'in this instance there is no doubt he has a good deal of right on his side and will have a good percentage of the public with him'.[77] On 11 April Lloyd George summoned Cunliffe to his flat for a working breakfast with the Dominion Prime Ministers in an effort to mollify Hughes and talk him round – to no avail.[78] 'He is a real terror to have anything to do with', Cunliffe observed of Hughes, 'when it is a matter of give and take.'[79]

Later that day, at a charged meeting of Dominion Prime Ministers attended by the Twins, Hughes again took up the cudgels. He reproached Cunliffe with abandoning the £24 billion figure which Cunliffe himself had recommended to the Hughes Committee. Cunliffe admitted frankly that he *had* changed his mind. He agreed that the latest figures under discussion were 'nearer to £12 billion than to £30 billion. It was true that in London he himself had given a much larger estimate, but as he had said at the time, this had really been little more than a shot in the dark.' But having now been 'incessantly engaged in these nego-tiations, he would stake his reputation that these were the best terms that we could hope to get'. Eleven billion pounds over 50 years 'repre-sented, in his view, the utmost that Germany could pay, including inter-est. That was his considered opinion.'[80] Sumner gloomily confirmed that the attitude of the Americans rendered 'hopeless' any further attempt to include war costs.[81] Protesting noisily to the last, Hughes was reluctantly persuaded to keep his own counsel.

Two months later, Lloyd George faced an opposite and still more serious challenge. This took the form of a profound crisis of confidence in the peace terms generally on the part of the British Empire delegation, which reviewed them at a series of meetings across the last weekend in May. At these critical sessions the Dominion Prime Ministers were joined by members of the British Cabinet, specially summoned from London by Lloyd George. While Hughes continued to protest that Germany was being let off too lightly, the overwhelming feeling among his colleagues was that, on the contrary, the terms were mani-festly excessive. The German counter-proposals, just received, included a counter-offer of £5 billion by way of reparations. This had made a considerable impression. The British delegation, beginning with Smuts, was virtually united in urging on Lloyd George the desirability of agreeing a fixed sum for immediate insertion in the treaty. The matter should be settled then and there, not left in abeyance and uncertainty.

Smuts's pleas received powerful support from three of the Prime Minister's most influential Unionist colleagues, Austen Chamberlain, Birkenhead and Milner. Most present were for meeting the Germans halfway.[82]

Despite the clear authority now invested in him to conclude a deal on reparations, however, Lloyd George stood out firmly against his colleagues, invoking Cunliffe's figures in justification of his own stand. At different times on the same day, Cunliffe and Keynes called on Lloyd George in his flat, Keynes to plead for moderate figures, Cunliffe to counsel rejection of the German counter-offer,[83] which, he wrote to the Prime Minister on 1 June, 'should not be entertained'. If a lump sum was to be named in the treaty, he maintained, it should not be less than £12 to £13 billion, over twice the American maximum.[84] As both Cunliffe and Lloyd George were well aware, agreement with the Americans on such a sum was out of the question. As between Keynes and Cunliffe, the Prime Minister came down squarely on Cunliffe's side. It was at this point that Keynes quitted the Conference, admitting final defeat at the hands of the Twins.

III

The traditional view of Cunliffe and Sumner is of an intemperate and domineering pair of reactionaries – 'the old fire-eaters', as Nicolson called them,[85] and Thomas Jones's 'stony-hearted men'[86] – whom Lloyd George rashly took with him to Paris to appease the 'hard-faced' Conservatives on his backbenches; that he was shocked and disconcerted by Cunliffe's figures – 'a wild and fantastic chimera', he later called them;[87] and would gladly have followed his natural instincts, which were generous and liberal, by settling for 'a reasonable figure',[88] had he not felt bound hand and foot by his electoral pledges to 'make Germany pay'; pledges which the backbenchers, to the baying of the Northcliffe press, kept ceaselessly in the public eye, with motions in the House, a stormy debate on reparations, and the open telegram to the Prime Minister.[89]

Most historians subscribe broadly to this version of events. It derives essentially from Keynes's *The Economic Consequences of the Peace*; from the chapter on reparations by Lamont in the American account of the Peace Conference entitled *What Really Happened at Paris*; and to some extent from Lloyd George himself in *The Truth about the Peace Treaties*. According to the accepted interpretation, then, Lloyd George was swayed against his better judgement into making wildly misleading pledges by temptations of electoral gain; while the Twins turned out to be mutually infected with *la folie à deux* and totally out of control: a pair of rogue elephants, yoked together and on the rampage, trumpeting for the moon. Lloyd George lacked the authority, or, some would say, the moral courage, to rein them in, preferring to career along on their backs in a rickety howdah, headlong but politically secure, than to risk being trampled underfoot in the mad stampede. At a decisive moment, say his critics, he took the easy way out and fell below the level of events; and his solution of the reparations problem by evasion and delay represented a historic failure of nerve. As Lamont observed to the President: 'with all respect to Mr Lloyd George, he is simply trying to postpone the evil day, as far as public opinion is concerned'.[90]

Without venturing on a wholesale revision of this account – for there is no denying that Lloyd George was much exercised at Paris with the task of matching parliamentary expectations and keeping, or appearing to keep, his electoral promises – a different perspective of Cunliffe – and of Lloyd George – emerges from a fresh consideration of the facts. Lloyd George certainly took care, twenty years later, to distance himself from Cunliffe and from what he called his 'strange lapse into megalomania'.[91] By the time he wrote *The Truth about the Peace Conference*, Cunliffe and Sumner were both dead and there was no one to defend them. Keynes's *Economic Consequences* had left its mark on the whole subject of reparations – and on Lloyd George. In defending retrospectively his own record at the Conference, Lloyd George found in Cunliffe a convenient lightning conductor to deflect criticism away from himself. At the time, however, whatever his private opinion of Cunliffe's figures – and he frequently voiced scepticism – he was of course fully alive to those figures before he sent Cunliffe to Paris to defend them. To profess surprise and incredulity after the event suggests extreme forgetfulness – or lack of candour.

According to Keynes, Lloyd George never had the slightest faith in Cunliffe's figures and retained him at Paris purely out of political opportunism. It is true that Lloyd George, in voluble and apparently earnest colloquies with Colonel House, with Davis and Lamont, and with President Wilson himself, left the Americans in no doubt of his total disbelief in Cunliffe's figures and his low opinion of his competence. Over lunch with Davis and Lamont, he led them to understand that he would willingly accept the £6 billion figure, or even, according to Davis, 'that he thought £5 billion would be all right and that it would be quite acceptable to him' if – but only if – they could persuade Sumner and Cunliffe to endorse it, the Twins' approval being essential, he said, to his own political protection and survival.[92] Without their endorsement, he told Colonel House, he would 'be crucified at home'.[93]

Much has been made of these remarkable avowals – one historian writes of the Prime Minister's 'astonishing frankness'[94] – and we may be sure that Lloyd George, at his buttonholing best, wished them to be taken with the utmost seriousness. But how seriously did he take them himself? Words for all occasions were his stock-in-trade as a past-master of persuasion; and the unique character of these apparent confidences should make us wary of taking them entirely at face value. Knowing the Twins as he did, their views, their personalities, their intransigence, the disagreeable impression which they made on the Americans, and the Americans on them – 'those d—d Yanks', Cunliffe exclaimed[95] – is it likely that Lloyd George ever supposed that the *Americans*, of all people, could win them round to the £6 billion figure or anything like it? More to the point, did he want them to accept it, was he really prepared to countenance it himself while there was still no agreement on the all-important division of the spoils, and while Sumner indeed, at his behest, was engaged in a scheme to double Germany's liability by adding to it the stupendous cost of Allied war pensions and separation allowances? When the unofficial committee first produced the £6 billion figure, Loucheur noted, '*Lloyd George se récrie devant la faiblesse de ces chiffres.*'[96] This sounds like a spontaneous reaction of disappointment and shock. One sees him wince. To settle for a total of that order even before Britain's share had been determined might, after all, be to accept a very undersized and scrawny pig in a poke.[97]

The episode between Lloyd George and the Americans suggests, on reconsideration, a tactical ploy, a feint to throw them off the scent, a confidence trick, a piece of play-acting. The strongest evidence that he saw the Twins as an insuperable obstacle was what he told the Americans himself; and though he appeared to convince them, this particular display of his persuasiveness is in itself no more proof of his sincerity than any other. Nothing could be more effective than Lloyd George's simulated earnestness: he, no less than Cunliffe, another old stager, was 'a bluffer – and enjoyed playing the part'. Even so, the Americans were not without their suspicions. They found him 'very shifty and clever' on reparations; as one of them said, like 'the bright boy that doesn't have to study'.[98] Yet the probability is that they did not see through his stratagem, if stratagem it was. In any event he only told them the half of it. Colonel House, a seasoned connoisseur of politics and human nature, was amused and disarmed by Lloyd George's cheerful cynicism; but House was perhaps the victim of a double-bluff. When Lloyd George confided, or apparently confided to him that 'he knew Germany could not pay anything like' the sums demanded, he stressed that 'he wanted the amount named to be large, even if Germany could never pay it'.[99] He did not add that naming a large amount would be better still if it turned out that Germany *could* pay. Yet this, it seems, was what he had in mind.

How far is it true that the Twins 'went off the deep end and refused to compromise at all'? We have seen, after all, that Cunliffe had already, within limits, shown himself far more flexible in the numbers game than he has been given credit for, dropping variously to one-half or even one-third of his original 'guess'. What is clear is that, as negotiations dragged on, the riddle of Germany's capacity found Lloyd George an ever more convinced agnostic. Blaming the stalemate on the Twins and pleading his own political vulnerability provided effective cover for his growing determination not to commit himself to any figure at all. The stakes for Britain were high, very high; yet none could say how high. In the current state of conflicting advice and total uncertainty about German capacity, he had everything to gain by caution and delay, much to lose by rash and premature agreement. When the Americans urged him to give the Twins their *congé* and, in Davis's words, to 'start quite afresh ... with some human beings' like Keynes and Montagu, Lloyd George did no such thing. He kept the Twins firmly in place at Paris, not only because their removal, and more especially that of Hughes, would have stoked up the furore at Westminster, perhaps beyond even his ability to quench it, but also, and more particularly, because Cunliffe and Sumner were irreplaceable pieces in his reparations strategy. It was Keynes and Montagu who were the pawns.

From the remarks which Lloyd George let fall, the Americans supposed Cunliffe to be as much a thorn in his flesh as he was in theirs. They were wrong. Cunliffe was no trouble to Lloyd George. He did not, like Hughes, make scenes, though he might privately threaten to do so.[100] He did not exceed his brief. He reported regularly to Lloyd George, he looked to him for instructions, he carried them out faithfully. It was Lloyd George who kept Cunliffe in line, with warnings against abandoning Britain's claim to indemnity.[101] Far from 'winding up the Commission' and sending Cunliffe home, Lloyd George hardly let him out of his sight. Cunliffe himself in vain requested leave of absence.[102] At the beginning of April, the reparations crisis at its peak, he leaped at the chance of a lift to England by air, the pilot offering to land near his house on Epsom Downs. 'The Prime Minister refuses absolutely to let me go', he noted ruefully, 'although I seem to be worse than useless here.'[103]

'Still dull', he wrote the next day, 'and absolutely nothing to look forward to, as the P.M. obstinately refuses to let me go home even for a day.'[104] A week later, 'L.G. will not let me get away and keeps us all dangling around from hour to hour.'[105] Cunliffe did himself less than justice. Far from 'worse than useless', he was, as has been seen, a key player in the Prime Minister's efforts to restrain Hughes.[106] More was to come. A week later Lloyd George required, indeed '*ordered*', the Twins to remain in Paris as delegates to the commission set up to levy reparations from Austria and Bulgaria.[107] Cunliffe heard that he was even thinking of appointing them to the permanent Reparations Commission – convincing proof, if it was true, of their exceptional usefulness in his eyes.[108] If the Twins really 'went off the deep end' at Paris, on whose authority did they take the plunge?

IV

If there is substance to this reinterpretation, then Lloyd George's representations to the Americans and his pleas for their understanding were a clever charade. He was never in thrall to the Twins: they were the obedient agents of his bidding. To suppose otherwise, to accept that he truly feared that his government might fall on the issue of reparations and that, as he warned the President, his place at the Conference table would be taken by Lord Northcliffe or Horatio Bottomley[109] – is to succumb to his own mesmeric rhetoric. To accept that a Prime Minister of such matchless ingenuity and resource, at the summit of his authority and prestige, enjoying an overwhelming parliamentary majority and the support of his Cabinet colleagues – to suppose that this prince of politicians lacked the skills to outmanoeuvre a pair of political outsiders like the Twins, and that his hold on power hinged on the ability of the *Americans* to talk them over – is to enter the realm of make-believe. That he appears to have woven a temporary spell over the Americans is a tribute to his powers of mystification. Fact rather than fancy, however, suggests that from first to last, before, during and long after the Conference, Lloyd George always intended, as he declared on the hustings, 'that Germany must pay the costs of the war up to the limit of her capacity',[110] whatever that might be; and that he sent the Twins to Paris and kept them there because he believed, and rightly, that they would fight for that limit as no one else would.

It was not simply, as Keynes complained, that Cunliffe 'was brought in for electioneering and parliamentary purposes',[111] though it is true that Lloyd George was determined not to lose face with his backbenchers by falling short of the expectations which he had aroused. It was rather that the slogans which he so effectively proclaimed at the hustings genuinely reflected the policy which he had adopted in the belief that it best served Britain's interests. However flexible or devious his tactics, he never lost sight of that policy. Its best chance of success lay, not with Keynes or Montagu, both moderates, both in fundamental agreement with the Americans, both anxious, like most of his colleagues in the end, to close with the Germans – but with the Twins, ever ready to stand up to the Americans, ignore the Germans and hold out for the uttermost. Cunliffe, blunt and brusque, made no bones about warning an indignant Lamont that his attitude to reparations was 'playing into Boche hands'.[112] With the Twins in post, faithful guardians of his cause, Lloyd George could also avoid descending personally into the fray and doing battle with Wilson or House. Rather he could engage their sympathies by dwelling on the embarrassment in which, he said, he was placed by the Twins' intransigence. In reality, as between the Twins and the Treasury, in Balfour's defining words, 'the Prime Minister has been largely guided by *their* opinion, and their view has often been right against the Treasury'.[113]

To concentrate, then, on what Lloyd George actually did: what emerges is that he adhered consistently to what may be called a 'hard line' on the principle of reparations, while remaining ever alert to the possibility of some plausible quick solution to the problem which, of the many challenges of peacemaking, he called 'the most baffling and perplexing of all'.[114] Nor did his strategy derive from mere imperialist greed, uninformed by broader considerations. The issue was not so much 'spoils to the victors' as the need to make up losses and redress balances. At his famous – or infamous – election speech at Bristol on 11 December 1918, with his pledge to 'make Germany pay', he went straight to the heart of the matter. The fact was, as he pointed out, that *vis-à-vis* Germany, 'the war has cost her less than it has cost us'. 'It is absolutely indefensible', he asserted, 'that a person who is in the wrong and who has lost should pay less than the person who was declared to be in the right and who has won.'[115] Even in the Fontainebleau Memorandum, that classic statement of his considered – and liberal – convictions, his thinking on reparations was dominated by an accurate perception of postwar geopolitics. 'In estimating Germany's capacity to pay', so ran a résumé of those views, 'the following considerations may be taken into account. Germany's indebtedness today is less than that of Great Britain and less than that of France when the devastation of her territory is taken into account. Her population, even taking new frontiers into account, will probably be 50 per cent greater than that of France or Great Britain.'[116] Britain's debts to America imposed 'a heavy handicap in commercial competition with the United States and other nations'.[117] Hence the need to exact 'as large an indemnity out of Germany as possible'.[118]

Here were hard facts, the determinants of postwar Europe. However much liberals might deplore it, 'make Germany pay' was as much an imperative of *raison d'état* as it was a populist slogan. However much or however little Germany might pay, Lloyd George was determined – how could he not be? – that Britain must have her fair share;[119] and his moves towards that end were directed as much against France and America as against Germany. From the start of Anglo–American wranglings, when President Wilson resisted the demand for war costs, Lloyd George warned Cunliffe not to yield. Finding Wilson immovable on that score, he first gave the Americans the impression of flexibility, of his willingness to accept a £6 billion or even £5 billion figure, conditional on endorsement by the Twins; but then veered round to an outright refusal, casting the blame on them. Even in the Fontainebleau Memorandum he avoided naming a specific sum; and while he did urge in that document a 30-year limit for payment, he abandoned this within days for the open-ended timescale of 50 years or more which Cunliffe had proposed from the start to prevent Germany from evading payment by procrastination or default.[120] The final crisis saw Lloyd George still refusing to name any sum despite his colleagues' almost unanimous pleas. He insisted that Britain should abate none of her claims. He echoed both Cunliffe and Sumner in pointing out that 'the Allies could have included much more' in their demands.[121] 'Why should the Allies surrender any part of their legitimate claim?' he asked. 'If Germany could not pay, it meant that the British taxpayer had to pay.'[122] If, crudely put, reparations were a game of 'beggar-my-neighbour' with the Germans, then Cunliffe had put it crudely from the start: 'it is rather a choice of who is to be ruined, we or them?'[123]

There was much to be said, and much was said, in favour of a fixed sum. Pressed by the Americans and by his own delegation and Cabinet colleagues to come to terms, to 'look at the matter from a large point of view', as Smuts pleaded, 'and not ask the impossible',[124] Lloyd George readily allowed that 'a great deal of criticism was founded upon the fact that the amount of Germany's liability was undefined. He agreed that it would be better to define it.'[125] As he pointed out repeatedly, however, it could not be in Britain's interest to accept the German counter-offer of £5 billion, if, as he said, invoking Cunliffe's totals, they might look to

Germany for 'somewhere between £5 and £11 billion'.[126] Keynes's credibility with Lloyd George must have been badly damaged by the counter-offer, which, as Lloyd George reminded his colleagues, exceeded the Treasury's highest estimate of German capacity by 40 per cent.[127] The Prime Minister favoured Cunliffe's £12 billion figure as a hedge against settling too soon for a sum which might not only prove less than Germany could afford, but would be largely or even entirely consumed by French and Belgian claims for war damage, claims already of a magnitude which he described as 'almost incredible',[128] and which, as matters stood, took precedence over Britain's war pensions, so that 'it would all be in favour of France and against the British Empire'.[129] To the protesting Barnes, he wrote an incisive statement of the essential dilemma:

> There is no doubt it would be better to fix a sum if we could agree on the figure. The difficulty is first of all to ascertain it; the next is to secure agreement amongst the Allies as to the amount; and in the third place to secure an arrangement as to the proportions in which it is to be distributed. If you have any plan that will meet these three difficulties you will have solved the most baffling problem in the Peace Treaty.[130]

These are trenchant and challenging words. They deserve the historian's respect.

In the light of later events, it might indeed have been well to set a final figure then and there. But hindsight is a poor guide to historical understanding. Knowledge on the salient issue was then conspicuously wanting. No one at Paris could foretell the long-term capacity of a revived Germany.[131] The answer was anyone's guess – so why not Cunliffe's? Lloyd George assured his delegation that all he sought was 'a reasonable figure'.[132] But in the current state of ignorance, this could mean anything. Under these circumstances, scepticism made good sense. 'He [Lloyd George] did not say that the Germans could pay a particular sum or could not pay it.'[133] The experts offered contradictory advice. He kept an open mind and kept open his options. What point was there in tying oneself to a purely notional figure, if Germany might subsequently prove able to pay more, perhaps much more? Rather than speculate, better to wait on events, leaving it to the permanent Reparations Commission to determine, year by year and in accordance with data as they became available, the actual limits of German capacity and to adjust the scale of payments accordingly, if necessary allowing postponement or even partial waiver. 'That', as he said, 'was on the assumption that Germany could not pay.' But, Lloyd George insisted, 'he was not prepared to accept that assumption', given the advice he was receiving from Cunliffe. 'We should not water down our claim just when we were being assured that Germany could pay.'[134]

Lloyd George took his decision advisedly, and in consciousness of the problems, inseparable from reparations, of international transfer and of competition from German exports.[135] Whatever economists might say – and they were not all of Keynes's mind – common sense suggested that Britain could hardly be the loser from an influx of cash and goods from Germany.[136] The alternative, to let Germany off lightly, was unthinkable, economically as well as politically.[137] If, as was the case, the deflationary policies recommended by Cunliffe as chairman of the Committee on Currency and Foreign Exchanges were accepted by the Treasury, where, in debt-ridden Britain, was money to be found for reconstruction and 'homes for heroes'?[138] The conundrum of reparations was complex and multi-dimensional. It involved momentous national and international issues. In the circumstances under which he arrived at it, Lloyd George's decision for postponement, however much affected by immediate political convenience, is also attributable to long-term views and has even been hailed as a triumph of pragmatism and good sense.[139]

V

Some of the Americans, in their post-Conference disenchantment, not only made a scapegoat of Cunliffe but even questioned his sanity. 'I think he was a bit mad', Lamont concluded: 'To everyone who knew him as intimately as I did…his conduct was simply inexplicable and inexcusable.'[140] For Keynes, contempt for Cunliffe came naturally. 'Who that knows him', he wrote, 'could suppose that his opinion as to Germany's capacity to pay was of the slightest value?'[141] Lloyd George himself, in *The Truth about the Peace Treaties*, chose to moralise on Cunliffe's 'ravings'. 'It is what happens', he pronounced, 'when men of natural and disciplined sobriety of mind suddenly lose control of their judgment.'[142] His censoriousness was disingenuous: at the time, as the record shows, for all the subtlety of the one and the bluntness of the other, their objectives were identical.

Later historians have been more open-minded than Keynes. Etienne Mantoux, famously, in 1944, in *The Carthaginian Peace or The Economic Consequences of Mr Keynes*, and others more recently, have argued, for what it is worth, that it was within Germany's capacity to pay the figures set in 1921, and more.[143] In 1919, reparations also involved broader considerations, transcending the single issue of capacity. To German protests at the inroads that reparations would make on their economy and standards of living, Cunliffe rejoined that it was not *German* territory that had been invaded and ravaged for four years, nor German factories, coal-mines and railways looted and dynamited to eliminate postwar competition. As he wrote to Lloyd George, 'I should like to say a few words after a recent visit to the devastated areas of France, but forbear.'[144] Furthermore, if the Germans paid nothing substantial before 1926, as was explicit in their counter-offer, this could only be to France's detriment and to the advantage of Germany, 'whose mills', as Cunliffe pointed out, 'are ready to start as soon as the raw material is available'.[145]

Cunliffe, Robert Cecil recalled, 'had courage and tenacity, but no intellect'.[146] Keynes sneered that Cunliffe 'evidently had the advantage of knowing his own mind, perhaps not a difficult mind to know'.[147] Whatever his limitations, he seems to have been an honest man. His letters suggest no great relish for peacemaking. 'Paris is still extremely dull', he wrote at the beginning of April, 'and nothing to look forward to but wrangling with Yanks.'[148] Next day: 'I'm not quite wishing that I never came, but am fast reaching that stage.'[149] He was 'sick to death of the job', he told Riddell.[150] Nevertheless, he showed a sense of historical responsibility[151] and of having lived up to it. 'If I had it all over again', he wrote, 'I should do the same and I have really nothing to regret.'[152] He simply felt that Britain, with her colossal war expenses and crippling debts, was entitled to maximum compensation and should not be thwarted by American scruples as to limitation; scruples rendered particularly invidious by the refusal of the United States Treasury to contemplate any waiver of war debts,[153] by Wall Street's zeal to invest in Germany rather than France, and by America's long insistence on retaining a wholly disproportionate part of Germany's merchant navy.[154] 'I never want to to see or hear another Yank!' he expostulated.[155]

Cunliffe, it was said, 'was often out of his depths in the refinements of complicated financial theory'.[156] He never denied it. 'I smile to think how I am mistaken for a financier', he wrote.[157] As Governor of the Bank his methods had been instinctive rather than ratiocinative. Asked how he knew which bills to approve, he replied, 'I smell them.'[158] Giving evidence to a royal commission and pressed to quantify the Bank's reserves, he would only repeat that they were 'very, very considerable'.[159] By the same instinct, he knew that the sums which Germany would be capable of paying in years to come were 'very considerable',[160] even if he did not know – and, as he repeated, 'I do not know, and nobody knows' – how much.[161] The figure of £24 billion, on his admission, was pure guesswork. He agreed that many would find the figure 'enormous, monstrous'.[162] Yet he quickly changed course for reality in his willingness within days to settle for less than half that amount. When Hughes, 'the ineffable Hughes', as Robert Cecil called him,[163] still held out for the full £24 billion and continued to urge defiance of America, Cunliffe pointedly reminded him that 'if the United States excluded German bonds from her market, they would become valueless, and the Allies would get nothing.'[164]

'You are ordered here and ordered there', Cunliffe complained to Riddell: 'Do this and do that. But no-one ever says, "Good dog!"'[165] The chance remark suggests a clue to his relationship with Lloyd George: for the role which lent him most value in Lloyd George's eyes was indeed that of a watchdog, an old mastiff, fierce and bad-tempered, but obstinate, loyal and a good sniffer. Lloyd George had trusted Cunliffe ever since the crisis of 1914. He described him to Riddell as 'a sagacious old boy'. 'When any proposal was made which L.G. thought doubtful, he turned to Cunliffe and asked his opinion. If he replied "I don't like it", L.G. knew that it would not be accepted and acted accordingly.'[166] At the end of the war, the Prime Minister again confirmed: 'He's a good old fellow, very inarticulate, but he has good judgment.'[167] 'I liked him', he recalled in his *War Memoirs*, 'I relied on his shrewdness, his common sense and instinct.'[168] In contrast to his later aspersions in *The Truth about the Peace Treaties* on 'the inflated estimates of Lord Cunliffe',[169] these earlier verdicts have the ring of truth. Lloyd George valued Cunliffe's advice because it was the advice he wanted to hear, an echo of his own wishes, a projection of his own policy. At the supreme crisis, when the Prime Minister's colleagues were almost all for leniency, Cunliffe said that the German counter-offer of £5 billion would not do.[170] Lloyd George agreed, and 'acted accordingly'.

Cunliffe urged his subcommittee to 'reckon something more indeterminate than capital', namely Germany's productive capacity, or what he called 'the credit of a hard-working, well-trained industrial population',[171] especially if, under the treaty's disarmament provisions, 'millions of men would be employed in useful work, and earning money, part of which could go to make good the damage done to the Allies'.[172] Cunliffe saw no reason to 'let the Hun down gently';[173] and neither did Lloyd George. 'He did not think', he told his delegates, 'that the time had quite come for letting Germany off anything.'[174] On reparations,

Lloyd George's moral indignation kept breaking through, just as it did over punishing the Kaiser. 'You must remember', he told the House of Commons, 'that Germany suffered less than her victims. Louvain is not in Prussia. France is not in Pomerania. The devastated territories are not in Brandenburg.'[175] This echoed what Cunliffe had written to him. It may be, as has been suggested, that Lloyd George was actuated by 'the streak of Calvinism in his soul which believed in retribution'.[176] If so, the belief was not unique to him. The nation as a whole believed that it had gone to war for justice' sake. The historian who looks down with Olympian detachment on such sentiments fails in the task of grasping the genuine, though short-lived conviction in Britain that to 'make Germany pay' was a fundamental act of restitution. As Lloyd George said: 'Those who ought to pay were those who caused the loss.'[177]

VI

Lord Cunliffe barely outlived the Conference. He died suddenly on 6 January 1920. His name, 'almost a household word', said the *Times*, was soon forgotten.[178] Keynes's *Economic Consequences of the Peace* had just appeared, to immediate and shattering effect. It tore to shreds Cunliffe's findings on the Hughes Committee and the Cunliffe subcommittee report.[179] It endorsed German complaints that Cunliffe's demands would reduce Germany to penury and ruin. 'My book', Keynes noted in March, 'has now been published in England for some three months, and, although it has been subjected to much criticism, no one has yet made a serious attempt to controvert my arguments as to Germany's capacity to pay.'[180] It was true.

At the moment when Keynes left Paris on his crusade against the treaty, Cunliffe too, though for different reasons, had also pondered the treaty's fate – 'another scrap of paper', he called it.[181] Another portrait, strangely potent, of Cunliffe, by Augustus John, very different from the Dodd caricature, conveys an unexpected image: the pensive, sad-eyed repose of an old man in prophetic contemplation. Shortly before his death, Cunliffe made a prediction: 'Keynes will write a brilliant book about the Peace Conference, which will do unfathomable damage.'[182]

3
The Treaty that Never Was: Lloyd George and the French Connection, 1919

Anglo-French treaty of alliance crucial to the Treaty of Versailles—collapse of treaty of alliance—Lloyd George's amateurism?—crisis over the Rhineland— Lloyd George's intervention—his unprecedented offer to France— qualifications—the Empire—the casus foederis—*relevance of the American guarantee—drafting of British guarantee—was Clemenceau aware? Lloyd George's strategy and tactics—Anglo-French disagreements over enforcement of Versailles*

> The argument that Monsieur Clemenceau was led, as regards the safety of France on her eastern flank, into a characteristic British trap, is one which . . . lies not far below the level of the French consciousness.
>
> Foreign Office memorandum, 9 May 1922

> We seek him here, we seek him there,
> Those Frenchies seek him everywhere.
> Is he in heaven? – Is he in hell?
> That damned, elusive Pimpernel!
>
> *The Scarlet Pimpernel*, chapter 12

The signing of the Treaty of Versailles on the afternoon of 28 June 1919: a scene sharply etched in popular memory. To the modern visitor to the Palace of Versailles, filing through the Hall of Mirrors, is pointed out, like some relic, the table on which the treaty was signed. Was it of historic interest, Balfour asked Clemenceau. 'No', Clemenceau replied, 'but it will serve'.[1] In the event, the table has outlasted the treaty . . . Little known, by contrast with the final act at Versailles, almost indeed of antiquarian interest only, it seems, is the meeting on the morning of the same day, at President Wilson's apartment in the Place des Etats Unis, of Lloyd George, Clemenceau and Wilson. Yet the occasion was of the utmost significance at the time, for there were signed the Anglo-French and Franco-American treaties of alliance, or guarantee treaties, equal in importance or secondary only to the Treaty of Versailles itself. Professor William Keylor rightly numbers them among 'the most neglected but important features of the peace settlement'.[2] The two collateral treaties supplemented, buttressed and indeed made possible the Treaty of Versailles. They represented 'the crowning glory of Monsieur Clemenceau's policy', in the words of his right-hand man, André Tardieu.[3] Of the two treaties, that with Britain was incomparably the more important. Versailles would never have come about – Clemenceau would not have agreed to sign it – had not Lloyd George first set his hand to a treaty of alliance with France stipulating that 'Great Britain agrees to come immediately to her assistance in the event of any unprovoked movement of aggression against her being made by Germany.'[4]

Ratification followed with speed and enthusiasm, Lloyd George steering it unopposed through the House of Commons as the Anglo-French Treaty (Defence of France) Act 1919. Clemenceau secured overwhelming approval in the National Assembly, Tardieu informing the Chamber of Deputies, on Lloyd George's assurance, that 'in a few months' time' the two countries would also be linked by a Channel tunnel.[5] Formalities between London and Paris were exchanged in November. All seemed set for a postwar era of Anglo-French cooperation, a renewal of the Entente, a revival of the late comradeship-in-arms and a solid guarantee of the peace of Europe. A month later, French policy lay in ruins. The guarantee to France, which Clemenceau described as 'nothing less than the ultimate sanction of the Peace Treaty' and 'the keystone of European peace', was a dead letter, an undertaking, in his mournful reproach, 'silently abandoned by England'.[6] The failure of the treaty marked a postwar parting of the ways between Britain and France. It prised open the cracks in the Entente that had emerged during the Conference. It widened the basic divergences in the policies of both countries towards each other and towards Germany. It led repeatedly to recrimination, confrontation and strife between all three.

Historians have mostly averted their gaze from what Philip Bell has called 'a disastrous episode',[7] or have consigned it to a half-forgotten footnote in the annals of the Peace Conference, an unlucky slip in Lloyd

George's foreign policy, a bold but ill-fated initiative, frustrated by circumstances beyond his control. The fault, if fault there was, lay with others. The failure of the alliance to materialise arose, after all, from the failure of the United States' Senate to ratify the analogous guarantee treaty which President Wilson had signed on behalf of America. Blame for the debacle therefore falls on Wilson for political ineptitude, or worse, for neglecting to secure or even to solicit senatorial approval – rather than on Lloyd George.[8]

There were, it is true, critics like Lord Hardinge, Permanent Under-Secretary at the Foreign Office. Nominally Organising Secretary of the Conference, but embittered by his effective replacement in that role by Colonel Hankey at Lloyd George's instigation, Hardinge, as a professional diplomatist, retained a lasting scorn for what he saw as Lloyd George's amateurism and lack of serious credentials as a peacemaker, his airy indifference to Foreign Office advice, and his ready resort to 'stunts' and improvisations. Thirty years after the event, Hardinge singled out the Anglo-French treaty as the most egregious of Lloyd George's attempts to run foreign policy as a 'one man band'. 'I doubt if any treaty of such vital and far-reaching importance', he reflected, 'has ever been negotiated in such a thoughtless and light-hearted manner.'[9] Now whether justified or not – and, as will appear, the evidence suggests that Lloyd George's underlying approach in the matter was neither thoughtless nor light-hearted – such criticism relates to the Prime Minister's methods, not to his policy as such. It concerns means, not ends. Whilst Lloyd George's volatility in the handling of foreign policy can scarcely be denied, in the matter of the Anglo-French alliance few historians have questioned his good intentions.

I

The Anglo-French treaty was devised by Lloyd George as a means of resolving the grave diplomatic crisis which divided the Conference over French claims on the Rhineland. The Rhineland issue had been quietly simmering since the armistice. It came to a head in February 1919. By mid-March it threatened the very continuance of the Conference. As Philip Kerr, temporarily deputed to handle the matter for Britain, reported to Lloyd George, the French demand was 'being pushed for all it is worth by Clemenceau'.[10] The question exposed fundamental and unbridgeable differences of principle between Britain and France. Its importance for France was succinctly conveyed to the Acting Foreign

Secretary, Lord Curzon, by Paul Cambon, France's ambassador in London. It was, Cambon stated, 'the main preoccupation of all Frenchmen'.[11]

For the French, the Rhine was not merely a natural strategic frontier or the culmination of a long historical process – *l'idée fixe de l'histoire de France*[12] – but the gage of their security, their ultimate protection against an inevitable resurgence of German power. It was a simple question of geography, manpower and logistics, set out with Euclidian precision in a series of memoranda variously drafted by Marshal Foch and André Tardieu. Foch indeed had framed the conditions of armistice with a particular view to the question. Since 1814, the left bank of the Rhine had served as a springboard for five successive invasions of France. In 1914, only Russia's intervention had permitted the 'miracle of the Marne' and prevented the fall of Paris. In 1918, with Russia out of the war, the Ludendorff offensive had brought the Germans once more within range of the capital. The postwar threat was all the greater to a France whose geopolitical inferiority to Germany was more, not less marked than in 1914. In a future war, unhindered and perhaps even abetted by Russia, Germany would once more hurl her storm-troopers across Belgium and northern France. Unless France acquired, if not sovereignty, then control of the Rhineland; unless Germany were deprived permanently of the use of the territory as a launching-pad for aggression – then France remained at Germany's mercy and the Great War had been fought in vain. As Foch protested with lucid intensity:

> There is no overriding principle which compels a victorious people, when it has recovered in a war of defence the means indispensable to its security – to restore them to its adversary. There is no principle which can oblige a free people to live under continual threat... To give up the Rhine barrier is to concede this unimaginable horror: that through our voluntary abandonment of the Rhine, Germany, even though defeated... would still be capable of recommencing her designs as if she had been victorious.[13]

In French eyes, then, the Rhineland was not so much a part of the spoils of war, as an absolute and irreducible necessity. 'There is no other way to ensure the security of France', said Clemenceau.[14]

Lloyd George and Wilson would not hear of it. So far as they were concerned, there was, despite Foch, an overriding and unanswerable objection: the Rhinelanders were Germans, as German as the Prussians or the Bavarians. The severance of German territory would be the most flagrant violation imaginable of the principle of national self-determination so often and so earnestly proclaimed by the President, the principle on which, as had been solemnly agreed with Germany at the armistice, peace was to be made. When the French disclaimed any plans to annex the Rhineland and argued simply for its independence, Wilson rejoined that independence could no more be forced on a people against their will than it could be forcibly withheld from them. As for the detachment of the Rhineland in any shape or form, 'nothing', Wilson declared, 'would induce him to consent' to it.[15] Lloyd George agreed emphatically. It would be, he said from the first and more than once repeated, the creation of an Alsace-Lorraine in reverse, the seed of a new war of revenge.[16] 'On the Rhineland question', Clemenceau recalled, 'Mr Wilson would shake his head ominously, while Mr Lloyd George assumed an expression of determined opposition.'[17] Between the imperative of French security and the imperative of national self-determination no compromise seemed possible.

Clemenceau had not raised the issue sooner with Lloyd George except fleetingly, during a visit to London shortly after the armistice, when he employed Foch as his mouthpiece. When Foch suggested that a Rhine-land detached from Germany would soon become reconciled to the blessings of French rule, Bonar Law pointed gloomily to England's centuries-old experience in Ireland.[18] Clemenceau had chosen not to cloud the immediate postwar goodwill, the cordiality of his reception in London or the genuine gratitude which France owed to her ally. His first and predominant object was to maintain good relations with Britain. For the sake of these, as he told the Chamber of Deputies, he would make every sacrifice.[19] He had already made concessions to Lloyd George in the Middle East in return for what he understood to be Lloyd George's acquiescence on the Rhineland. He had been reproached for delaying to put forward France's principal demand. He now made up for this bluntly and with vigour. He rejected, he told Kerr on 7 March, 'the principle of self-determination which allowed a man to clutch at your throat' whenever it suited him; nor was he disposed to set any time limit to the 'enforced separation' of the Rhineland from Germany.[20]

Matters came to a head on 12 March. Tardieu, representing Clemen-ceau, pointed to the broader considerations of *raison d'état*, the balance of power and the peace of Europe, which were allowed to override Ger-man claims to self-determination in the case of Danzig, Austria and the

Sudetenland. Why, he asked Kerr, did these same principles not apply, and with equal or still greater validity, when it came to protecting France 'not from a theoretical danger, but from a known danger, a danger which epitomises the entire history of the last war'.[21] Reporting to Lloyd George, Kerr recommended strenuous defiance: 'I would resist the Tardieu proposition to the end.'[22]

That afternoon, Clemenceau himself angrily sought out Lloyd George, to have it out directly. Lloyd George declared that he would never agree to a separate Rhineland, adding that since Germany was to be disarmed, the Rhineland was superfluous to French needs. Clemenceau retorted that for his part he would never give up the Rhineland. 'I am not yielding on the point', he assured President Poincaré afterwards.[23] A Cabinet colleague recorded Clemenceau's view: 'Lloyd George is very fickle: quick-minded but shameless. Lloyd George promises a thing, gives his word and goes back on it, gets out of it the next day. Having assured Clemenceau that he would support his policy on the left bank of the Rhine, he told him that he did not agree with him and had reservations.'[24] The Conference was deadlocked and near to collapse.

Two days later came Lloyd George's dramatic intervention.[25] At noon on 14 March, President Wilson arrived in Paris on his return from Washington, where he had been obliged to attend the opening of Congress. Immediately on reaching his residence, he was visited by Lloyd George on a matter of the highest urgency and confidentiality. Precisely what arguments Lloyd George employed in this private interview, we do not know. No record was kept of their discussion, nor of the further colloquy held the same afternoon at the Hotel Crillon, where the two leaders asked Clemenceau to meet them for an immediate exchange. No official or secretary was present at either of these top-level encounters, held, as Colonel Hankey records, 'under very "hush-hush" conditions'.[26] What is known is that, then and there, Lloyd George made to Clemenceau the offer of a defensive alliance with Britain in the form of a guarantee pact against Germany. Wilson for his part undertook to put an identical proposal to the Senate. On the strength of these pledges, Clemenceau eventually and reluctantly abandoned his demand for the separation of the Rhineland, though he maintained across six weeks a stubborn and in the end successful struggle for its temporary occupation by the Allies and its permanent demilitarisation by Germany. Alliance with Britain and America replaced the Rhine frontier as the basis of French policy at the Conference. Lloyd George's initiative had broken the deadlock and enabled the work of peacemaking, gravely imperilled, to resume.[27]

II

The importance of Lloyd George's role cannot be exaggerated: not only because it resolved the immediate crisis but also because it determined all that followed. Lloyd George had broached the issue boldly and on his own authority, without apparently consulting any of his colleagues, whether in the Empire delegation or in the Cabinet. He appears not even to have informed Balfour until several weeks later; and even then he treated his Foreign Secretary as a mere drafting amanuensis.[28] The Anglo-French alliance was Lloyd George's own brainchild, the progeny of that fertile and astute imagination; a striking gesture of solidarity, a solemn act of state. It was, as Clemenceau recalled, 'an unprecedented historical event'.[29] The treaty was rightly understood as an extraordinary departure in British foreign policy, 'an astounding innovation', in the words of Tardieu.[30] 'It is not usual', Palmerston observed in 1841, 'for England to enter into engagements with reference to cases which have not actually arisen.'[31] Here was Lloyd George, in peacetime, offering a renewal of the wartime Entente in the shape of an unconditional military guarantee. 'What a stroke of fortune for France!' Clemenceau exclaimed.[32] The offer was irresistible:[33] it was meant to be. Lloyd George understood that nothing less than a full and unqualified promise of commitment could persuade Clemenceau to abate his claim to the Rhineland. 'It was proffered', he agreed, 'as an answer to those who claimed that the left bank of the Rhine should be annexed to France';[34] and he coupled his offer with the no less striking undertaking to construct a Channel tunnel for the rapid transfer, in the contemplated emergency, of British troops to France. Clemenceau, we are told, was 'much moved'.[35]

In the days and weeks that followed until final signature of the pact, Lloyd George followed up his offer with a variety of supplementary assurances. He expressed Britain's readiness, in the event of a German attack on France, 'to place all our forces at her disposal'.[36] His words suggest the kind of unified command entrusted in 1918 to Marshal Foch. He hinted at Anglo-French military conversations on the pre-war model.[37] His overall message to Clemenceau, frequently, volubly and eloquently articulated, was clear and unequivocal: 'you may count on us'. He proclaimed it in his Fontainebleau Memorandum, that manifesto of his policy.[38] Amid terse wranglings on the future of the Saarland, Clemenceau arguing obstinately for its annexation to France, Lloyd George invoked the inviolability of his plighted word. Clemenceau must understand, he loftily asseverated, that Britain and America could no more break their word to Germany over self-determination in the Saar than they could renege on their promise to defend France.[39] When Clemenceau responded to the Fontainebleau Memorandum with a counter-argument of some acerbity, Lloyd George irately reminded him of 'the pledge I offer on behalf of Britain to come to the aid of France if the invader threatens'.[40]

As for formal undertakings: on 22 April, Lloyd George assented to a written memorandum of agreement with Clemenceau, incorporating the fundamentals of an Anglo-French convention,[41] offering, two days later, 'to publish in full our agreement with France to guarantee her against the risk of invasion'.[42] On 6 May, he formally handed to Clemenceau a protocol of alliance, signed by himself and Balfour the day before; and its existence was announced by Tardieu later the same day at a plenary session of the Conference.[43] Two weeks later, when Clemenceau complained of British bad faith in the Syrian question, Lloyd George indignantly retorted. 'I do not think that France has the right to complain of Great Britain's loyalty', he declared; 'British opinion freely offers to place the whole of Great Britain's strength at France's disposal if she is in danger.'[44] What more could he have said or done by way of assurance?

III

And yet there was more to Lloyd George's assurances than met the eye. Or rather, as it turned out, there was less. A cloud of qualifications and reservations crept slowly across the clear horizon of his original undertaking. How long, to take an elementary stipulation, was the treaty to remain in force? It appeared to be of unlimited duration.[45] The protocol of 5 May stated that the treaty would remain in force until the contracting parties agreed that the League of Nations afforded France 'sufficient protection'.[46] In view of Clemenceau's well-known scepticism towards the League, this suggests that the treaty would last for as long as France considered it necessary. Addressing the Empire delegation the same day, however, Lloyd George told a different story. The treaty, he said, would last 'for a period of fifteen years, coterminous with the military occupation of the Rhineland'.[47] 'Had the Prime Minister intended to deceive?' Professor Nelson speculates. 'Or had he inadvertently revealed a private misunderstanding, or was he simply confused?'[48] Forgetfulness or confusion seems the most likely explanation, since the plain words of the draft were there for all to hear; indeed Lloyd George read them aloud to his delegates. Even so, the incident suggests a certain casualness towards a salient term of the promised alliance.

When Lloyd George pledged Britain to defend France, what did he mean by 'Britain'? On the face of it there could be no doubt. Britain meant the British Empire; and 'the British Empire' is specified both in the Fontainebleau Memorandum and in the Anglo-French treaty itself. Britain's declaration of war in 1914 was automatically binding on the Empire, a single constitutional entity. But the war had brought demands for a looser relationship with the mother country. When Lloyd George informed the Empire delegation on May 5 that 'Clemenceau desired the Dominions to join in his guarantee', the Prime Ministers of Canada and South Africa at once demurred. Lloyd George thereupon assured them that the Dominions would *not* be bound by the treaty.[49] In the signed protocol which he presented to Clemenceau the next day, a clause was appended stating that 'the obligation imposed under this treaty shall not be binding on the Dominions of the British Empire until the treaty is ratified by the Parliament of the Dominion concerned'.[50] On the eve of final signature, he explained to Clemenceau that he was not authorised to sign for the Dominions.[51] The implication seems to have been, not that the Dominion Prime Ministers would not sign in due course; merely that, as British Prime Minister, Lloyd George could not, from a constitutional point of view, sign for them. It was just a matter of form. Given the strong expression of Dominion feeling against the treaty, this suggests a degree of disingenuousness. In the event, Canada, South Africa, Australia and New Zealand, whose sons had fought on French soil in their tens of thousands, were exempted at a stroke of the pen from Lloyd George's pledge to Clemenceau, implied and express, of immediate aid from a worldwide Empire.

The definition of a *casus foederis* also turned out to be less clear-cut from the gloss which Lloyd George put upon it to his delegation than appeared in his promise of instant succour. The treaty laid down that British intervention would be activated 'in the event of any unprovoked movement of aggression' on the part of Germany; and 'movement of aggression' was defined in terms of specific acts of violation of the demilitarised Rhineland. At that same meeting of the delegation, how-ever, chaired by Lloyd George, Bonar Law observed that 'the words "unprovoked aggression" protected *us*'. Whether an 'aggression was provoked or not' would be for Britain to decide.[52] Bonar Law would not have given such an emphatic assurance without Lloyd George's approval. And indeed, in a letter to General Botha, the South African Prime Minister, on 26 June, two days before signing the guarantee, Lloyd

George confirmed that 'we ourselves shall be the sole judge of what constitutes unprovoked aggression'.[53]

We have noted Lloyd George's repeated assurances to Clemenceau, spoken and written, of Britain's commitment. His overall pledge was unequivocal: if Germany attacked France, Britain would go to France's defence. However much whittled down in detail, that much, at least, was clear; and for Clemenceau, it was enough. Urged by Poincaré to press for details, to demand a formal military convention, above all on no account to renounce the claim to the Rhineland before the British and American guarantees were ratified, Clemenceau contemptuously refused. Was he to demean himself, undermine his negotiating authority and sow irritation and mistrust by legalistic cavils?[54] 'In politics', he declared, 'and above all in diplomacy, promises must be sacred'.[55] He had the word of the British Prime Minister. He had given his own. At a Cabinet meeting on 25 April, his ministers gave formal approval both to the Anglo-French alliance and to the Treaty of Versailles. Whatever misgivings they expressed outside the council chamber of the Elysée – and there were bitter exchanges in the corridors – France was committed.

IV

During the sixteen weeks from 14 March, when Lloyd George first made his offer of alliance, to 27 June, the eve of signature, at no time did he suggest that the Anglo-French treaty might be in any way contingent on the attitude of the United States. Writing to Bonar Law on 31 March, he stressed the unilateral nature of Britain's pledge, adding, 'Wilson is inclined to join if he can persuade the Senate.'[56] Certainly Wilson never intended any connection between the two pacts. On the contrary, he was particularly anxious to dissociate them, since any such link with Britain would be anathema to the Senate, Republican-dominated, isolationist, and likely to oppose the American guarantee in any event.[57] Colonel House, while doubtful that the Senate would ratify, noted that 'England was resolved to give this guarantee, whether the United States did or not.'[58] His informant? Lloyd George, who had told him so on 12 March, two days before making his offer to Clemenceau. Moreover, when announcing to the Empire delegation on 5 May the existence of the British guarantee, and admitting that he was 'apprehensive lest the United States might refuse' to ratify Wilson's counterpart, Lloyd George gave no indication that he regarded the two treaties as in any way connected other than in their subject-matter.[59]

Clemenceau too was under this impression. While grateful to Wilson, he set far greater store by Lloyd George's promise: 'The American agreement was secondary', he wrote.[60] In the event of a German invasion, only British troops could reach France, with or without a Channel tunnel, in time to help stem the aggression. Clemenceau was clear in his mind that the British and American proposals comprised two distinct offers, of related but unequal weight. 'Do not forget', he recalled, 'that it was Mr Lloyd George who had made the original proposal, offering to do all he could to induce the American President to agree to it. Mr Wilson merely came in in the second line as the defender of interests less immediately concerned with us.'[61] The same, for that matter, applied to the Dominions, whose forces, like those of America, would be unable to reach France until later. It was Lloyd George's guarantee, then, which really counted. Wilson's, if it materialised, would be a welcome bonus that would guarantee the eventual outcome if the worst came to the worst. Lloyd George confirmed Clemenceau's understanding. When, on 21 May, Clemenceau pointed out how much France had conceded at the Conference, Lloyd George replied: 'If Monsieur Clemenceau has agreed to sacrifice certain claims, it is because England has promised to come to France's aid if she were attacked.'[62] Lloyd George acknowledged – and correctly acknowledged – that the overriding consideration for Clemenceau, the condition *sine qua non* of his renunciation of the Rhine frontier, was the alliance with Britain.

While drafted in similar terms, therefore, the two treaties, British and American, were distinct, separate and independent. How, then, did the British guarantee come to be linked with the American? The signed protocol of alliance which Lloyd George handed to Clemenceau on 6 May contained a clause stating that the British treaty 'will be in similar terms to that entered into by the United States and will come into force when the latter is ratified'.[63] An innocent provision on the face of it, signifying no more than that the two parallel treaties, British and American, both having the same purpose, both containing virtually identical terms, would come into effect simultaneously. It was essential to stipulate when the British treaty would become operative, and it was reasonable to synchronise that date with ratification of the American treaty. There was no other obvious or necessary link between the two treaties. Yet President Wilson dropped a curious remark. Lloyd George, Wilson observed to one of his delegates, 'had slipped a paragraph into the British note about ratification by the United States and . . . he did not think Clemenceau had noticed it'.[64] What was it that required notice by Clemenceau?

The answer becomes startlingly clear if we turn to the final draft of the treaty, which Lloyd George produced in the late afternoon of 27 June, the day before that treaty and the Treaty of Versailles were to be signed. Wilson, Lloyd George and Clemenceau were in session at the President's house, engaged in miscellaneous last-minute items of business. At 4.30 p.m. they broke off and, together with Clemenceau's Foreign Minister, Pichon, withdrew briefly to an adjoining private room. Maurice Hankey was present as secretary. Lloyd George called in Cecil Hurst, legal adviser to the Foreign Office, who, he explained, 'had prepared a text' of the Anglo-French alliance.[65] After discussion of some minor alterations, which were duly agreed, Hurst's amended version of the text was 'read to and approved by' the three leaders.[66] The final draft, then, of which there was at this stage only one copy – Hurst's – was read aloud, in English, presumably by Hurst. Into this draft a word had been added – the word 'only'. The operative clause now read that in relation to the American guarantee, the Anglo-French alliance would come into force *'only* when the latter is ratified' (emphasis added).[67] One word transformed the sense of Lloyd George's undertaking, making it wholly contingent on the fate of its American counterpart. If the Senate failed to ratify, then the Anglo-French treaty would also lapse, or rather would never come into being. At a word and in the twinkling of an eye, Lloyd George's promise vanished

> Into the air, and what seemed corporal melted
> As breath into the wind.

> Shakespeare, *Macbeth*, I, iii, 81–2

This slight though crucial amendment, notes Clemenceau's biographer, took place 'without objections from Clemenceau at the time'.[68] How could this be? Clemenceau's English was excellent; what about his attention? Did Clemenceau or Pichon even notice the introduction of the fatal qualification? Pichon we may dismiss as a timid and insignificant acolyte. 'Pichon is frightened to death of the old boy', Lloyd George noted.[69] What is inconceivable is that Clemenceau would have wittingly assented to the final draft or have signed the engrossed treaty the following morning had he had the slightest inkling of this momentous addition. But Clemenceau was a man of his word, as Lloyd George well knew. 'Clemenceau had already accepted our proposals', he recalled, 'and he never went back on an arrangement to which he had assented – however reluctantly.'[70] Having signed, moreover, it was too late for Clemenceau to retract. It was politically impossible for him to admit that he had been hoodwinked by Lloyd George, not least because his domestic critics believed that he had.[71]

V

Lloyd George's manner of negotiating the treaty with France, his repeated assurances to Clemenceau, and the reservations with which he hedged them once Clemenceau had acted on the strength of those assurances, cannot but raise suspicions. Tardieu soon voiced his. While acquitting Wilson of any taint of sharp practice, he added: 'I am not so sure of the good faith of Lloyd George. Why should he have made the assistance of Britain contingent upon ratification of the pact by Washington?'[72] Why indeed?

Answers are not hard to find. If the Senate ratified Wilson's pledge, then, in the event of an attack on France, Germany would confront both Britain and America. Indeed, as Lloyd George put it to Foch, the certainty of Anglo-American retaliation made such an attack unlikely in the extreme. In all probability, then, Britain would never be called on to fulfil Lloyd George's promise.[73] On the other hand, if war did come, then not only France but Britain too could count on American support. In this sense Wilson's pledge was as much a commitment to Britain as to France. If, however, the Senate failed to ratify, then, thanks to Lloyd George's last-minute interpolation, Britain would not be left to act alone. Britain would not be bound to do anything at all. She would be discharged altogether from the obligations of the alliance – paradoxically by the terms of the alliance itself. Lloyd George would be absolved from what one historian rightly calls his 'solemn pledge',[74] while the blame could be laid at the door of the United States. As Lloyd George confirmed to the House of Commons in December: 'If there should be such a possibility as the United States not ratifying that compact, undoubtedly we are free to reconsider our decision.'[75] Either way, Britain's liability to France was limited. Meanwhile Lloyd George's promise had served its immediate purpose of resolving the impasse over the Rhineland. It did more: it put paid to French claims to permanent control of the Rhineland. Whatever the outcome in Washington, Clemenceau's abnegation of the Rhine frontier, confirmed by the Council of Ministers on 25 April, was final and irrevocable. Subsequent attempts by French governments to revive the issue by encouraging Rhineland separatism were clandestine and embarrassed: they could never be openly avowed.

Did Lloyd George at some stage positively wish the Anglo-French alliance to come to nothing? In terms of realpolitik it was not wholly to Britain's disadvantage to distance herself from France. To break with France was to regain freedom of action. The war once over, Clemenceau recalled, Lloyd George began to adopt an attitude of antagonism towards France.[76] Deep differences at the Conference frayed the wartime solidarity, especially over reparations and Middle Eastern mandates. Above all, over differing perceptions of postwar Germany. Lloyd George told his delegates that 'he did not think that the British Empire would allow the future peace of the world to be tied to the chariot of French fury.'[77]

What, then, was in Lloyd George's mind when he made his offer to Clemenceau? Let it be assumed that the offer was sincere. Certainly he persuaded the Commons to approve the treaty without a division, using language of passionate moral conviction.[78] Why, then, did he contrive to make the British guarantee contingent on America's? The same insistent question confronts us at every turn. It was common knowledge that the Senate might not ratify Wilson's offer. The Republican majority was deeply suspicious of the League of Nations. They opposed Wilson's overseas commitments under the covenant of the League as a breach of American neutrality and even of the constitution. Lloyd George knew that the main object of Wilson's return to America in February had been to arrest this isolationist trend, and he knew that Wilson had failed.[79] He told the Empire delegation so. 'He was apprehensive', he told them on 5 May, 'lest the United States Senate might refuse the guarantee.'[80]

'Had the Prime Minister intended to mislead?' asks Professor Nelson.[81] Whether Lloyd George had decided all along that the British guarantee should hinge on Wilson's ability to sway the Senate, or whether this was an inspired afterthought, made no difference to the outcome for France. Either way, Clemenceau had reason to complain of *Albion perfide*. He staked all on the treaty with Britain – and he lost all – the American alliance, the British alliance and the Rhine frontier, a triple debacle soon to contribute to his political demise. 'I trusted Lloyd George', he admitted later, 'and he got away from me.'[82] As Birkenhead reflected: 'the man who enters into real and fierce controversy with Mr Lloyd George must think clearly, think deeply, and think ahead. Otherwise he will think too late.'[83] More important were the consequences for Anglo-French relations. More than any other consideration, it was the failure of the guarantee treaty which accentuated French feelings of vulnerability and alarm at the inadequacies of Versailles.

Was Lloyd George ever serious about the alliance? His original state of mind is crucial to an understanding of this episode. At one stage or other he decided to go back on his word to Clemenceau. Was it before or after he gave it? And was it a question of innocent, or, as Nelson asks, of fraudulent misrepresentation? Was Lloyd George a deep tactician, who plotted from the start to deprive Clemenceau of the Rhineland in return for a worthless pledge? Or was he a casual opportunist, who played the game by ear, adapting his next moves in response to shifting circumstances and emerging temptations? In support of the latter view, it may be argued that in making his original offer to France, Lloyd George acted in good faith, hoping that renunciation by Clemenceau of the Rhine frontier would remove that stumbling-block permanently from the Conference agenda. When Clemenceau then insisted on a prolonged Allied occupation of the Rhineland – the demand which aroused the most strenuous opposition in the British Empire delegation as likely to drag Britain into fresh hostilities[84] – Lloyd George changed tack and determined to qualify his original commitment.

Even if this is the correct interpretation, it follows that Lloyd George held out as inducements to Clemenceau a set of pledges which, once Clemenceau had acted on them, were each summarily whisked away. Lloyd George offered the support of the British Empire; he then exempted the Dominions. He pledged instant retaliation against specific acts of 'aggression', while confiding that it would rest with Britain to define that 'aggression'. He dangled before Clemenceau the prospect of military conversations and a Channel tunnel; the airy visions faded away. Above all, having held out the guarantee–treaty as independent and free-standing, by a last-minute sleight-of-hand he made its existence hinge on the dubious outcome of American politics. Whether he devised an elaborate hoax from the start, or whether he sprang the final trap on a last-minute impulse, made no difference to France. And if Lloyd George meant what he said, why, when it failed to become legally binding, did he not recommend acceptance of what on his own admission remained a powerful moral obligation?[85]

The suspicion of premeditated guile must be strong. Is there evidence to substantiate it? There is the evidence of Lloyd George himself. First, the negative evidence: the absence in *The Truth about the Peace Treaties* of any explanation or even any mention of the outcome of his promise to Clemenceau. His silence on the point in that eloquent and otherwise circumstantial apologia, is in itself suggestive: the dog that did not bark in the night. But there is positive evidence of his intentions. It was on 4 March 1919 that he first aired the notion of an Anglo-French treaty. 'If the United States and ourselves would guarantee France against invasion', he told the Cabinet, 'she would be satisfied.' 'This, however', he continued, 'was impossible, as the President would not hear of any entangling alliances, as he put his faith in the League of Nations.'[86] At this stage, then, Lloyd George contemplated a solution to the Rhineland problem in terms of an Anglo-American undertaking to France, but was sceptical that Wilson would agree to it. Nothing suggests that he had changed his mind ten days later when he put the proposal to Wilson himself. Indeed by that time he was certain of American opposition to Wilson's policy. In other words, when, on 14 March, both Lloyd George and Wilson made their offers to Clemenceau, Lloyd George knew that there was a more than even chance that Wilson's would come to nothing.[87]

Why, then, bring Wilson into the matter at all? Why make a point of awaiting the President's return from America and securing his offer of an American guarantee on 14 March before making his own pledge to Clemenceau in the afternoon, unless he intended all along that the two offers should be linked? He admits as much in *The Truth about the Peace Treaties*: 'I then conceived the idea of a *joint* military guarantee by America and Britain', he wrote (emphasis added).[88] This retrospective account is corroborated by his words at the time. On 23 March, in a secret policy statement, he specified 'a *joint* guarantee by the British Empire and the United States' (emphasis added).[89] When he wrote that, he had good reason to believe that Wilson's promise would come to nothing, and that consequently so would his own. The Anglo-French treaty was a masterpiece of legerdemain, a contradiction in terms, a 'joint guarantee' in the sense that it was underwritten by America, but not severally binding on Britain: so that when the underwriter backed out, the principal guarantor could also default. It was an illusionist's trick – now you see it, now you don't – and its disappearance represented not the failure but the consummation of Lloyd George's policy towards France.

So Britain was free to do as she wished. Lloyd George delighted in Macaulay's essay on Machiavelli and the wiles to which the statesman may resort.[90] No doubt he found in it recognition rather than revelation. Dissimulation was second nature to him. It was part and parcel of his repertoire, his stock-in-trade as a political escapologist. 'His mind', Milner noted, 'like the knight in chess, jumped in two directions at once, both unexpected.'[91] He gloried in such agility as marking 'the chief difference between ordinary and extraordinary men. When the extra-ordinary man is faced by a novel and difficult situation', he told Riddell, 'he extricates himself from it by adopting a plan which is at once both daring and unexpected. That is the mark of genius in a man of action.'[92]

VI

With the renunciation of the Rhine frontier and the failure of the Anglo-French alliance, the French were forced back on the Treaty of Versailles as their sole protection, and on the alternatives of enforcing it or seeing it whittled away. As it was, the treaty seemed to them precarious, lacking the 'certainties' to which they felt entitled. A profound sense of fore-boding overcame them when they contemplated it. '*C'est la paix boche*', was the verdict of Berthelot, Secretary-General of the French Foreign Office.[93] 'This is not peace', echoed Marshal Foch, adding, with proph-etic insight, 'it is an armistice for twenty years'.[94] Clemenceau's fear was not so much of imminent German attack – that was something to be guarded against in the years ahead – but of the treaty's gradual unravel-ment, its systematic non-fulfilment by the Germans.[95] There could be no resting on laurels, he warned the Chamber of Deputies. The treaty must be 'a peace of vigilance'.[96] They must not let the Germans defy it even in small particulars, lest they be emboldened to take greater liberties, and worse should follow. The French thus adopted of set purpose an attitude of strict adherence to the letter of Versailles, treating every infraction as a sufficient reason for retaliation.

The rejection of the Treaty of Versailles by the United States Senate in November 1919 and again in March 1920 struck a second colossal blow at the peace settlement. It represented a seismic shift in the balance of power, and it led to a further hardening of French attitudes. Versailles had been premised on American cooperation. America's defection left Britain and France as sole guarantors of the treaty, apart from Italy; and with France and Germany continually at loggerheads, Lloyd George was the only spokesman for a policy of leniency or flexibility towards Ger-many. 'If only we could get rid of Germany', Clemenceau muttered to Lloyd George, 'there would be peace in Europe.'[97] Lloyd George warned against killing the goose that laid the golden egg.

The Treaty of Versailles came into force on 10 January 1920. Diplo-matic relations with Germany were resumed for the first time since 1914, Clemenceau mastering his repugnance at having to shake hands with a German representative. 'I spat on the place in order to commem-orate it', he told Lloyd George.[98] It was almost his last act as Prime

Minister. Within a week, France and Britain were at odds. Lloyd George, first and most fervent of the advocates of prosecutions for war crimes and avid for the trial of the Kaiser, demanded his extradition from Holland; but when the French produced their own list of wanted men, headed by Bethmann-Hollweg, Ludendorff and Hindenburg, Lloyd George was furious, and complained of wanton provocation.

In April, when civil unrest broke out in the demilitarised Rhineland, the German government sent in 20 000 troops to restore order. This was in clear breach of the Rhineland provisions of the Treaty of Versailles, so doggedly fought for by Clemenceau. The French retaliated by despatching their own troops into Frankfurt and Darmstadt. Britain was neither consulted nor forewarned. The presence of Moorish and Senegalese contingents in the occupying forces added to British as well as German indignation; for it was against France, not Germany, that British anger was directed. Lloyd George denounced the annexationist plans for the Ruhr which he suspected the French of hatching. The French complained of the loss of the Rhine frontier.[99] Lord Curzon, now Foreign Secretary, summoned Paul Cambon, and subjected the veteran ambassador to a tirade of almost unbridled ferocity. Cambon's successor, the Comte de Saint-Aulaire, was to characterise Anglo-French relations as a *mésentente cordiale*. The British chargé d'affaires in Paris agreed. 'A marked hostility towards us is frequently evident', he reported, voicing a reciprocal and spreading British perception of France: 'The Versailles treaty', he wrote, 'has laid the foundation of a very great French Power in the future.' There was, he claimed, not 'the slightest military danger to France from Germany in our life-time at any rate, and I personally think for a much longer interval'. A French occupation of the Ruhr would 'have Germany at their mercy for all time; and then, as sure as winter follows summer, they, feeling themselves absolute masters of the Continent, will turn round on us.'[100]

Lloyd George shared this view. 'He was very anti-French', Riddell noted, 'that is, suspicious of French military tendencies and designs.'[101] He too believed that the cause of European unrest was not German recalcitrance, but French neuroticism. He saw a need for a fresh start, in which he would play the leading part, to smooth relations between France and Germany. At the San Remo Conference later in April, he sought to cut the Gordian knot of reparations by holding direct negotiations with the Germans – something which he had ruled out the year before. Millerand, Clemenceau's successor, agreed that the Germans should be invited to a conference at Spa, but fuelled British suspicions by broaching the possibility of occupying the Ruhr to secure payment of reparations. After the Boulogne Conference in June, Lloyd George reflected: 'You cannot trust the French altogether. Who knows but some day they may be opposed to us?'[102] It was true that at Spa in July, when the Germans were given their first opportunity to put their point of view, their conduct, like that of Count Brockdorff-Rantzau the year before, was stereotypically provoking. General von Seeckt, Commander-in-Chief of the Reichswehr, in full dress uniform, with iron cross and monocle, agreed with soldierly directness that Germany had not disarmed. The large and abrasive coal-magnate, Hugo Stinnes, deputed to speak on reparations, lost his temper and roared that the Allies would get nothing out of Germany.[103] Even Lloyd George grew hot under the collar at Stinnes: 'a real specimen of the jack-boot German', he said.[104] Nevertheless he was persuaded that German uncooperativeness derived ultimately from French intransigence. After the Hythe Conference in August, Riddell noted that Lloyd George's 'antipathy to the French' was 'very marked'.[105]

Jules Jusserand, French ambassador at Washington, contrasted French and British attitudes to Versailles with pointed clarity. Advising the Quai d'Orsay to stand firmly by the treaty, he castigated 'the policy of the English revisionists, who would have the Germans believe that all they need to do in order not to have to carry out the treaty is not to carry it out'. This he contrasted with 'the policy of France, which is to grant no concession whatever without proof from the Germans of a genuine change of heart'. France's policy was 'the only right and proper policy', the only one 'capable of preventing ... Germany from starting all over again'.[106] Lloyd George differed in his assessment of how to treat Germany. Riddell recorded:

> The official British point of view is that the German nation were not responsible for the war, that the Junkers have been ejected, that the German government should be supported, that German industries should be revived and that, generally, the Germans should not be regarded with suspicion.[107]

These were brave words on both sides; and Lloyd George, though hesitating between coercion and Appeasement and alternating both in practice, moved closer towards a policy of holding a balance between France and Germany for the remainder of his premiership.

As expressions of a joint Anglo-French policy towards Germany, however, such statements of intent were altogether at odds, contradictory and incoherent: there *was* no joint policy. Between the upper and lower millstone of Anglo-French discord, the ability and the will to enforce the Treaty of Versailles was gradually ground down. To outward appearance, and to the superficial observer, the treaty stood firm for a dozen years, the citadel of Allied victory, with an imposing array of battlements, ramparts and revetments in the shape of occupation, reparation and a military control commission. Lacking the mortar of Anglo-French solidarity, however, it was a crumbling façade, built on sand and of sand: a sandcastle, to be washed away with the incoming tide of German resurgence. By 1927, a weary Clemenceau, despairing equally of Britain and of France, foresaw from Anglo-French disunity one certain outcome: the Germans would again invade – 'in six months, in a year, in five years, ten years, when they like, as they like'.[108]

4
The Worm in the Bud: 'Appeasement' at the Peace Conference

'Appeasement' a phenomenon of the Paris Peace Conference—stages in Appeasement—the British Empire delegation—'tactical' and 'moral' revisionists—General Smuts—Lloyd George's ambiguous attitude—anti-French feeling—criticism of the treaty—the Fourteen Points—'Pro-Germanism'—the Germans at Versailles—background of the 'appeasers'—religion and conscience—disenchantment

> We looked for peace, but no good came.
>
> *Jeremiah*, 8: 15

> I am filled with disappointment and grief.
>
> General Smuts, 2 June 1919

The legend of Versailles as a settlement doomed from the first dies hard. No amount of historical analysis seems able to dent its popular perception as a byword for harshness and injustice.[1] But perhaps that is as it should be: for the perception itself – one of the main psychological consequences of the peace – was a decisive part of inter-war reality. General Smuts insisted at the time that Versailles contained 'the roots of war' and would lead to war;[2] and his diagnosis became a self-fulfilling prophesy. The treaty not being automatically self-enforcing, but dependent for its fulfilment on the will of the victors – what they thought of it, or came to think of it, was bound to affect and did profoundly affect its fate. Whether the treaty was too severe or too mild, or 'too mild for its severity',[3] may be beside the point, if what matters is what thinking people in Britain came to believe. The historian must accept as a premise, a given fact of the utmost import for the future of the peace, the sorry reputation which it acquired so soon after its conclusion. The real question for him, therefore, is how and why did Versailles acquire this reputation?

Smuts took it for granted. 'A great revulsion will set in', he predicted, 'and a favourable atmosphere will be created in which to help the public virtually to scrap this monstrous instrument.'[4] Herbert Fisher agreed: 'There will be an appeasement',[5] he confidently predicted. But the aspirations of Smuts, Fisher and the rest were, after all, frustrated at the Conference. 'I am slipping away from this scene of nightmare', Keynes wrote to Lloyd George, 'I can do no more good here';[6] while Smuts admitted: 'I return to South Africa a defeated man.'[7] The treaty signed on 28 June 1919 and ratified a few days later in parliament by a huge and enthusiastic majority, was a far cry from what these men had hoped. It was, to use Smuts's expression, 'a rotten thing, of which we will all be ashamed in due course'.[8] The contrast between instant public acclaim followed by rapid loss of faith calls for elucidation.

As far as public reaction is concerned, we need look no further than Maynard Keynes's *The Economic Consequences of the Peace*, though liberal opinion against the terms was beginning to harden during the Conference itself, in the press and even at the polls. But it was Keynes who, on leaving Paris, deliberately set out, as he told Smuts, 'to make the treaty, or much of it, a dead letter';[9] and who six months later duly dealt it a massive ideological blow. 'I send you for Christmas Keynes's book', Violet Bonham-Carter wrote to a friend, 'which I think *quite* brilliant: an unanswerable indictment.'[10] Six weeks later, her father, the former Prime Minister, Herbert Henry Asquith, publicly lamented that Versailles was not the longed-for 'clean peace'.[11] There is no need to enlarge here on the epoch-making impact of Keynes's polemic.[12]

But while *The Economic Consequences of the Peace* brilliantly distilled the personal disenchantment of one individual at the Conference, Keynes's 'strictures', as Elisabeth Glaser puts it, 'appeared more excessive than the others' only in that he opted to make them public'.[13] Keynes's feelings were not unique: they were shared by most of Lloyd George's delegation. Alfred Zimmern wrote: 'Paris disgusted and depressed me more than I can say.'[14] To Arnold Toynbee, the Conference was 'a soul-destroying affair'[15]; to James Barnes it was 'a madhouse'.[16] Appeasement as a feeling, a mood, a temper – and it is these intangibles with which the historian of the lost peace has to deal – emerged at the Conference itself. 'Even at this late hour', Smuts pleaded to Lloyd George, 'I would urge that we revise our attitude towards Germany.'[17] The 'late hour' was

26 March, less than half-way through the Conference. Five weeks later, just before the draft terms were presented to the Germans, he wrote: 'I wish fifty per cent of this peace treaty could be scrapped.'[18]

Appeasement was even institutionalised at the Conference. On May 30, at the British delegation headquarters, was founded the Institute of International Affairs, a body implicitly critical of the treaty. Chairing the crowded inaugural meeting of Conference delegates, Lord Robert Cecil stated as a fact: 'There is no single person in this room who is not disappointed with the terms we have drafted.'[19] Harold Nicolson confirmed this a week later: 'There is not a single person among the younger people here who is not unhappy and disappointed at the terms.'[20] Another three weeks, and James Headlam-Morley re-echoed the common verdict on the treaty: 'I have not found one single person here who approves of it as a whole.'[21] That Appeasement was also recognised at the time as a political fact of the first importance is clear from the elaborate apologia which Lloyd George delivered in presenting the treaty to the House of Commons. Time and again he turned to the moral, as opposed to the practical criticisms of the treaty, to address the burning question: was it just?

Appeasement was a phenomenon of peacemaking, a collective malaise which soon became an epidemic. It was spread through shared feelings and misgivings, communicated in letters, conversations and discussions, formal and informal, in and outside the Conference rooms. The best evidence is in the Conference records and in diaries and correspondence, published and unpublished; in spontaneous contemporary reaction rather than in measured reminiscence: in Nicolson's diary, for example, rather than in his classic analysis, *Peacemaking 1919*, to which the diary is annexed (though *Peacemaking* itself, published in the fateful year 1933, is proof of the durability of impressions received at Paris). The fullest and most striking record, however, a personal yet also a representative account, is to be found in the day-by-day correspondence of General Smuts; and for that reason among others Smuts may be ranked first among the appeasers. But Appeasement, it must be emphasised, was a general disability: it afflicted the British delegation, in one strain or another, almost to a man. In the words of Robert Vansittart, who was also there and was himself not untouched, they were 'smitten by meaculpism'.[22]

The very term 'Appeasement' was part of the language of peacemaking, a standard of judgement and of reproach. In the *Manchester Guardian* of 10 May 1919, C.P. Scott called for 'a peace of appeasement'. Smuts, appealing to Lloyd George for generosity towards Germany, called for 'her appeasement now'.[23] Lloyd George himself assured a worried Archbishop of Canterbury of his hopes of 'early appeasement'.[24] The word twice finds its place in an official document, the Allied reply to the German counter-proposals. This extensive commentary on and rationale of the treaty, authorised and approved by the Big Three, while rejecting German complaints and refusing further concessions, looked forward to 'early reconciliation and appeasement' and 'that process of appeasement which all desire'.[25] Implicitly, then, the Big Three themselves conceded the truth of Smuts's charge, contained in the press statement that he released immediately after the signing of the treaty, that 'the real work of peace will only begin after this treaty has been signed'.[26] This view of Versailles was epitomised the next day in Garvin's editorial in the *The Observer*, headed 'Peace without Appeasement'; in a further communiqué by Smuts on 18 July regretting the 'failure of the Peace Conference to bring about the real and lasting appeasement of the nations to which we had been looking forward';[27] and in his still more striking assertion that 'in our policy of European settlement the appeasement of Germany... becomes one of cardinal importance'.[28]

The keynotes of Appeasement, then, are unhappiness and guilt, and a sense of the Conference as a road to Calvary. The contrast between Smuts and Lloyd George in their reaction to the Conference is instructive: to Lloyd George it was the 'happiest', to Smuts 'the unhappiest time of his life'.[29] Smuts expressed the elegiac and cosmic perception of Versailles as 'a tragedy of almost infinite dimensions, the poignancy of which is often more than one can bear'.[30] He wrote of 'my own bitter reflections and self-reproaches'.[31]

I

Five distinct but connected stages may be traced in the evolution of Appeasement at the Peace Conference:

1. Growing dissatisfaction with lack of progress in the first six weeks of peacemaking and with particular aspects of it, notably reparations.
2. These feelings accentuated in early March by the contrast between astronomical reparations demands on the one hand, and on the other, reports of famine in Germany. The doubts spread. On March 8, Nicolson writes in his diary: '*Are* we making a good peace? Are we? Are we?'[32] On March 26 Smuts protests to Lloyd George against what he already calls 'an impossible peace'.[33] Such feelings find reflection

in Lloyd George's own Fontainebleau Memorandum, calling for re-appraisal of many of the terms.

3. The presentation of the draft terms to the Germans on 7 May marks the moment when victors as well as defeated see the treaty for the first time *in toto*; and marks the point of maximum shock and alarm. The terms are perceived as 'impossible', almost as incredible. 'Every-one I have talked to', James Headlam-Morley records, 'agrees that the treaty as a whole is quite impossible and indefensible.'[34] 'The cumu-lative effect of it is to put on Germany disabilities of such a nature that no nation could be expected to acquiesce in them.'[35]

4. An increase in the volume and intensity of protests by the appeasers in May, brought to a head at the end of the month by the German counter-proposals, which, as Sir Henry Wilson admits, 'drove a coach and horses through our terms'.[36] These counter-proposals make a powerful impression on the British Empire delegation and British Cabinet, summoned in special session to consider them on the week-end of Friday 30 May to Sunday 1 June. Smuts takes the lead in urging change. Herbert Fisher notes in his diary: 'We all condemn the Treaty and agree that it should be modified.'[37] Smuts is only partly success-ful: but the delegation authorises Lloyd George to press for revision of Germany's eastern frontier, for a reduction in the duration of the Rhineland occupation and for Germany's immediate admission to the League of Nations. This long weekend marks a milestone in the genesis of Appeasement. The Empire delegation identifies and speci-fies what it regards as indispensable amendments. Their juniors also take action. On 30 May, the plenipotentiaries having agonised at the Hotel Majestic throughout the day, Lord Robert Cecil and others convene there in the evening to launch the Institute of International Affairs, a focus of opposition to Versailles within the Foreign Office, which includes James Headlam-Morley, Harold Nicolson, Arnold Toynbee, Allen Leeper and Edgar Abraham.

5. Lloyd George's last-minute revisionism is only partly successful and not all wholehearted; and he virtually ignores his delegation's pleas for the immediate settlement of reparations. Failure to achieve radical revision leads to the final crisis of Appeasement at the Con-ference. Smuts dismisses Lloyd George's eleventh-hour amendments as 'concessions which I consider paltry'.[38] Keynes resigns to write *The Economic Consequences of the Peace*. Smuts and Barnes threaten not to sign the treaty, and though they do so in the end, Smuts issues his public statement, which in effect repudiates what he has set his hand to.

These, then, are the main stages of Appeasement across the six months of the Conference. But they are largely the artificial convenience of historical periodisation: they were not seen as clear-cut at the time. Rather there was a gradual overclouding of original high hopes, a growing sense of accumulated grievance, communicated in private meetings and in correspondence, a mutual cross-fertilisation of discontent. Examples of this occur before and in the intervals of the crucial sessions of the Empire delegation. Summoned from London by Lloyd George to discuss the German counter-proposals, Edwin Montagu, Austen Chamberlain and Herbert Fisher study them en route to Paris. Montagu notes: 'We were all in agreement that the Germans had made out a case requiring considerable modification of the treaty.'[39] That evening the same three dine with Lloyd George, Birkenhead and Churchill; and, Montagu continues, 'the whole drift of the conversation was unanimous'.[40] Discussion in the same vein was resumed next morning at breakfast before the formal meeting of the delegation.

Appeasement was an Anglo-American phenomenon. 'The Majestic and the Crillon were full of uneasy and heartbroken men', wrote Alfred Zimmern.[41] There was anguish and foreboding in the French delegation, of equal, perhaps greater intensity; but not on the score of the treaty's harshness. Jules Cambon, the one professional diplomat in Clemenceau's delegation, pondered resignation because the Rhineland had not been severed from Germany and because he feared that the Anglo-American guarantee to France would prove delusive.[42] There was nothing comparable to the unique Anglo-Saxon sense of culpability. 'We do not have to beg pardon for our victory', Clemenceau exclaimed at the litany of Anglo-Saxon lamentations.[43] There were French accounts of the Conference, like André Tardieu's *La Paix* and Clemenceau's own *Grandeurs et misères d'une victoire*, written to justify the treaty; there were critiques, notably *Les conséquences politiques de la paix*, Jacques Bainville's subtle and prophetic analysis of the treaty's failure to solve the German problem. No Frenchman in 1919 was moved to write that Versailles was unfair on Germany.

Nor are we here concerned with the American appeasers, influential though they later became. This is because, with America's refusal to ratify Versailles, it fell to Britain and France to determine how far to enforce or not to enforce it; and British Appeasement at once became fundamental to the decline and fall of the peace settlement. Moreover, as it became clear even at the Conference that America might not ratify, an element of anti-Americanism itself entered into Appeasement. The British appeasers originally got on well with their counterparts in the

American delegation. But when Wilson's Treasury officials at Paris advised him to reject Keynes's scheme for American investment in Europe's rescue and regeneration, Keynes turned on them. Not merely was Wilson 'the greatest fraud on earth',[44] but the American colleagues with whom he had cooperated since America entered the war, were, like the President, 'broken reeds'.[45] Smuts too, having hoped that Wilson would implement or at least stand by his principles, found him in the end an arid revivalist.

Returning, then, to the British appeasers, it is instructive to focus on the British Empire delegation, the body which having played its part in drafting the terms of peace, was, together with members of the British Cabinet, charged with their review. What is remarkable about their lengthy debate on the terms is the difficulty of finding anyone with a good word for them. When called on individually by Lloyd George to comment, the Cabinet were almost uniformly negative. Churchill was earnestly for meeting German objections half-way. Milner, Birkenhead and Austen Chamberlain said little, but that little was hostile to the treaty. 'On the whole', as Milner recorded, 'the opinions expressed were strongly critical of the peace treaty.'[46] The question almost becomes: given the strength of anti-treaty feeling on the British side, how did the treaty come to be accepted at all? The answer is that by many, perhaps most, in Lloyd George's delegation, it was *not* accepted in more than a formal sense.

II

Professor Michael Fry draws a useful distinction between what he calls 'tactical' revisionists and 'ideological' revisionists[47] (though the term 'moral' revisionists may be more appropriate here). 'Tactical' revisionists were pragmatists, who favoured amendments to the draft treaty in order to induce the Germans to sign. 'Moral' revisionists were the idealists who sought revision in order to bring about a just peace. The former had practical doubts and favoured changes of detail, the latter had moral qualms and yearned for a change of heart. It is these whom I designate the 'appeasers'.

Most with influence in the British delegation, and especially the plenipotentiaries, were tactical revisionists. But not even the hard men, like Hughes of Australia or his fellow reparations delegates, Lords Sumner and Cunliffe, showed much confidence in Versailles. Among Lloyd George's close advisers, Hankey and Philip Kerr were 'tactical' revisionists (though Kerr, as Lord Lothian, underwent in after years a notorious conversion to full-blown 'moral' Appeasement). Together with Henry Wilson, another tactical revisionist, Hankey and Kerr helped to draft the Fontainebleau Memorandum. Bonar Law was a tactical revisionist, not because he thought Versailles was wrong, but because he thought it would not work. Even the hard men were to some degree tactical revisionists. Hughes looms large in the demonology of Versailles; but even Hughes favoured revision of Germany's eastern frontier. Massey of New Zealand was all for punishing the Kaiser; yet he said 'he would give up a good deal to get a signature'.[48] Sir George Foster of Canada is a good example of a tactical appeaser. He made no bones about admitting that he 'hated the Germans'. Nevertheless, like most, he argued for a reparations settlement then and there, because 'it was necessary to meet practical questions in a practical way';[49] and for the same reason he favoured Germany's admission to the League. Churchill, Birkenhead and Austen Chamberlain were tactical revisionists, with moral overtones.

The case of Keynes and Nicolson might suggest that 'moral' Appeasement, like the Spanish influenza, afflicted the thirty-somethings with particular virulence. 'I really feel that this bloody bullying peace is the last flicker of the old tradition', Nicolson wrote to his wife, 'and that we young people will build again.'[50] Such embittered idealism certainly brings out the polarisation between these 'angry young men' of their time and the 'terrible old men' incarnated in Lords Sumner and Cunliffe. Other like-minded young or young middle-aged appeasers included, from the Political Intelligence Department, Arnold Toynbee, Alfred Zimmern, Rex and Allen Leeper, Edward Hallett Carr, Philip Noël-Baker and James Barnes. Edgar Abraham, of the Conference secretariat, is an interesting and less well-known adherent. An outspoken appeaser, he was accused by a visiting British politician of being a pacifist. Abraham, a war veteran, replied: 'When there's a war on, I'm warlike, but when there's a Peace Conference on I *am* a pacifist.'[51]

But guilt at Versailles spanned the generations. That was one of its strengths. Appeasers in their forties, fifties and sixties included members of the Empire delegation and the British Cabinet, notably Smuts, Milner, Robert Cecil, George Barnes, Edwin Montagu and Herbert Fisher. Lord Milner had shown his colours even before the armistice, when his call for a moderate peace drew heavy fire from the Northcliffe press. Half a year later, on 23 March 1919, he noted dyspeptically in his diary: 'My birthday. I am 65. A year ago we were in the middle of the Great German Offensive. Now there is "Peace". But I am not sure that the outlook for this country and the world is not even blacker today than it was then.'[52]

To Milner, indeed, is attributed the world-weary description of Versailles as 'a peace to end peace'.[53]

The leading appeaser was Jan Christian Smuts. One of the two South African plenipotentiaries together with Louis Botha, and recently a member of Lloyd George's War Cabinet, Smuts, almost alone, had the standing and moral authority to confront Lloyd George and Wilson, and repeatedly to present his misgivings in terms that demanded a reply. Smuts was serious and singleminded and was taken seriously as a dissenting force in the Empire delegation. 'I have fought this peace from the inside with all my power', he told C.P. Scott.[54] He was also a conduit between officials like Keynes, Nicolson and Headlam-Morley and senior politicians like Milner and Robert Cecil. He spread the word by circulating among the delegates copies of his impassioned letters to Lloyd George. 'I hope you will allow me to say', Headlam-Morley wrote in acknowledgment, 'how glad I am that someone has said what many are thinking.'[55]

At the advisory level just below the top political echelons, Headlam-Morley himself provides a reliable barometer of opinion among the appeasers. Assistant Director of the Political Intelligence Department and head of its German section, an authority on German history, he had no illusions about German war-guilt, on which he had written the official account for the Foreign Office – *The History of Twelve Days*. 'Rational, detached, objective', in his daughter's words,[56] Headlam-Morley is in his way more significant than Keynes or Smuts precisely because of his calm sobriety, his level-headedness, his aversion, in E.H. Carr's description, 'from any emotional indulgence'.[57] Keynes might be written off by the hard-headed men as Bloomsbury, neurotic and frankly disloyal; even Smuts might sometimes seem holier than thou; Headlam-Morley, in and of the establishment, could not be faulted in terms of temperament.[58]

Yet Smuts remains the inspirational figure, by virtue of his towering integrity, the principled consistency of his critique of Versailles and his ceaseless efforts to modify and humanise it. 'A splendid, wide-horizoned man', Nicolson wrote.[59] 'His sense of values takes one away from Paris and this greedy turmoil.'[60] Smuts's powerful statement of protest on 28 June prefigured Keynes's *Economic Consequences of the Peace*. It was Smuts who encouraged Keynes to write the book and who coined the damning description of Versailles which Keynes made his keynote – 'the Carthaginian peace'.[61]

Lloyd George, as ever, is a special case, ambiguous, elusive and protean, weaving back and forth from 'hanging the Kaiser' and 'making

Germany pay' to provisioning Germany and drafting the Fontainebleau Memorandum in favour of concessions to the Germans. 'If they can establish a just case for modification', he assured the Archbishop of Canterbury, 'I am sure modifications will be made.' Ultimately, however, he stood by the treaty as an instrument of redress, restitution and even of retribution, upholding the punitive clauses and unyielding on reparations. 'We should not', he told the Primate, 'weaken the fundamental principles which underlie the peace' or 'refrain from imposing on their country the conditions which justice demands.'[62]

But Lloyd George must also be considered functionally, for his objective effects on Appeasement, which were important though often oblique. His pride in the treaty as artist and creator coexisted with a receptiveness to his colleagues' misgivings, an anxiety not to drive Germany into Bolshevism and a fear of the consequences of a refusal to sign. This led him to instigate some tactical revisionism once Britain's main demands had been met. Key stages in his contribution to Appeasement are the Fontainebleau Memorandum and his eleventh-hour openness to partial concessions. Lloyd George was a catalyst of Appeasement, both in what he said and did and in what he did not do. He read aloud to Wilson and Clemenceau, on the day he received it, Smuts's first great letter of protest.[63] His priority, he assured the Empire delegation, was 'an absolutely just peace';[64] but having thus articulated the appeasers' chief concern, he then gravely disappointed their expectations. He spoke their language with fluency, but he did not always mean the same thing, or perhaps anything at all; and at heart he was riled by their criticism. He reflected moral impulses which he fully understood but did not fully share, or share for long: they shimmered momentarily on the surface without stirring the depths below. Lloyd George was a carrier of Appeasement, not a fellow-sufferer. It is clear, moreover, that he was irked and goaded by Smuts. Would Smuts, he asked mischievously, care to set an example of high-minded Appeasement by restoring German South-West Africa to the Germans?[65]

The appeasers were markedly critical of the French, Smuts the most hostile. 'There was far too much of the French demands in the settlement', he told the Empire delegation.[66] On this there was general agreement. Headlam-Morley too considered that 'we depended far too much on French opinion; and whatever merits the French may have, that of understanding Germany does not seem to be included among them'.[67] Headlam-Morley thought his French counterparts narrowly opportunistic, grasping and vindictive. 'They seem completely defective in all sense of justice, fair play or generosity', he declared;[68] and he held them responsible for some of the most objectionable aspects of Versailles. Reacting to French demands for the Rhineland, he wrote: 'if our people have any guts, they will take the opportunity of giving the French rather a sharp reminder that they cannot do this kind of thing'.[69] On the choice of a high commissioner for the Saarland, Headlam-Morley looked in vain for 'a Frenchman whom one could trust to behave with absolute impartiality and, if necessary, hold his own even against the French Government. We in England have plenty of people who are accustomed to this sort of thing; my impression is that the very conception of such an attitude is very rare among the French.'[70] There was some understanding, theoretical rather than heartfelt, of France's continuing fears of Germany, offset by the ready assumption that these were exaggerated and by constant irritation at French tactics. 'The truth is', as Headlam-Morley put it, 'that the French are so frightened of the idea of a great Germany with nearly double the population of France, that they will resort to any manoeuvre or intrigue in the attempt to break off little fractions of it.'[71]

There was mistrust of Clemenceau's chief negotiator, the brilliant André Tardieu. Headlam-Morley thought him slippery and untrustworthy. Of French officialdom generally, he complained: 'they bargain like Jews and they generally are Jews'.[72] The delay in lifting the blockade was blamed (unfairly, since British and even German policy was also responsible) on Clemenceau's finance minister, Lucien Klotz, on whom Lloyd George retaliated in a devastating exploitation of popular prejudice. Even when French interests were indisputably paramount, as with the retrocession of Alsace-Lorraine, Headlam-Morley objected that 'the French, of course, put up claims which seemed to me politically very foolish, and in many details quite unjustifiable'.[73] French triumphalism in the Hall of Mirrors was much resented. 'The one thing which was forced on one by the whole scene', wrote Headlam-Morley, 'was that it was the revenge of France for 1871.'[74] What has been said of anti-French sentiment was also true of the appeasers' attitude to Britain's other Continental allies. Balfour recognised that the British delegation 'had been driven into a peculiar state of mind by the greed of France, Belgium and Italy'.[75] By 'a peculiar state of mind' he meant that counterbalancing disposition to sympathise with Germany which lies at the heart of Appeasement.

There were few provisions of Versailles with which the British delegation did not take issue. Emphases differed; but there was something in it to trouble almost every one of them. Headlam-Morley found the territorial provisions more or less acceptable, including the controversial

'A terrible outcome of all our professions.' – General Smuts

Figure 4.1   The Treaty of Versailles is delivered to the Palace of Versailles by the Secretary-General of the Peace Conference, Paul Dutasta, 28 June 1919

Saar and Danzig settlements to which he himself largely contributed; but he regretted the lack of a plebiscite in Alsace-Lorraine. Smuts on the other hand – and he spoke for most – was sweeping in his condemnation of Danzig, the Polish Corridor, Memel, the Saar and the Rhineland. 'I am simply amazed at all this', he wrote to Lloyd George on 26 March, 'Are we in our sober senses, or suffering from shell-shock? What has become of Wilson's Fourteen Points?'[76] Smuts struck a common note of incredulity and indignation at perceived violations both of the Fourteen Points and of the Pre-Armistice Agreement, essentially a British document, which underwrote the Fourteen Points as the contractual basis on which peace was to be made – 'a Wilson peace'. As Smuts repeatedly told the Empire delegation, 'he had always looked upon those declarations as bedrock and as governing any peace treaty which would be made'.[77] The treaty was thus 'a terrible outcome of all our professions'.[78] (See Figure 4.1)

Adherence to those professions, then, was seen as the test of Britain's good faith; and the fallings-away from them stood out as grievous and mortifying transgressions. As Headlam-Morley pointed out, while the Pre-Armistice Agreement 'specifically determined the nature and extent of the reparation to be paid by Germany, this is categorically violated in the reparation clauses'.[79] Exception was taken to the internationalisation of the German rivers, seen, together with the occupation of the Rhineland, as flagrant breaches of German sovereignty, at variance with the Fourteen Points and intolerable in themselves. To remove from German control regulation of traffic on the Rhine was, for Headlam-Morley, 'preposterous',[80] and to Keynes, 'humiliating and interfering'; while the disarmament and demilitarisation terms alone, wrote the latter, 'go beyond what any self-respecting country could submit to'.[81] 'The most shocking of all', Smuts told Lloyd George, was the Rhineland occupation. Occupation by French troops 'must shock every decent conscience'; while the the indictment of German officers for war crimes 'could not honourably be accepted by any Government'.[82] Smuts held Versailles to be a travesty of Wilsonism, both outside and contrary to the Fourteen Points; and he was unmoved by Lloyd George's sly assurance that Wilson himself was satisfied that it did conform with the Fourteen Points; for the President's credibility in the appeasers' eyes had long since plummeted. Edgar Abraham, prefiguring *The Economic Consequences of the Peace*, contrasted the purity of 'the Wilsonian gospel' with what he called the 'Woodrovian casuistry' of the treaty.[83]

To return once more to that defining moment in the crystallisation of Appeasement: the Empire delegation's discussions across the long weekend at the end of May. Here, at the highest executive level, was the clearest expression of misgiving and antipathy to the draft treaty. In addition to Lloyd George and Balfour, there were present on 1 June: Smuts, Botha, the representatives of Australia, New Zealand and Canada, and seven leading members, Liberal and Conservative, of the British Cabinet: Churchill, Secretary of State for War, Milner, Colonial Secretary, Lord Chancellor Birkenhead, Austen Chamberlain, Chancellor of the Exchequer, Edwin Montagu, Secretary of State for India, Herbert Fisher, President of the Board of Education, and George Barnes, for the working man. They represented opinion across the Dominions and across the broad spectrum of the Downing Street coalition – in President Wilson's unjust but understandable reproach, 'united in their funk'.[84]

The consensus against the treaty was felt to be, and was, remarkable. Even before detailed discussion began, 'each member said that he was in favour of making some concessions'.[85] Smuts led vigorously with a root-and-branch attack on the terms, and struck a common chord in demonstrating their harshness and incompatibility with the Fourteen Points. Austen Chamberlain agreed that 'it was certain that Germany could not keep the peace proposed'.[86] Most of those present, certainly, were tactical revisionists; and Smuts felt that he had failed to move them at the profound level of moral principle at which he sought amendment, warning prophetically against a settlement that might hereafter be morally repudiated by Germany. It is also true that Lloyd George shrewdly undercut the force of his colleagues' remonstrances by reducing them to those important, but from the appeasers' view, minimal concessions which he was willing to urge on Clemenceau and Wilson. These were not the radical changes sought by the moral revisionists, 'the very drastic course' which Smuts pressed on Lloyd George, 'that the peace treaty should be recast and transformed'.[87] This Lloyd George rejected as constituting 'such far-reaching concessions as to amount to a general reconstruction of the whole treaty'.[88] That was precisely the point. The gulf between Smuts's demands and what Lloyd George was prepared to concede marks at its widest and sharpest the measure of dissent and disappointment.

III

The epithet 'pro-German' is a little crude. At the Conference it was a term of abuse. Lloyd George himself, denounced as pro-German in the Northcliffe press, exclaimed 'That is a libel' and contemplated suing.[89]

But he also complained that his delegation had 'erred rather on the side of consideration for the enemy';[90] while Balfour warned them not 'to fix the mind on the lamentations of the Germans and their misfortunes'.[91] The comment was shrewd. Balfour noted as part of that fixation the uncritical conviction 'that Germany was repentant, that her soul had undergone a conversion and that she was now absolutely a different nation'.[92] The observation pinpoints a certain loss of emotional and intellectual balance about Germany. Even Headlam-Morley believed the German revolution to be 'as thorough, complete and sincere as any revolution of which there is any record'.[93]

Then there is Keynes's famous admission that during his face-to-face encounters with Dr Melchior, his German opposite number, 'in a sort of way I was in love with him'.[94] No one else went quite that far, though few others took part, like Keynes, in the negotiations for the renewal of the armistice and for famine relief, where personal contact with 'the enemy' formed the unique and cathartic experience which made it impossible to continue to regard them as such. The absence at Paris of face-to-face negotiations, the seemingly pharisaical ostracism of the German delegates, left its mark on the appeasers. Smuts and Botha, the Boer rebels of twenty years before, were already poignantly predisposed to identify with the Germans. As Botha reminded the Empire delegation on 1 June, by chance the anniversary of the Treaty of Vereeningen, 'he understood the position and feelings of the Germans because he also had had to make a peace'.[95]

A by-product of pro-Germanism was, as has been seen, antipathy towards Britain's Allies: France, Belgium, Italy and even, in the end, America. To this may be added disdain for Poland. Smuts shared the common German attitude for the Pole as half-child, half-savage. He not only dismissed Poland as 'an historic failure',[96] but in his disgust at Polish excesses, exclaimed: 'Kaffirs, that's what they are!'[97] For the Weimar Republic, by contrast, he called publicly for 'encouragement and support from this country', stressing 'the supreme importance' of 'having a stable, moderate and democratic republic in Germany'.[98] Lewis Namier, vehemently disenchanted with the new Poland when independence produced pogroms, veered over to a qualified respect for the Germans. 'No-one in this office dislikes them as thoroughly as I do', he admitted to Headlam-Morley; nevertheless he thought that the Weimar Republic would be 'an enormous asset for order and progress in Europe' and that 'everything possible should be done to give them a fair chance'.[99] Headlam-Morley agreed on the need to conciliate the new Germany. The treaty should be such as to 'appeal to the German Liberal and Socialist opinion'.[100] Germany's admission to the League would be the moment to revise the punitive clauses or at least the war-guilt clause.[101] Cecil proposed that the League should review the entire treaty after five years and amend it by majority decision.[102] Headlam-Morley regretted that on the Danzig question 'there was no one appointed specially to consider things from the German point of view'.[103] Smuts agreed, in relation to the treaty generally. He proposed to Lloyd George that a three-man subcommittee be appointed to talk directly to the Germans and in effect to renegotiate the terms. 'The very fact of listening to and considering the German case', he pleaded, would help to remove from the treaty 'all appearance of one-sidedness and unnecessary dictation'.[104] This was a prophetic attempt to undo and transform the *Diktat.*

The blockade aroused profound unease. Keynes saw the German children – 'tiny faces with large dull eyes, overshadowed by huge, puffed, rickety foreheads, their small arms just skin and bone'.[105] The suffering could not be denied, since it was attested by military intelligence officers not given to Germanophilia, by General Plumer of the occupying forces, and by observers like the veteran Berlin correspondent George Saunders, now a member of the Political Intelligence Department. Saunders and the other German experts, Headlam-Morley, Edwyn Bevan and Alfred Zimmern were stirred to their depths. At the beginning of March, once the extent of the catastrophe was borne in on him, Headlam-Morley begged Kerr to apprise the Prime Minister of Germany's desperate need. 'To this everything else is subordinated', he wrote.[106] Robert Cecil, formerly Minister of Blockade, was likewise 'oppressed', in his own word, by the enemy's plight. In early April he begged Lloyd George to make immediate peace and to lift the blockade.[107] He objected, he wrote six weeks later, to 'starving their children to force them to accept terms which, as you know, I am by no means sure about myself'.[108]

But supplies did not start to reach Germany until the end of May; and the prolongation of suffering lay heavy on the appeasers' consciences. Headlam-Morley, again, is a useful index of feeling. 'Cannot you imagine the feelings of the Germans', he wrote to his brother, 'when month after month went by after the Armistice and no step was taken towards bringing about peace or allowing food into the country, and they saw children and other people slowly dying from want of proper food?'[109] Famine still worse in Vienna also evoked their distress, while their anger was aroused by the reparation demands made by the Twins – Lords Cunliffe and Sumner – on a broken and impoverished Austria. Smuts and Nicolson saw conditions there for themselves. 'Never in my life', wrote Smuts, 'have I seen such a load of despair.'[110] Nicolson begged his father to use his influence to promote famine relief, 'as it is the one way in which we can mitigate the moral responsibility of the blockade'.[111] On the streets of Vienna, he reflected, 'I feel that my plump pink face is an insult to these wretched people.'[112]

Then there was the cold-shouldering of the German delegation, peremptorily summoned to Versailles to receive the preliminary terms. Headlam-Morley was troubled by the ostentatious denial of diplomatic nicety. 'People will not realise how important it is to observe external forms in dealing with people like the Germans', he wrote.[113] There was shame at their confinement to a hotel whose grounds, at French insistence, were palisaded like a prison camp, Parisians and American doughboys gaping at them through cracks in the fencing. 'The wretched Germans are caged like criminals', Nicolson noted.[114] There was pained sympathy at the presentation of the draft terms on 7 May, notwithstanding the truculence of Count Brockdorff-Rantzau, head of delegation, in denouncing the war-guilt clause and remaining seated while he did so. A British military representative, Colonel Beadon, records that before Brockdorff-Rantzau and his colleagues entered the Trianon Palace Hotel where the grim little ceremony took place, there was discussion among the Allied officers on duty outside as to whether or not the Germans should be saluted. The French refused outright. The others were in doubt. When the moment came, the British alone saluted. 'The most ordinary courtesy', wrote Beadon, 'demanded a salute to the vanquished foe.'[115] Despite the general show of indignation at Brockdorff-Rantzau's performance, Beadon confessed to 'a certain admiration for the manner in which they were endeavouring to "hold up their ends" under circumstances intended to humiliate them'.[116]

Still more painful was the final act in the Hall of Mirrors. Smuts regretted that not one of the Big Three thought to speak to the two German signatories, Dr Müller and Dr Bell, isolated and ignored. 'No word of sympathy for them at the end', he wrote, 'when one little word from Clemenceau or George or Wilson would have meant so much.'[117] This is echoed by Sir Esme Howard, an experienced career diplomat and a pronounced Germanophobe. 'They seemed to me intolerably lonely', he recalled. 'I felt then that I should have liked to get up and shake them by the hand.'[118] When all was over, Nicolson recorded: 'I find Headlam-Morley standing miserably in the littered immensity of the *Galerie des Glaces*. We say nothing to each other. It has all been horrible.'[119]

IV

Revisionism necessarily meant changes in Germany's favour; but the appeasers' view, or at any rate Smuts's view, of Germany, went far beyond that. He accepted as a fact of postwar life German predominance in Europe, pointing out that 'the seventy odd million Germans represent the most important and formidable national factor'.[120] This was something which he welcomed. From the outset he called for the 'generous treatment of Germany as a vital factor in the restoration of human civilisation'.[121] He spelled this out in his letter to Lloyd George of 26 March: 'Instead of dismembering and destroying Germany, she ought in a measure to be taken into the scope of our policy... She ought not to be despoiled and treated as an international pariah, but rather to be taken in hand by the Allies and helped to her feet again.'[122] He argued that German cooperation was essential to the succession-states – the new states of central and eastern Europe – which could not survive 'without German goodwill'; and that 'her appeasement now' would make Germany a 'bulwark' of civilisation against Bolshevism.[123] There was no sense of Germany as a continuing or even a latent threat; or if there was, it was fear of what would happen if the treaty were not revised. The Empire delegation's overriding fear was of being drawn into fresh hostilities by France through her attempts to enforce the treaty to the letter, and probably through some Rhineland imbroglio. Here, then, already, are the broad outlines of British foreign policy in the 1920s: a certain distancing from France, a sense of Germany as as a civilising force in a chaotic eastern Europe and a rampart against Bolshevik anarchy.

How are we to explain the appeasers, their immediate failure, followed within six months by general acceptance of their doom-laden view of Versailles? Keynes's book, of course; but it fell on fertile ground. Douglas Newton argues that the weakness of the appeasers was political; that without the backing of a political party, Smuts and Barnes were lone moderates in a Conservative-dominated delegation, whose peace terms 'were based', as Montagu complained, 'not on brotherly love, on the healing of wounds, or international peace, but on revenge on our enemies, distrust of our Allies and a determination for swag'.[124] This explanation is partly true. Smuts had entered the War Cabinet without having been elected to parliament and Barnes was shunned as a renegade by the Labour Party. It is also true that many appeasers were Liberals of the Asquithian persuasion, at a time when their parliamentary representatives were in eclipse. But political allegiance is not the whole answer: as has been seen, Appeasement transcended political barriers. Appeasers in the Cabinet included Liberals like Montagu, Fisher and Churchill, and Conservatives like Milner and Austen Chamberlain.

The appeasers belonged to a social and intellectual elite with tenacious roots in British society. Nicolson's father had been Permanent Under-Secretary at the Foreign Office. Headlam-Morley's brother was Regius Professor of divinity at Oxford and a future bishop. A public school education, Oxbridge and a Church of England affiliation were the norm. Keynes, Zimmern, Toynbee and Headlam-Morley were or had been Oxbridge dons. Fisher was Warden of New College. Two-thirds of the British delegation staff were Balliol men.[125] Headlam-Morley, in the words of E.H. Carr, was 'the strongly marked product of a classical education and of the British civil service in its heyday'.[126] A respect for German achievements in the arts and sciences also formed part of their common background. Members of the Edwardian establishment, the appeasers brought with them from the nineteenth century certain values and assumptions, cultural and ethical, clear-cut and durable, which coloured their responses to the treaty, and which, once expressed by Keynes, found ready reflection among the educated public. Christianity, or at least Christian ethics, are relevant here. Headlam-Morley, son and brother of clergymen, was a practising Anglican. Edwin Montagu and Alfred Zimmern were assimilated Jews. Zimmern, in anguish during the Coupon election, bearded the Archbishop of Canterbury at Lambeth Palace, passionately to condemn the morality of the government's policy on reparations. Cecil, the high Anglican among the appeasers, was sought out by the Archbishop: Cecil encouraged the Primate to urge Lloyd George along the path of revision.[127]

Again, the transcendent, sage-like figure is Smuts. Smuts followed a spiritual philosophy of his own, which he named 'holism', eclectic but much influenced by Christianity and by Quaker and pacifist friendships. From the outset he called for Germany to be treated with 'pity and restraint'; and as for the treaty – 'to eliminate from it all traces of petty spite and ill-feeling'.[128] He felt for the broken body of postwar Christendom, of nations ideally members one of another, but manifestly not healed by a deformed treaty born of human imperfections. He invoked 'the great Christian qualities' for the making of a true peace that should follow the inadequate efforts of the politicians.[129] The very cast of Smuts's mind was biblical, his communiqué of 28 June a sermon in prophetic vein. The hopes of the peoples, he declared, 'are not written in this treaty, and will not be written in treaties'; and, quoting St John, he pronounced: ' "Not in this Mountain, nor in Jerusalem, but in spirit and in truth," as the Great Master said.'[130] He called for 'a new heart . . . a contrite spirit, a spirit of pity, mercy and forgiveness for the sins and wrongs which we have suffered'.[131]

On the same day, his blood-brother, General Botha, after reluctantly signing the treaty, was moved to write on his agenda paper as if in a kind of sin-offering: 'God's justice will be done righteously to all peoples under the new sun; and we shall persevere in the prayer that it may be done unto mankind in charity, peace and a Christian spirit.'[132] Such exalted conceptions of peace on earth and goodwill among men were half-cynically paraphrased in the House of Commons by Lloyd George, who could quote Scripture with the best of them. The appeasers' idea of peacemaking, he said, was to dismiss German wrongdoing with a simple: '*Go and sin no more*'.[133] At a level only slightly less emotional than that of Smuts, religion, ethics and chivalry combine in Headlam-Morley, who stood for gentlemanly punctilio in peacemaking, and epitomised the qualms of most appeasers: 'Ultimately the problem is not so much a question of what Germany deserves, but of what it is consistent with our own respect and honour to do...There are certain elementary principles of humanity and Christianity which seem to me too much forgotten.'[134]

For victors no less than vanquished, revisionism was a moral and psychological necessity; but while German revisionism was fuelled by the heady oxygen of self-righteous indignation, the roots of Appeasement were watered by tears of remorse. 'I am troubled in my conscience', Smuts wrote, 'about putting my name to such a document.'[135] Hence the Allied reply to the German counter-proposals, intended by the Big Three to regain the moral high ground by predicating the treaty on German war-guilt, failed to move the appeasers; for it was the appeasers themselves who felt guilty. Though decision-making at Paris rested with their political masters and was often contrary to their advice, they all shared a sense of complicity. The more so Smuts because of his high position, his ideals and his strenuous but unavailing efforts. 'I cannot look at that draft treaty without a sense of grief and shame', he wrote.[136] 'I am grieved beyond words', he wrote to Wilson and Lloyd George;[137] and though he also gnashed his teeth at the Big Three, admitting that, 'like Job, I cursed the whole lot of them',[138] he sadly concluded: 'I feel I am no better than the others, and that I must stand in the dock beside them. And God be merciful to us poor sinners.'[139] In the hearts of the appeasers Versailles was something unclean, 'an abomination'[140] and 'a rotten thing'.[141] Their revulsion was almost physical. 'I felt sick in the pit of my stomach', James Barnes recalled.[142] Their only comfort was that Versailles was too bad to last. 'It will and must all soon collapse anyway', Smuts predicted.[143] Headlam-Morley, like Keynes, felt that the reparation clauses would simply not work: 'revision will be almost inevitable'.[144]

Nor did pointing the finger at French or American transgressions assuage their consciences. Edgar Abraham wrote that before blaming the French, the Anglo-Saxon delegates, 'who claim to be of straiter sect than their neighbours, should closely examine their own cases, lest they be found to have fallen from grace'.[145] Abraham indeed admitted a personal responsibility for the 'war-guilt' clause.[146] Headlam-Morley drew the same moral from the reparations clauses: 'If we do this sort of thing, we have no right to accuse the Germans of want of good faith.'[147] The expression 'a scrap of paper' was much in evidence, reflecting a perceived abandonment of principle comparable to any offence by Germany. Thus Headlam-Morley to his brother: 'You speak of the German behaviour under the armistice', he wrote.

> I think that our own action under the armistice is equally or more reprehensible. One of the conditions of the armistice was that we should let Germany have sufficient food. Four months elapsed before any food of any kind got into Germany; and the blockade, instead of being to some extent relaxed, was made even more strict than it was during the war... It is, I think, an action, or rather an inaction, as indefensible as anything I have ever heard of.[148]

Disappointment in the Political Intelligence Department weighed the heavier because its members had spent the last years of the war preparing for peace, for a new diplomacy and a new Europe. They believed that the task to which they had dedicated themselves, the studies in which they had made themselves expert, would enable the statesmen to go intellectually equipped to the Conference and to reach decisions that were informed, rational and just. At a time of slaughter beyond imagining they had looked forward to the Conference as a vindication of the Allied cause. They felt the times to be millenarian because of the scale of suffering. Only a regenerative peace, 'a Wilson peace', could hallow such carnage. Lloyd George himself in the House of Commons proclaimed his desire 'to consecrate the sacrifices of millions to the permanent redemption of the human race from the scourge and agony of war'.[149] And now the transcendant ideal, the grail which had inspired and sustained them all, was exposed, in Toynbee's words, as a 'pathetic illusion'.[150] 'At times', we are told, Smuts 'wondered whether the millions of lives had not been shed in vain.'[151] This sense of Versailles as a betrayal of the dead and a desecration of the cause was reflected in a bitter despondency. Keynes, and even Smuts, cursed an indifferent fate that played out its cosmic jest on their generation. Smuts wryly recalled the Kaffir prayer that it was time for God to come to earth in person, not send his son, as it was no time for children.[152]

Something of this spirit is captured by the war artist, William Orpen. In his well-known tableau of the signing of the treaty, the participants, though individually differentiated, are depicted in a sardonic spirit of detachment: insubstantial, hollow, trivial men in the Hall of Mirrors, dressed in a little brief authority, dwarfed and mocked from behind and above by the massive gilded pillars, the iridescent glass, and the pall of tragedy which looms over them.[153] And this was the official picture! In the beginning of Versailles was its end.

5
The Magic Mountain: Lloyd George and Hitler at the Berghof, 1936

Lloyd George's visit to Hitler—Lloyd George traditionally cast as Hitler's dupe—Ribbentrop—Lloyd George as Baldwin's unofficial emissary—arrival at the Berghof—the first Hitler–Lloyd George conversation—the second visit—talk of the armistice—Anglo-German understanding—perceived symbolism of the visit—Britain's place in Hitler's foreign policy—Lloyd George and Hitler—elective affinities

> *Conticuere omnes intentique ora tenebant* (everyone fell silent and listened intently)
>
> *Aeneid*, II, i

> Suddenly we all found ourselves listening to a talk between Mr Lloyd George and Hitler. It is difficult to describe the atmosphere. It seemed to become all of a sudden almost solemn... Everybody listened intensely and it was a moving experience.
>
> T.P. Conwell-Evans, Notes, 5 September 1936

> [We strained] to miss no word of the dialogue of two men whose word had settled the fate of two nations and whose power for good and evil was not yet spent.
>
> Thomas Jones, diary, 5 September 1936

In the autumn of 1936, Lloyd George paid a visit to Germany. He had first been there 28 years before, in 1908. Now as then, his ostensible purpose was to study social and economic conditions, on this occasion to see for himself the radical measures that were spectacularly solving unemployment and that were so similar to his own proposals for a 'New Deal' in Britain. He welcomed a meeting with the man who in three years had transformed the face of Germany. Furthermore their converse could not fail to broach the paramount issue of Anglo-German understanding, which had been the real object of his earlier journey, when as Chancellor of the Exchequer he hankered unsuccessfully after an interview with the Kaiser. Lloyd George's visit to Hitler is invariably represented as an exercise in folly and bamboozlement, Lloyd George the innocent abroad, the deluded, or self-deluded victim of Nazi propaganda. His effusions in the press on his return, of Hitler as the 'George Washington' of a peace-loving Germany, determined never again to go to war with Britain, are an embarrassment to his admirers and were discouraged even at the time by his advisers as hostages to fortune. Of all of Hitler's British visitors, Churchill pronounced, 'no one was more completely misled than Mr Lloyd George'.[1]

This magisterial verdict commands general assent and stamps a seemingly indelible image of Lloyd George at Berchtesgaden as the man whose wonted intuition for once badly failed him. Yet Churchill's verdict came nine tremendous years after the event, another World War away. In his sweeping history-cum-autobiography, *The Gathering Storm*, Churchill enjoyed, from his postwar Olympian height, the clear-seeming vantage point of hindsight, from where past events were iron links in an indissoluble chain of causation, a clear line leading from the advent of Hitler straight to European catastrophe. The year before Lloyd George's visit, however, Churchill himself had published an account of Hitler, more incisive, more critical, and more sombre, to be sure, than Lloyd George's encomium, but not without a shared note of admiration for the patriot and leader of his nation. No more than Lloyd George could Churchill then foretell 'whether Hitler will be the man who will once again let loose upon the world another war, or whether he will go down in history as the man who restored honour and peace of mind to the great Germanic nation and brought it back serene, helpful and strong, to the forefront of the European family circle'.[2]

By 1936, the Germans were once more master in their own house, and it was apprehended that they had the ability to become masters in others', though it should be emphasised that they had not done so. Whether they would do so would depend at least as much on British intentions as on Hitler's. Three years in power, Hitler had repudiated the disarmament clauses of the Treaty of Versailles, reintroduced conscription and inaugurated the Luftwaffe. In March 1936 he ordered his troops into the Rhineland, demilitarised under the treaties of Versailles and Locarno, demolishing at one blow the last remaining buttress of the security system set up in 1919 to contain Germany, but at the same time giving out assurances of peaceful intentions, and disorientating British opinion by both denouncing the Treaty of Locarno and proposing a fresh Locarno to replace it. The Foreign Secretary, Anthony Eden, was keen to follow up this initiative with Germany. 'It is in our interest to conclude with her as far-reaching and enduring a settlement as possible while Herr Hitler is still in the mood to do so', he told the Cabinet.[3]

Equally enthusiastic to seize the moment was Lloyd George, now, at 72, an elder statesman of independent views, unrivalled experience and undiminished dynamism. Though out of office for 14 years, he was neither out of sight nor out of mind, and had by no means despaired of returning to power. The Father of the House was the *enfant terrible* of British politics and the *bête noire* of those who had taken care to keep him out of Downing Street since 1922, notably the Prime Minister, Stanley Baldwin and his Chancellor of the Exchequer, Neville Chamberlain. Lloyd George had excoriated both men in the Commons in July 1936 in a legendary denunciation of the failure of their foreign policy over Abyssinia, which left the front bench blenched and reeling and showed that he had lost none of his parliamentary prowess. Backed by the enormous private resources of the 'Lloyd George Fund', he had a private secretariat in London and a solid political base in his north Wales constituency – he had been the member for Caernarvon Boroughs uninterruptedly for almost half a century. Nominally a Liberal, he was in effect an independent force, a one-man band, almost a one-man opposition. He received the largest post-bag of any British politician.[4] Across the country he could command audiences of 10000. In 1935, he had appeared to come close to power. His energetic campaign for a 'British New Deal', promoted by a 'Council of Action', won enough cross-party support to worry the National Government. Baldwin pondered whether to offer him a Cabinet post, though well aware that any Cabinet with Lloyd George in it would find him the cuckoo in the nest. Lloyd George offered himself as Foreign Secretary, in which capacity, he said, he 'might be of some use in placating Germany'.[5] He was invited to Downing Street to present his New Deal proposals, he was politely received and patiently heard. When in November, however, the National Government was comfortably re-elected with a huge majority, Baldwin could cautiously relax, and Lloyd George found himself as far as ever from Downing Street. He was casting about for other opportunities to maintain himself in the public eye when he received the invitation from Hitler.

The other leading actors in this drama were Joachim von Ribbentrop, Hitler's newly appointed ambassador to London, and Thomas Jones, the former Cabinet secretary, who had served both Lloyd George and Baldwin and remained a close confidant of Baldwin. Baldwin's spectre, genial but wary, hovers equivocally in the background of this entire episode. With Ribbentrop as his host and intermediary, Jones had already flown to Germany in May 1936 as Baldwin's unofficial emissary, to meet Hitler and hear from his own lips of his fervent desire, repeatedly expressed, of a meeting with Baldwin; and the practicalities of that meeting were still under consideration when the invitation was diverted to Lloyd George. Lloyd George for his part had persuaded Jones to be of the party. This was, he said, in order to avoid the appearance of upstaging the Prime Minister;[6] but Jones's presence on the embassy was bound, on the contrary, to lend an air of official authority to an ostensibly private visit. Jones was the potential conduit between Lloyd George and Baldwin in the event of a promising outcome. Whatever the outcome, a meeting between Lloyd George and Hitler could not be other than an event fraught with interest and expectations.

The invitation, though originating with Hitler himself, was conveyed by Ribbentrop. As Hitler's roving envoy, Ribbentrop had triumphantly pulled off the Anglo-German naval agreement the year before, and on Hitler's terms. Since then he had endeavoured, through Jones, to impress on Baldwin Hitler's overwhelming desire for a meeting. Hitler had come to a point in the evolution of his foreign policy where its future direction hinged on relations with Britain. He sought to build on the naval agreement to achieve with Britain a more far-reaching and comprehensive settlement. Baldwin had snuffed and rooted around the idea in his usual dilatory manner, half-tempted, largely suspicious; but whether through habitual indolence or a canny sense of self-preservation, he was not in the end to be persuaded to hazard his reputation as his longed-for retirement approached, to cross the grain of his character by so dramatic a gesture as a flight to the Reich, or even to alter his holiday plans by substituting a German spa for the annual cure at Aix-les-Bains. While Baldwin was making up his mind, Hitler considered Lloyd George a highly acceptable substitute, as well as a statesman whose wartime leadership he had held up to admiration in *Mein Kampf*. When Ribbentrop set his cap at him, Lloyd George, having, as he felt, nothing to lose, did not play hard to get. He had none of Baldwin's inhibitions. The invitation tickled his vanity, and it appealed to his dramatic as well as to his political imagination. He shared Hitler's preference for the face-to-face discussion with the man at the top. No one indeed was more experienced in it than he. Baldwin, no doubt, did not begrudge him the chance to burn his fingers.[7]

It is a measure of the importance that Hitler placed on the visit that instead of leaving for his posting in London, Ribbentrop remained in Germany to superintend arrangements, and took up his ambassadorial duties only after the visit, which was organised and paid for by the German government. In that sense it was something of a state visit. The intermediary between Ribbentrop and Lloyd George was Thomas Conwell-Evans, a visiting professor of international relations at the University of Königsberg and joint secretary of the Anglo-German Fellowship. An intimate of Ribbentrop, Conwell-Evans too had had an audience with Hitler. Ribbentrop and Conwell-Evans organised the travel and accommodation arrangements, Conwell-Evans making several flights from Germany to England and back to finalise details with Lloyd George at Bron-y-de, his country home at Churt in Surrey. Conwell-Evans told Lloyd George that he was 'the only man who understood Hitler' and 'the only man for whom Hitler had any respect on this side'.[8] The mutual interest of the two protagonists was unfeigned.

I

The party which assembled expectantly at Berchtesgaden on 3 September 1936 – by chance three years to the day before Britain and Germany again went to war – consisted of Lloyd George, accompanied by his son, Gwilym, and daughter, Megan; his private secretary, A.J. Sylvester; Thomas Jones and Conwell-Evans. They were joined by the distinguished physician, Lord Dawson, who was medical adviser to Lloyd George and happened to be in Germany. On the German side were Ribbentrop and his wife; Baron Geyr von Schweppenburg, military attaché in London, an old-school diplomat whom Ribbentrop had detailed to escort the party through Germany; and Dr Schmidt, Hitler's interpreter. Unlike the shuffling, gout-ridden and elegiac Baldwin, yearning for rest, Lloyd George was in the pink, with an energy, curiosity and exuberance which, Jones observed, 'took thirty years off his seventy-two',[9] brimming with all 'the qualities which the Cabinet so much lacks – vision, initiative, force'.[10] Ever his active self, he was full of the last volume of his *War Memoirs*, which he was busy completing en route – indeed he hoped to interview Field Marshal von Ludendorff in the course of the visit – yet wholly in the present and on the alert, lively and loquacious, immersing himself in a sea of English newspapers. He was also 'soaking up information about Germany', Sylvester noted admiringly, 'like a dry sponge soaks up water'.[11] 'He lives more in a day', echoed Jones, 'than the average minister in a week.'[12]

At dinner in the Grand Hotel there were effusive exchanges across the table, but they were more than flummery. Lloyd George said how much he looked forward to meeting Hitler. Ribbentrop, ever his master's voice, replied that 'The Führer has been looking forward to this opportunity of meeting you for many years.'[13] Lloyd George described Hitler, as far as Germany was concerned, as 'the resurrection and the life'.[14] Politics, past and present, were broached, Ribbentrop steering the conversation to what lay behind the visit, the course of Anglo-German relations. Germany's great blunder at the turn of the century, he said, had been the failure to take up Joseph Chamberlain's offer of alliance. 'I know that Hitler agrees with that view', he declared.[15] Flying another kite, Ribbentrop lambasted Czech discrimination against the Sudeten Germans. Lloyd George obligingly commented that 'he did not trust Beneš in his sight, let alone out of it. He had behaved very badly at the Peace Conference.'[16]

Next morning saw a preparatory tête-à-tête between Lloyd George and Ribbentrop. Emboldened by the previous evening's success, Ribbentrop pressed for Britain's participation in 'a great anti-Bolshevik front'.[17] Lloyd George was taken aback and, according to Sylvester, 'rather worried'.[18] 'That is going much too far', Lloyd George reported, 'We couldn't do anything of the sort.'[19] Ribbentrop had raised Hitler's crusading scheme too bluntly and too soon. Dawson commented that he had never met 'anyone more unlike an ambassador'.[20] Jones agreed that Ribbentrop spoke 'with the most intense seriousness, unrelieved by any human or light touch'.[21] At lunch, the talk was of the armistice, Lloyd George fresh from the details of his *War Memoirs*. Ribbentrop regretted Germany's capitulation as a 'stab-in-the-back'. Lloyd George said that 'he could not understand why the Germans had signed the armistice. That had certainly been a mistake on their part.' Ribbentrop replied that 'Hitler would not have signed it.'[22] He again reverted to the underlying theme of the visit, emphasising that what Hitler desired above all else was a 'complete understanding' with Britain.[23] They were still talking, Lloyd George in full flow, when Hitler's private limousine arrived to convey him, together with Ribbentrop, Conwell-Evans and Schmidt, on the ten-minute drive to the Berghof.

High in the Bavarian Alps, and built partly into the pine-clad mountainside, the Berghof was Hitler's legendary redoubt, his mountain eyrie. Here, amid spectacular views across the Obersalzberg into his native Austria, he communed with himself and dictated policy. As the car drew up, a stately quadrille ensued (see Figure 5.1). Hitler descended the great flight of granite steps beside the house, to greet his guest. Lloyd

'The Great War leader of the British Empire and the great leader who had restored Germany to her present position were meeting on a common ground. One seemed to be witnessing a symbolic act of reconciliation between the two peoples'. – T. P. Conwell-Evans

Figure 5.1 Hitler welcomes Lloyd George to the Berghof, Berchtesgaden, 4 September 1936 (Photo: Kurt Huhle. Immediately to Lloyd George's left is Joachim von Ribbentrop, German ambassador-designate to Britain. Between Lloyd George and Hitler is Thomas P. Conwell-Evans, secretary of the Anglo-German Fellowship)

George, leonine and beaming broadly, advanced, holding his hat at a courtly angle. Hitler, two steps above, bowed smilingly. They shook hands warmly, Hitler clasping Lloyd George's right hand within both his own. Conwell-Evans, doffing his fedora, discreetly interpreted the pleasantries. Ribbentrop alone did not smile. He stood apart, his arms at his sides, solemn and deferential, the Führer's faithful acolyte. Then Hitler led Lloyd George up the steps and into the Berghof, along corridors capped with vaulted stone ceilings, like some 'cathedral crypt', noted Jones,[24] to his fabulous subterranean drawing-room, a large cavernous hall tunnelled into the rock and illuminated at the far end by an enormous window, which stretched the length and height of the wall and overlooked the mountains. On another wall hung a portrait, which Lloyd George, to Hitler's surprised approval, recognised as that of Frederick the Great as a boy.

At Hitler's invitation, Lloyd George opened the dialogue. He had thought hard about what to say and was in masterly form, 'the polished diplomat speaking with exquisite politeness',[25] gliding dextrously to the heart of the matter. He harked back to his visit to Germany in 1908, stressing 'how, ever since that visit, I had been convinced of the necessity of a good understanding between our two countries'.[26] He declared that he had done his utmost since the war, both as Prime Minister and after, to promote good relations with Germany, which were necessary for the sake of 'Western civilisation itself'. Nor could Anglo-German rapprochement be the object of some remote aspiration. The time was ripe for action, which 'should be taken to bring about agreement within the next few months'. 'If not', and Lloyd George spread his hands in an expansive gesture, 'England and Germany would drift rapidly apart.' Hitler was clearly delighted at the instant rapport. 'I agree with all my heart', he rejoined emphatically.[27] He too, since 'his earliest days in politics', indeed, since before the war, had *always* desired the closest co-operation between the two kindred nations. 'Since the last war that had been his aim and his ideal.'[28] He instanced the conclusion the previous year of the Anglo-German naval agreement as 'proof of his eagerness to respect British vital interests'.[29] Britain too, he went on, must understand 'the aims, aspirations and requirements' of Germany.[30]

Lloyd George urged Hitler to rejoin the League of Nations and to engage in serious discussion with Britain, France, Belgium and Italy at the proposed Conference to renegotiate the Treaty of Locarno. Hitler agreed on the need for a new Locarno and a new series of mutual guarantee pacts, in which the recognition of German equality was 'an indispensable condition'.[31] Germany was 'perfectly content with the present territorial settlement in Western Europe', he said.[32] This was probably true. It was to the south and east that he had set his sights. Was he prepared to conclude an air pact with Britain and France, Lloyd George asked. This was an objective long sought by the British Government and one often held out by Hitler. 'Yes', Hitler replied, adding more obscurely, 'provided the three powers were able to reach a common defensive position.'[33] He was clearer and more positive about his attitude to Britain's role as a world power. The naval agreement, he stated, 'secured Britain's supremacy on the High Seas' and proved that 'Germany was not unmindful of the interests of the British Empire'.[34] Unfortunately France had rejected his proposals in 1934 for a Franco-German arms ratio on land, and – referring to his Rhineland coup – he had been 'compelled to take action to protect the frontiers of my country'.[35] Czechoslovakia too threatened Germany through her alliance with Russia.

This led Hitler to the leitmotif already sounded by Ribbentrop, Hitler enlarging at length and with growing emotion on the universal menace of Bolshevism. He conceded, with a smile, that Bolshevism might be thought to be 'an obsession with him'.[36] 'At the cost of being regarded as a fanatic',[37] however, he saw it as his mission to warn against its inroads, of which he had personal experience in Germany. A victory for Bolshevism in the Spanish Civil War would leave Europe defenceless. Germany would be encircled. The advent of Bolshevism he considered to be a historical phenomenon as momentous as the invasions of Islam. Only the alignment of Britain and Germany could stem the tide. Lloyd George was non-committal about Spain, and denied that communism would triumph in France. The powers should remain neutral in the Spanish Civil War.

They adjourned for coffee in the great drawing room, 'which looked like some great hall in an old castle'.[38] At the far end, advancing to the huge, floor-to-ceiling plate-glass window, they took in the stupendous mountain views, which, wrote Conwell-Evans, 'almost took one's breath away'.[39] Hitler spoke of his reconstruction programme, the great motorways, along one of which Lloyd George had sped from Munich to Berchtesgaden the day before, and the four-year plan which he would announce at the Nuremberg rally the following week. He invited Lloyd George to attend the rally, but Lloyd George sidestepped this awkward proposal. He had not come to Germany for politics, he told Hitler, but to study social institutions, 'and above all your solution to the unemployment problem'. 'If I went to Nuremberg', he explained, 'England would be offended'. Hitler expressed disappointment.[40]

Lloyd George returned from the Berghof in a state of elation, enraptured at the success of the talks and infatuated with Hitler, returning to the subject again and again. 'He is a very great man', Lloyd George asseverated, ' "Führer" is the proper name for him, for he is a born leader, yes, and statesman.'[41] 'From the very start we got on like a house on fire.'[42] They had covered all manner of issues. 'We talked about everything', Lloyd George related, 'I talked with great bluntness and frankness and the Führer liked it'[43] and responded in kind: 'In his conversation he had had the directness of a cannon ball.'[44] This was much to Lloyd George's taste. The question of the Nuremberg rally came up again next morning. No doubt Ribbentrop had raised it with Sylvester, who told Lloyd George that he would probably be pressed again to attend. Jones had suggested that Lloyd George might adopt a low profile by sitting 'in the 2s 6d seats' rather than in the visitors' box. Sylvester dismissed the absurd suggestion. It was 'quite impossible – L.G. would be instantly recognised'.[45]

The first visit to the Berghof had been partly in the nature of a dress rehearsal, or rather an experiment. Had it not been to Hitler's liking, no doubt a convenient excuse would have been found to avoid a sequel. But all had gone well for both sides. That afternoon, the second act, was a more public performance, with cameras at the ready: for Lloyd George's entire entourage was invited for tea. Sylvester brought along his colour cine-camera. As the fleet of cars reached the top of the winding gradients and Lloyd George alighted, Hitler, 'smiling happily',[46] hastened once more down the steps to welcome him. (A blessing for the world, the reader may reflect, had he tripped and broken his neck.) Sylvester filmed them as they remounted the steps together. High tea again in the drawing-room; Hitler animated, Lloyd George genial and exceedingly polite. Ribbentrop sat stiffly between them, as solemn and po-faced as ever in his sense of the occasion and of the presence of the 'All-Highest'. He 'might have been Savonarola', Jones noted, 'if he had a better nose.'[47]

Through the great panoramic window, lowered to let in the mountain air, the sun was setting behind the Alps. Candles on the tea table flickered in the breeze. A bust of Wagner glowered in the dusk. For a time there was general conversation. Suddenly all voices save two were stilled. Hitler presented Lloyd George with his signed photograph, set in a silver frame. Lloyd George immediately rose and took Hitler's hand. With a sob in his throat, he declared how honoured he was to receive the gift from 'the greatest German of the age'.[48] 'It was a great moment', Sylvester noted.[49] Pathos was relieved by humour; but it was Hitler who provided it. Would Hitler object, Lloyd George asked, if he were to place the photograph on his desk at Bron-y-de, side by side with those of the war leaders, Foch, Clemenceau and Woodrow Wilson? Hitler had no objection, he said, provoking laughter, as long as it was not placed anywhere near those who signed the armistice in Germany's name – the 'November criminals'.

These reminders of the armistice roused Hitler to further reflection. The inspiration of his political career, the Damascene conversion, the vision of himself as Germany's saviour, came, after all, with the spectacle of Germany's collapse. Yet instead of the tirade that might have been expected, Hitler appeared inwardly calm, mellow and philosophical. 'The fact that Germany lost the war does not matter now,' he said.[50] There was no disgrace, except in the conduct of the 'November criminals'. Of them he spoke with bitterness; but 'I am only too glad to say now', he continued, 'there is no hatred of our former enemies.' He turned Germany's defeat into a gracious compliment. The victory of 1918 was 'due to one statesman, a great statesman, yourself, Mr Lloyd George. It was you who rallied the people and gave them the determination for victory.' He had always held to that opinion and he welcomed the opportunity to pay tribute to Lloyd George in person. Lloyd George returned the compliment with skill. Hitler had restored Germany's honour, her equality among the nations. The one desire of the British people was 'a better understanding and a closer cooperation between our two nations'.[51] Hitler replied that he was 'passionately interested in the furtherance of Anglo-German understanding'. That was his purpose in sending to London his 'best man', Ribbentrop, whose departure on this mission was imminent.[52] Lloyd George urged Hitler himself to visit England. 'Tell him', he said to Conwell-Evans, 'that he would be welcomed by the British people.' The words were translated. Hitler said nothing, gave a dismissive gesture, 'expressing he wished it might be true', and pursed his lips. 'Ah well', Lloyd George said affably, 'The time will come, and possibly quite soon.' 'Possibly', Hitler muttered non-committally.[53]

II

Who fooled whom in this Alpine encounter? It is important but difficult to separate the layers of reality at which it took place and to penetrate its underlying significance. There was a level of symbolism and a palpable emotional dimension, not to be ignored. 'It is difficult', Conwell-Evans wrote, 'to describe the atmosphere. It seemed to become all of a sudden

almost solemn.'[54] This was no meeting between conventional statesmen, however outstanding, such as had been the stuff of Lloyd George's
life as Prime Minister. Rather, it seemed the encounter of two elemental
national forces, Goth and Celt, Wotan and Merlin, 'the dialogue', as
Jones reflected, 'of two men whose word has settled the fate of two
nations and whose power for good and evil was not yet spent'.[55] All
present, including both protagonists, were affected, overwrought even,
by the dramatic overtones of the occasion, enhanced by the romantic
grandeur of the surroundings. 'One realised', wrote Conwell-Evans, 'that
the great War Leader of the British Empire and the great Leader who had
restored Germany to her present position, were meeting on a common
ground. One seemed to be witnessing a symbolic act of reconciliation
between the two peoples.'[56]

Both main actors were consummate showmen, deep in statecraft.
Each combined extraordinary assimilative capacity with profound,
almost occult visionary intuition; each exerted the mesmerising char-
isma which inspired others to do their bidding and was the mainspring
of their political genius; both related to the people, from whom they
sprang, yet both were also isolated and apart. Both too, though political
realists to their fingertips and without illusion about others, were to
some degree in thrall to the persona which each had created and the
myth which he cultivated. Both shared an unshakeable belief in self, a
unique sense of mission. 'I go with the certainty of a sleepwalker along
the path laid out for me by Providence', Hitler had told the ecstatic
crowds after the Rhineland coup.[57] Lloyd George, in 1920, at the height
of his fortune, confided: 'I feel there is work for me to do. Fate, Providence, or what you will, has ordained me for the purpose. It is my
destiny and I must fulfil it.'[58] Across the intervening sixteen years, he
had not lost that sense of destiny.

Hitler of course was on home ground in this Alpine Valhalla, amid his
household gods and icons: the Frederick portrait, the Wagner bust, the
awesome Teutonic panorama. Beneath the Untersberg flanking
the Berghof, Barbarossa was deemed to sleep. For the spectators, the
atmosphere was both human and numinous, prosaic and reverential.
Tom Jones, observing the Führer dapper in lightweight Sunday suit,
toying with Zwieback and petit beurre, mused that this was the man
who, two years before, had had his former henchmen butchered in the
'Night of the Long Knives'. Sylvester recalled Hitler's indefinable attraction – 'magnetic, masterful, electrical'.[59] Of Hitler in full spate, Jones
noted, 'he lifted his eyes and looked into the distance like a prophet
possessed'.[60]

For both Hitler and Lloyd George it was an opportunity to sound out the other; and both, though relaxed and masterful from the moment of their first encounter, and playing a role that came naturally, were also on their best behaviour. Hitler was modest, pleasant and *gemütlich*, 'neither fierce nor savage'.[61] He waxed earnest and eloquent, speaking 'with a grave and sincere animation',[62] but there was no ranting or raving. 'His head has not been turned by adulation', Lloyd George observed.[63] Of the two, however, Jones reflected, 'I don't think Hitler would be specially singled out if we met him in a general company.' It was Lloyd George who 'easily dominates any company';[64] and Conwell-Evans noted that from the first Hitler gazed at Lloyd George with eyes full of benevolence and admiration. 'He showed a veneration for his visitor and could hardly keep his eyes away from him.'[65] At the end of the visit he took Lloyd George by the arm and escorted him once more down the steps. He had long since paid feeling tribute to him in *Mein Kampf* as the war leader whose 'genius' had 'opened the hearts of his people and made these people carry out his will absolutely'.[66]

Hitler, who had earthshaking ends in mind, was out to please as well as to probe. Hence, Jones noted, it was 'only when he has been talking for some time that one observes the latent passion of the man emerging, the mystical view of Germany, bordering on fanaticism'.[67] It was a success for both that the meeting took place at all. Lloyd George succeeded with Hitler where he had failed with the Kaiser. Hitler succeeded with Lloyd George where he failed with Baldwin. Even had Baldwin been induced to meet Hitler, such a rapport as emerged between Lloyd George and Hitler seems almost unthinkable. Hitler, Dr Schmidt somewhat fatuously recalled, was 'obviously delighted by the recognition implied in this visit from the world-famous statesman'.[68] But recognition of that kind was the least of it. What each recognised in the other was a kind of doppelgänger.

At the political level what was at stake was war and peace. Hitler stood at a crossroads in his foreign policy. He had long since decided on the inevitability of conflict with Russia, the struggle for the attainment of *Lebensraum*. That was laid down in *Mein Kampf*, something fixed prophetically for the future. What he sought to determine now was whether to continue the quest for the understanding with Britain which was equally a priority in *Mein Kampf*. Baldwin, wary of the power of 'a dynamic force', be it a Lloyd George or a Hitler, was not to be drawn into Hitler's magnetic field. Both Eden, his Foreign Secretary, and Vansittart, the Permanent Under-Secretary, opposed a meeting between Hitler and the Prime Minister. No move would come from Britain.

Much therefore would depend on Ribbentrop's embassy to London. This, as we know, would turn out a disaster, summed up in the nickname which the ambassador gained in consequence – 'Von Brickendrop'. Affronted by his reception, Ribbentrop would persuade Hitler that Britain, having rebuffed the Führer's generous overtures, was ingrate and betrayer. Hitler would lose his patience, and write Britain off, together with France, as *Haßgegner* – 'hate- inspired antagonists'. But this was not for another year.[69] Meanwhile, in the new reckoning the fluid international possibilities released by the remilitarisation of the Rhineland and the looming option of the *Drang nach Osten* – was Britain to be counted friend or foe? That, for Hitler, was the question. That was the purpose of the Lloyd George visit.

It was Hitler's dream to enlist Britain in the anti-Bolshevik alignment, the anti-Comintern pact, which Ribbentrop concluded two months later with Italy and Japan. Hitler desired a settlement with Britain; but he wanted it, as he wanted everything, on his own terms. What he sought was a free hand for Germany in Eastern Europe and acceptance of German predominance on the Continent, in return for which he offered friendly coexistence with Britain and her Empire. 'Each country could recognise the vital interests of the other', he told Lloyd George. 'These interests did not conflict.'[70] 'Every German welcomed a strong British Empire.'[71] This was to ignore France, as Lloyd George reminded Jones, to whom he suggested that in the negotiation of an Anglo-French understanding with Germany, the new Locarno which he pressed on Hitler, he himself would be better suited than Baldwin to broker a deal and complete the circle of pacification.[72]

Hitler, however, was not interested in a new Locarno. He had, after all, just destroyed the old one. Talk of a new Locarno had been a smoke-screen to tide him over the Rhineland coup. What concerned him now was expansion eastward, and Britain's attitude to that. Both Hitler and Ribbentrop dinned the Russian alarm into Lloyd George's ears; but Lloyd George, who fully expected the onslaught, was not to be drawn on what he rightly called 'Hitler's pet subject of Bolshevism',[73] and riposted both that the Russian danger was exaggerated and that an anti-Russian coalition was of no interest to Britain. To Ribbentrop he stressed 'the advantages which could be derived by co-operation between England and Germany, as against the organisation of an anti-Bolshevik front'.[74] Thus far he kept clear of Hitler's wider influence; and the policy which he advocated was that of the British government – a fresh multilateral security pact in the west. Hitler might imagine that where her own interests were concerned, Britain would ignore France, since that was how the Anglo-German naval agreement had been reached: behind France's back and on the anniversary of Waterloo. Insofar then, as Lloyd George made it clear that, however much she desired an understanding with Germany, Britain would not purchase it at the price of abandoning France, he performed a responsible service. Likewise, by making it clear to Ribbentrop that however little sympathy Britain had for Bolshevism, she would never join the anti-Comintern pact or agree to give Germany a free hand east or west. 'I told him quite bluntly', he said, 'that we would not have anyone make a wanton attack upon either Germany or France or any other nation for that matter.'[75] British interests and British foreign policy rested as ever on the preservation of a balance of power.

Yet there were things Lloyd George should not have done. Euphoria made him indiscreet in his contemptuous dismissal of Beneš, though aversion to the Czechs and their President was common in the Foreign Office. Hitler could surmise from this how Britain would react to German pressure on the Czechs in favour of the Sudeten Germans, whose cause he now openly championed at Nuremberg. Lloyd George's indiscretions also extended to British politics. He joked about Churchill to Ribbentrop. Later he gave the Hitler salute to Megan. The gesture was half in fun, a characteristic piece of clowning. His German onlookers were convulsed with laughter. But it was a public gesture; and it was unwise, as was his fulsome encomium of Hitler afterwards in the *Daily Express*.

Lloyd George was never a Nazi sympathiser. He admired Hitler's achievements, but never the measures he used to enforce his rule. In an interview with the *News Chronicle* the week after his return, he deplored Hitler's political and religious repression, 'a terrible thing to an old Liberal like myself'.[76] 'I need hardly say that I am no advocate of the immuring of political opponents in concentration camps.' He agreed that the persecution of the Jews was 'a grave and deplorable thing' and warned that its renewal 'would wither incipient goodwill in other lands'.[77] The Liberal tradition, however, was to encourage good relations with foreign states whatever their political complexion. Their internal problems were for them to resolve 'in their own way'. That was how Cobden and Gladstone had viewed relations with Napoleon III. The same principle applied to Hitler. 'That is why', he explained, 'I advocated a good understanding with him even after his sanguinary coup d'état', the Night of the Long Knives.[78]

Lloyd George learned little from Hitler that he did not know already. The visit confirmed what he came to see. The pilgrim goes to the shrine in the faith that his expectations will be fulfilled. In the man of destiny who now ruled Germany, Lloyd George saw a reflection of his own qualities, past and present. A strong man, both had agreed, a true leader at the helm in Germany and in Britain, would have prevented the catastrophe of 1914 – '*Ja, ja, ja*', Hitler exclaimed.[79] Lloyd George's *War Memoirs* dismissed the Kaiser as a fatuous bungler, and devoted sustained invective to the limp and fatal passivity of Sir Edward Grey. A strong man could have prevented war then, a strong man could prevent it now; and while Lloyd George saw that Hitler was bent on further consolidating German power and prestige, he was convinced that his policy towards Britain was positive and amicable. Insofar as Hitler was concerned with the ingathering of Germans lost at Versailles, Lloyd George had given warning at the Peace Conference. Memel and Danzig, he said now, 'are as German as Hull is English, and much more so than Cardiff is Welsh'; and as far as Danzig was concerned, 'the sooner the Germans cleared up that situation, the better'.[80] Union with Austria he thought natural and inevitable. The creation of a greater Germany he saw as the limit of Hitler's ambition, an object wholly compatible with British interests. Moreover, Hitler was 'a leader who would bring about complete understanding and friendship with Great Britain'.[81] This was, or could have been true, provided that Hitler appreciated that the unchanging principles of British foreign policy would never permit the grandiose division of spheres which he proposed. Lloyd George denied that Hitler intended war with Russia and believed that 'he has no desire to absorb millions of Slavs, whom he despises and would regard as an offence to the doctrine of racial purity'. Here, of course, he was grievously mistaken.[82]

Hitler was enacting at home the very social and economic policies which Lloyd George, as he ruefully told him, had urged, unsuccessfully, on the British government the year before, when it seemed possible that he might return to power to implement them: road building, land reclamation, agricultural settlements. 'Hitler is a builder', he enthused, 'a man who not only plans, but can put his plans into execution. He is the saviour of Germany, a great and wonderful leader.'[83] Was it not, as far as it went, undeniably true?

Certainly there were elective affinities between them. Lloyd George, Hitler told him, was 'one of the very few people in England today' who understood his aims.[84] He later said that Lloyd George was 'the one man in England whom he could point to as a genius': of all the Britons he had met, 'Lloyd George had made the greatest impression on him'.[85] Hitler readily identified with the qualities of 'the man who won the war' by embodying his people's will to victory. 1918 represented a year of fate for both men. 'I am convinced', Hitler told him, 'that had I been in power then, I could have prevented Germany's downfall.'[86] Looking back on the visit in 1942, he also believed that in 1936, 'if Lloyd George had had the necessary power, he would certainly have been the architect of a German-English understanding'.[87] Frances Stevenson agreed. 'I still believe', she wrote 30 years later, 'that had L.G. been given a say in the affairs of Britain during those years preceding 1939, with power to approach Hitler and negotiate with him, the Second World War would never have happened.'[88]

Lloyd George never doubted that an understanding with Hitler could have been reached. 'He made us two or three offers', he wrote to Conwell-Evans a year after the visit, 'which I urged the Government to act upon promptly.' Blame lay with 'the hesitancy and the nervelessness of the Baldwin Administration. They never saw an opportunity until it was too late to act upon it.'[89] If Hitler was determined on a war for *Lebensraum* come what might, then this was wishful thinking and no Anglo-German agreement could have prevented it. Yet if it was wishful thinking, Lloyd George was not alone in indulging in it. In December 1938, in the calamitous aftermath of Munich, another statesman lambasted the Baldwin administration. 'Three years ago we might have had a lasting settlement with Germany if real energy had been shown.' The speaker? Winston Churchill.[90]

On his return from Germany, Lloyd George had the library windows at Bron-y-de ripped out, the wall demolished and replaced by an enormous plate-glass window, overlooking his arbours and fields to the Surrey hills and 40 miles around from Sussex to Hampshire. 'A wonderful view', wrote Sylvester. 'It is an inspiration.'[91]

6
'A Conference *Now*': Lloyd George, Chamberlain and Churchill, 1939–40

A.J. Sylvester's accounts of Lloyd George—Lloyd George and Neville Chamberlain—the fall of Poland, 1939—Lloyd George agitates against Chamberlain—Hitler's peace offer—Lloyd George's Caernarvon speech—support for peace in 1939—Lloyd George and Chamberlain's resignation—Lloyd George, Chamberlain and Churchill—the fall of France

> The man stands head and shoulders above the present crew of British politicians. He foresees the deep crisis of the Empire. Hence his plain speaking.
>
> Goebbels, reporting Hitler's remarks on Lloyd George,
> 10 October 1939 (*The Goebbels Diaries 1939–1941*)

> I am going to try to stop this war before the Empire is smashed.
> Lloyd George, in conversation with
> A.J. Sylvester, 3 October 1939

We last met A.J. Sylvester at the Berghof, capturing Lloyd George and Hitler with his cine-camera, and then enthusing at the view from Brony-de. Sylvester was Lloyd George's private secretary from 1921 until the latter's death in 1945. In 1947, he published a book of reminiscences entitled *The Real Lloyd George*. Based on Sylvester's private diaries, it included an account of the visit to Hitler and touched on Lloyd George's attitudes to the Second World War. The book was outspoken for its time. Churchill had on this account cut Sylvester in the House of Commons. He later changed his mind – his curiosity was too much for him – and read Sylvester's revelations with alacrity. 'I wanted to find out what happened when Lloyd George met Hitler', he explained.[1] Even so, Sylvester was relatively discreet. He warned that he had not 'told the whole story of the Second World War'.[2]

In 1975, nearly 30 years later and in a less deferential age, Sylvester authorised publication of more substantial diary extracts under the title *Life with Lloyd George*. These revealed considerably more than the earlier book. In daily contact with Lloyd George for nearly a quarter of a century, Sylvester was uniquely placed to observe and analyse him. A brilliant stenographer, he took down Lloyd George's remarks verbatim, conveying a rare immediacy. Another 20 years on, in the National Library of Wales, the present writer came across a collection of unpublished letters from Sylvester to his wife. Among the most interesting of these relate to the opening months of the war.[3] Eighteen in number, they supplement the diary entries, and vice versa. Together the three sources provide a remarkably full account of Lloyd George's day-to-day reactions from the 'phoney war' to the fall of France.

They are far from being an impartial record, however. Sylvester held strong views, and his attitude towards Lloyd George clearly partook of a love–hate relationship. Veneration for what he called 'a very wonderful man' alternates with revulsion at aspects of what he saw as a flawed and complex character. Admiration for Lloyd George the spellbinding orator is tempered by anxiety for his career and his reputation. 'At the moment', he wrote, only a week after his earlier effusion, 'I am so contemptuous of him I have hardly any patience.'[4]

The reason for Sylvester's ambivalence is simple; and for many, perhaps most readers, it may be damning and conclusive. Within days of the outbreak of war, Sylvester became convinced that Lloyd George was a 'defeatist': that he did not believe that Britain could win, and that he favoured coming to terms with Hitler. Sylvester's own sentiments were straightforwardly patriotic. They prefigured the national bulldog spirit of 1940. He uses the word 'patriot' to describe what he plainly regarded as the only acceptable attitude. 'What about the patriot', he complained, 'standing up to a man who has said that he will swallow us?'[5] Of some pessimistic comments from Lloyd George to an American journalist he commented, 'I think it is *terrible.*' 'If news of them got out', he wrote, 'he will be shown not to be a patriot.'[6] Negotiation with Hitler 'would mean dishonour', and for Lloyd George to associate himself with it would be 'to disgrace the British Empire'.[7] These are heavy charges.

I

Before considering them, we must go back a little in time in order to note the state of relations between Lloyd George and Neville Chamberlain. These dated back to the Great War, when Lloyd George appointed Chamberlain as Director of National Service. He proved a failure, and Lloyd George dismissed him. 'It was not one of my successful selections', he told the world in his *War Memoirs*, explaining why in some detail and with obvious relish.[8] Chamberlain was a proud and sensitive man. His peremptory treatment and those candid reminiscences rankled. As he rose to second place in Baldwin's administration, becoming Conservative heir-apparent by the early 1930s, he made a point of blocking any opportunity of Lloyd George's taking office. In 1935, when Baldwin considered offering Lloyd George a Cabinet post, Chamberlain told him that he would not sit at the same table with him.[9] In May 1937 Chamberlain became Prime Minister.

By this time, Lloyd George had thought better of the pact with Hitler of which he had had such high hopes the year before; or rather he saw that circumstances were no longer propitious. While he never ceased to regard Hitler as a genius and to regret that a unique opportunity had been missed, he soon came to appreciate the threat to peace posed by Hitler's Germany. Hitler's blatant intervention on Franco's side in the Spanish Civil War despite his adhesion to the Non-Intervention Pact, in Lloyd George's eyes put a question mark over his good faith. He agreed with Churchill that it must be made plain to Hitler that aggression would be resisted. Lloyd George's apparent volte-face accorded with the realities of a rapidly deteriorating situation. A month after his return from Germany, he declared himself, so far as Hitler, Mussolini and Franco were concerned, 'against dictatorships out and out, root and branch, lock, stock and barrel'.[10] A deal with Hitler must wait until such time as Hitler had been taught a lesson, links with France strengthened and overtures made to Russia. Such was Lloyd George's attitude when Chamberlain entered 10 Downing Street. Chamberlain saw things the other way around: an accord with Germany, by which he meant concessions to Germany, would make Hitler more reasonable and warlike alignments with other states unnecessary. Hitler would learn that he could satisfy his territorial grievances through peaceful accommodation with Britain. Chamberlain wanted nothing to do with Russia and favoured Germany as a bastion against communism.

Lloyd George, who had a life-long belief in phrenology, pointed to the shape of Chamberlain's head as visible proof of his incompetence: 'Look at his head', he exclaimed on the day war broke out. 'The worst thing Neville Chamberlain ever did was to meet Hitler and let let Hitler see him.'[11] Phrenology aside, Lloyd George's diagnosis was accurate. Chamberlain lacked neither courage nor forcefulness, but he was blinkered, complacent, and in the pursuit of his foreign policy impervious to any view other than his own. Since he lacked all insight into Hitler's character and his policy was based on a complete misreading of that character, his predictions were consistently wrong and his policy invariably failed. Chamberlain never established the slightest credibility with Hitler, who held him in contempt; yet he prided himself that he had won an ascendancy over him. Lacking instinctive flair, he learned nothing from experience: failure only inspired him to try again. As the international situation slipped increasingly out of control in 1939, his final attempts to alternate Appeasement with a show of firmness were contradictory and misleading.

To his dying day Chamberlain never questioned the rightness of his policy. He was a profoundly obstinate man with a hard vein of conceit, and his inner vanity was stung by the successive attacks which Lloyd George launched at him from the day he became Prime Minister. 'I despised him and felt myself the better man', he wrote after one bruising encounter.[12] The antipathy was mutual. On the eve of Chamberlain's resignation, Thomas Jones noted, Lloyd George 'made no disguise of his contempt for Neville'.[13]

Lloyd George placed himself in the forefront of the opposition to Chamberlain's foreign policy. After Churchill, the leading advocate of a 'Grand Alliance', Lloyd George was Chamberlain's most persistent, incisive and unsparing critic. He was adept at needling, and he did not scruple to twist the knife. In June 1937, in his first foreign affairs speech as Prime Minister, Chamberlain spoke of the need to keep cool heads. 'Any fish can have a cool head', Lloyd George retorted. 'These dictators are very clever men, very daring men, very astute men', he observed, adding, 'They are taking at the present moment rather a low view of the intelligence and the courage of our Government – very low. I wish to God I could say it was too low.'[14] In the debate following Eden's resignation in February 1938, Lloyd George said that Chamberlain's political naivety made him unfit 'to deal with these Machiavellian dictators. He is only fit for a stained-glass window.'[15] These mocking interjections were not only wounding – and Chamberlain disliked being laughed at – they were also to the point. During the Munich crisis, Lloyd George repeated the charge that Chamberlain was out of his depth: 'Mr Chamberlain has not the experience, the breadth of mind, the imagination, nor the shrewd understanding of human nature which would fit him to face the most astute, subtle and audacious rulers.' 'He is no match for these astute, crafty, ruthless, unscrupulous dictators.'[16] Lloyd George understood his enemy; Chamberlain never did.

Chamberlain's sudden pledge in March 1939 of a guarantee of Poland's independence left Lloyd George incredulous and appalled at an act of supreme folly. Unsupported by any understanding with Russia, it was a terrible failure of judgement and comprehension, misconceived in every particular. Without Russian backing, it was bound to seem a bluff, and one which Hitler was likely to call. It immeasurably increased the risk of war. Yet Chamberlain persuaded himself that it would stop Hitler in his tracks. Like Churchill, Lloyd George lambasted Chamberlain's wilful and persistent neglect of the one element which might have put teeth in the guarantee and deterred Hitler. He railed against 'the supreme diplomatic imbecility of snubbing Russia'.[17] Chamberlain's rooted hostility to Russia, his obstinate refusal to come to terms with her, not only revealed his failure to grasp the realities of European power politics, but, as Lloyd George predicted, led inevitably and directly to catastrophe.

Chamberlain remained blind to the depths of his self-delusion. On 31 March, after announcing the guarantee to Poland in the House of Commons, he asked Lloyd George to come and see him. He wished to find out how Lloyd George would react in the coming debate. Had he not now done what his critics called for? He had sent Hitler a clear warning. He had drawn a line beyond which Hitler would not venture. Germany, he told Lloyd George, would not fight on two fronts. 'What is there on the other front?' Lloyd George asked. 'The Polish army', replied Chamberlain. Lloyd George dismissed this. Poland's poorly equipped army was no match for Hitler's Wehrmacht, and Poland had no air-force. Could the Prime Minister still not see that the key to the whole situation was Russia? Chamberlain expressed the view that 'Russia would come in ultimately.' Lloyd George warned that 'this was a very reckless gamble'. Chamberlain repeated his belief that 'Hitler would recoil when he realised that he was being confronted with a war on two fronts.'[18] The Prime Minister was inwardly upset. Lloyd George, as ever, riled and distressed him. But events soon proved which of them was right.

In the debate on the Polish guarantee on 3 April, Lloyd George trenchantly publicised his objections. 'If we are going in without the help of Russia', he warned, 'we are walking into a trap.'[19] Chamberlain's policy was 'a frightful gamble', leading straight to war. He called on Chamberlain 'to take immediate steps to secure the adhesion of Russia',[20] without which, he declared on 8 May, the guarantee to Poland was 'madness'. That guarantee and the guarantees which Chamberlain went on to give to Rumania and Greece were, he said, 'the most reckless commitments that any country has ever entered into'. They were 'demented pledges, that cannot be redeemed'.[21] Obstinately, Chamberlain had long refused to countenance negotiations with Russia:

> You need Russia, but you do not want Russia. Without her, there are two alternatives. If you are called upon to redeem these pledges, maybe in a few days or perhaps in a few weeks, you have two alternatives – to face certain disaster or to skulk from your pledge.[22]

Three months later, Lloyd George's forebodings were vindicated when Hitler concluded the Ribbentrop–Molotov non-aggression pact with Russia which made war a certainty. Chamberlain had believed such a realignment of ideological enemies to be impossible. He did not realise that it was his own attitude which provoked this diplomatic revolution. Nevertheless when war was declared on 3 September, Lloyd George pledged his support under 'any Government that is in power'.[23] He may have been fishing for a place in the Cabinet. If so, his hints fell on deaf ears. He may have been hinting at the need for a fresh administration, a Government of National Unity. But while Churchill was at once brought into the Cabinet, no invitation came for Lloyd George.

II

Lloyd George's attitude to the war quickly changed with the collapse of Poland, under relentless attack from Germany, and then, under a secret provision of the Ribbentrop-Molotov pact, invaded by Russia. Barely ten days after Britain declared war, Lloyd George was convinced that Poland was doomed. From the time of the Paris Peace Conference he had been sceptical of the quality of Poland's leaders and had denounced their territorial greed. In the Fontainebleau Memorandum he warned against including within Poland 'large masses of Germans, clamouring for reunion with their native land'.[24] In 1920 he had deplored Poland's seizure from Russia of lands far beyond her ethnic limits.

Now the whirligig of time had brought in his revenges. With Germany and Russia once more in possession of their lost territories, the international situation had radically and in Lloyd George's eyes irreversibly altered. Insofar as the problem of Poland's frontiers had occasioned the war, he saw that problem as capable of solution only by the acceptance of a fait accompli, but a fait accompli not unjustified in terms of national self-determination. He had in mind the reconstitution of an 'ethnic' Poland. To accept this, however, would mean a revision of Britain's policy of war with Germany; and it would mean distancing Britain from the existing Polish government.

Lloyd George now set out to discredit that government. On 24 September, he published an article in the *Sunday Express* sharply critical of the Polish regime. This provoked the next day what Sylvester called 'a snorty letter'[25] from the Polish ambassador, which appeared in the *Daily Express* on 27 September. Lloyd George drafted an immediate reply and charged Sylvester with its circulation to pressmen and parliament. Sylvester noted: 'Today I have been busy with the reply, getting it out to the Press, and I have just made arrangements...at the House to reproduce it and send a copy to every member tonight.'[26] Lloyd George's reply was to the point. It trounced the Polish regime and the policies which had led to Poland's ruin. 'I am sure', he wrote, 'that the people of Britain are not prepared to make colossal sacrifices to restore to power a Polish regime represented by the present Government.' Britain, he declared, would not fight 'to force back under Polish rule people of another race who objected to the imposition and were subjugated by the force of Polish arms, nor for the restoration of a particular régime which has failed in the hour of its country's distress'.[27]

His message was clear. Britain had gone to war for the old, overextended and overweening Poland of the 'colonels'. That Poland was gone forever and Britain had no interest in fighting for its restoration. There must be urgent reconsideration of British policy, a complete reappraisal of war aims. What, in effect, he asked, was Britain fighting for? His thinking was given particular point the next day, 28 September, when Ribbentrop and Molotov issued a joint communiqué calling on Britain to accept the status quo. There was, they declared, no reason for the war to continue.

The collapse of Poland led to political crisis in Britain. Discontent with Chamberlain was rife among MPs of all parties; and Lloyd George, 'the man who won the war' in 1918, was one obvious figurehead for those who sought more vigorous leadership. Sylvester believed that Lloyd George, by his experience, his authority and his parliamentary brilliance, was well placed to voice that discontent and to agitate for change. He shared Lloyd George's opinion of Chamberlain. 'The sooner Chamberlain goes, the better', he commented on 20 September, 'but he will take something like dynamite to shift him.'[28] Sylvester hoped that Lloyd George would provide that something. Lloyd George was nothing loath.

He had broadened his Council of Action into an all-party group of MPs, including such young progressives as Robert Boothby, Harold Nicolson and Eleanor Rathbone. On 27 September he addressed what Sylvester called a 'very representative' audience of some 25 members. Sylvester put it to Lloyd George that he should demand a secret session of parliament.[29]

Sylvester hoped to see in Lloyd George a re-emergence of the national leader of World War I, around whom 'patriots' of all parties could rally, the spokesman for change who would force the issue at Westminster. Sylvester's purpose in urging him to demand a secret session was 'so that he could speak his mind; and if he would only speak his mind, he would be voicing 90 per cent of the views of all parliamentarians'.[30] 'The ultimate idea', Sylvester confirmed, 'is, of course, to unseat this Government.'[31] He noted enthusiasm among Tories for such a strategy. At the same time, however, he sounded another note, revealing his doubts about Lloyd George's underlying commitment to victory. 'I would be happier if I could see some drive in him, some fixity of purpose, some definite policy. His is merely guerilla warfare [that is, against the Government], with no application.' He concluded: 'That does not sound to me as if he could fight a war. Perhaps I am wrong. I hope I am.'[32] From now on these misgivings were uppermost in Sylvester's mind. Was Lloyd George for war? Or for peace? He had told the Action Group that if the chances of victory were less than even, peace should be made.[33] The political editor of the *Daily Mail* told Sylvester that if Lloyd George was for peace, 'he ought to be bloody well locked up'; and if not, that 'he ought to make a statement in the House to clarify his position'.[34]

On 3 October, Poland surrendered. Chamberlain in the Commons declared Britain's resolve to fight on. Lloyd George followed with a speech in which he sounded a different, though carefully modulated note. He urged that if, as he believed, a peace initiative might be forthcoming, 'I think it is very important that we should not come to too hurried a conclusion.' He raised the prospect of a revision of the Versailles settlement, the discussion of specific German grievances and the future of eastern and central Europe, including Poland and Czechoslovakia. The question of peace, he stressed, 'needs very careful consideration'.[35]

The speech caused a sensation.[36] It was the first open suggestion that the war might be stopped without the defeat of Germany or the overthrow of the Nazi regime. Lloyd George was at once denounced in the House by Duff Cooper as a defeatist, his words 'a suggestion of surrender'.[37] But Lloyd George had chosen his words deliberately. Another MP told Sylvester the next day: 'When I heard his speech, I thought it was "bloody". When I read it in Hansard this morning, I wondered why I had thought so.' 'Precisely', commented Sylvester: 'He created the *impression* without saying so in so many words. Clever.'[38]

Sylvester himself did not doubt what Lloyd George had in mind. 'He has made a speech in the House', Sylvester wrote, 'which will cause some concern in the country, for it is a peace speech.'[39] The next day he described the impact that the speech had made: 'He let loose his speech in the afternoon, since when I have not stopped working, and the telephone was ringing until well after midnight. There is violent criticism on the one hand, and support on the other.'[40] Sylvester's own immediate reaction as a 'patriot' was on the side of Duff Cooper. 'Duff Cooper made a hot speech', he wrote, 'especially when he charged him with surrender. I thought he [Lloyd George] was very slashed up and jittery when he rose to say that that was the first time he had been charged with surrender. Later, however, he got cocky again, and now he says he is going on with it.'[41] Going on with what, one asks? With ostensibly advocating the vigorous prosecution of the war on the one hand while simultaneously extending peace feelers on the other.

While he described Lloyd George's pronouncement as 'a peace speech', Sylvester's atttitude was, all the same, not wholly condemnatory. He felt that it was the timing of the speech as much as its message that was at fault. 'Many people say it is ill-timed, and that, I think, is my judgment', he wrote on 3 October.[42] The next day he remained sceptical but relatively open-minded: 'Personally I cannot see that we can expect anything but defeat if we make peace now, with Germany on top; but it all depends upon the terms.'[43] 'If we knew the terms, it would be something; but we have little idea what they will be; and until we know, what is the good of talking anyhow?'[44] What continued to worry Sylvester was his belief that Lloyd George was at heart a 'defeatist'. However much he might palliate his addresses to the Commons or to the Council of Action, his remarks in private showed the real direction of his thoughts. 'It is his private conversation which I don't like', Sylvester noted. 'He said yesterday to me that "we are going to lose this war"; "I am going to try to stop this war before the Empire is smashed".'[45]

Sylvester perceived in Lloyd George a mixture of aims and motives: desire for office, rooted dislike of Chamberlain and contempt for his record of failure, alarm at Britain's military prospects and a conviction of his own grasp of the crisis, and the vision, energy and experience to confront it. Sylvester himself, as we have seen, was no admirer of Chamberlain; but he sensed a lack of principle in Lloyd George's unremitting hostility towards him. Sylvester complained that Lloyd George was inconsistent and animated by personal pique. 'It is only a few months ago that Neville C[hamberlain] was trying to make peace. Then "he" was criticising him for doing so. Now we are at war and "he" wants us to make peace *now*. What he really wants is to bring this Government rolling down in the muck. It's all wrong because he is not there at the head.'[46] Here Sylvester was unfair. There was no inconsistency in Lloyd George's criticism of Chamberlain's pre-war policy, which had failed to prevent war, and of his guarantee to Poland, which had brought it on.

Lloyd George was enjoying, at this time of crisis, the excitement of indulging, with effect, his taste for the dramatic intervention and the consciousness of provoking a major political sensation. His speech in the Commons was making the nation sit up and listen. He had gained the initiative. He had upstaged the Prime Minister and had hinted at a radical alternative policy. He was articulating what many wanted to hear. For the first time since 1922, he was in some measure the man of the moment. Who could tell what might fall within his grasp? Sylvester condemned his attitude as irresponsible and vainglorious. 'He is like a peacock with his tail in full show', he noted, adding, in a somewhat mixed simile, 'gloating over the fact that he has put the cat among the pigeons. He has done that all right.'[47] Lloyd George's self-esteem was massively inflated by the letters of support which came flooding in daily at the Commons and at Bron-y-de. Sylvester had never known him to receive so much mail in London. 'He has had an enormous post', wrote Sylvester, three days after the speech, 'but that is *nothing to what we have had at C[hurt]*.'[48]

On 5 October Sylvester again assessed the repercussions of the 'peace speech'. He conceded that it had polarised opinion at Westminster. It was no longer a question of Lloyd George's agitating for the more active prosecution of the war, but of definitely manoeuvering for peace. 'There is a new situation in the war caused by "his" speech', Sylvester wrote. 'There are violent expressions of abuse, and those who agree, the latter at the moment being in the minority, but it is a strong minority.'[49] The angry reactions of Lloyd George's critics showed that his intended message had gone home. They were not slow in making their feelings known. 'I have never in my life had such abuse thrown at me as I have in the Lobby since that speech', wrote Sylvester. 'Some will hardly speak to me.'[50] Sylvester returned again to the divergence in the speech between appearance and sub-text. 'When you read his speech, there is nothing much in it other than what the P. M. has said, but then I know privately and *sub rosa* that he thinks we are "licked"; that he means to do all he can to stop the war before we are "bust" completely ...Although he says he will fight if the terms are not satisfactory, nevertheless he has started a rather defeatist feeling throughout the country, though he would not call it that or admit that that is what he meant.'[51]

Lloyd George's speech could hardly have come at a more dramatic moment. Three days later on 6 October, Hitler himself, speaking in the Reichstag, offered peace. He said that he saw no reason for the war to continue. The Treaty of Versailles was null and void. He expressed his readiness to attend a peace conference, to discuss disarmament, the German colonies and a reconstituted Poland. He denied any hostility to Britain: 'I believe even today', he declared, 'that there can only be real peace in Europe and throughout the world if Germany and England come to an understanding.'[52] Hitler's speech gave immediate and sensational relevance to Lloyd George's. Lloyd George at once seized on it. In an article published in the *Sunday Express* on 8 October, he appealed for Hitler's offer to be given earnest consideration 'in view of the terrible prospect opened out by the rejection of a Peace Conference'. He was in exultant, jubilant mood, believing himself to be on the crest of a wave of public support and anticipating that his moment would not be long in coming. 'This is the most popular move I have ever taken in my life', he told Sylvester.[53]

Lloyd George remained buoyed up by the deluge of letters that came with every post. Sylvester himself was taken aback. '*Thousands and thousands* have written to him on *peace*', he wrote on 11 October.[54] Meanwhile, Lloyd George, though excitedly aware that a critical moment in his career was impending, had not yet decided how to proceed. 'He has not made up his mind publicly', Sylvester wrote, 'though I know what it is privately. I'll wager he doesn't dare let his private opinion become public. There would be damn little support for him if he did.'[55] What *was* his private opinion? Sylvester recorded his understanding of it on 9 October, repeating his habitual charge. 'He said on the phone today that no one could call him a pacifist. No, but what is not realised is that privately he is a defeatist, which is worse.'[56]

On 12 October, in the House of Commons, Chamberlain rejected Hitler's offer in language of bitter recrimination. Lloyd George was present but said nothing. He did not wish to jeopardise his burgeoning campaign and again be branded as unpatriotic in a hostile Chamber by an attempt, however guarded, to question Chamberlain's show of defiance. That evening, however, at a meeting of the Council of Action, he voiced cautious but clear reservations at the Prime Minister's apparently uncompromising response, raising the question whether Chamberlain intended to be taken literally. 'It may be', he said, 'that the door will be left open. I sincerely hope it will.'[57] While leaving this question hanging in the air, Sylvester reported, he deftly combined it with a telling attack on Chamberlain's record of incompetence both before and during the war, giving the clear impression that the time was right to consider an alternative. 'He made one of the most brilliant speeches ever on the general situation', Sylvester reported, 'What led to the present unfortunate situation, the chances we missed. That was admirable.'[58] What Lloyd George undoubtedly sought, Sylvester agreed, the goal to which he was irresistibly leading, was – 'a conference *now*'.[59]

Sylvester noted that Lloyd George's address had a marked impact on the Council of Action. 'At that meeting', he wrote, 'there was a definite cleavage.'[60] The cleavage, moreover, was over the means, not the end: it was between those in sympathy with Lloyd George's wish to respond at once to Hitler's offer, and those who, like Sylvester, took the view that 'we could only go into a conference *now* on Hitler's terms; that would mean we were the defeated Power. We could not agree to that.'[61] Lloyd George himself refused to accept these stark alternatives. Ever open to the variety of possibilities in a given political situation, he sought to exploit the circumstances to Britain's advantage. He invoked his own record of manoeuvre at international conferences. Sylvester would have none of it. As he saw it, any settlement was bound to be dictated by Hitler. 'He has never faced that', wrote Sylvester, 'but burked the question of the conference by saying: "Ah, I have great experience of these things. Once you get into a conference, you talk, and you could never afford to let a conference break down once it had started".' 'That', Sylvester observed, 'is pure concentrated bosh.'[62]

Lloyd George decided to follow up the sensation created by his Commons speech with an address in his own constituency of Caernarvon Boroughs. Here he would test in the public arena the proposals which he had adumbrated in parliament and the press. This led him, however, into a dilemma as to what he should say and how to say it. Even in the Council of Action he had been worried and embarrassed by the fact that a policeman had been detailed to keep an eye on him. 'The idea that the Father of the House, the man who won the last war, should be watched, upset him', Sylvester noted.[63] It was one thing to divulge his thoughts among sympathisers in the Council of Action. It was another to hazard the entire situation by speaking out before a large and possibly hostile audience.

At Sylvester's suggestion, one of Lloyd George's political staff, Walter Belcher, went ahead to Caernarvon to sound out local opinion. For several days before the meeting, Lloyd George continued to be agitated by the problem of how to rally opinion in favour of peace while ostensibly encouraging the war effort. On 17 October, Sylvester confided to his wife: 'I am amused. He knows he is up a gum-tree, so, at Caernarvon, according to what he told me on the phone this morning, he is going to talk about *war aims*.' Sylvester continued, with laboured irony, 'something, my dear, which is beautifully obscure, but away from the conference, although he will doubtless *just mention* that, but away from the question of *conference*'.[64]

The next day, Belcher telephoned Sylvester from Caernarvon to report that Lloyd George's constituents expected him to speak in support of Chamberlain and for the prosecution of the war. 'They think that "he" should support the man at the wheel, and that the country should be united the same as it was under him when he was at the helm.'[65] Given the strength of local feeling, it was even thought advisable that 'policemen should be in the meeting, as there might be a rumpus!'[66] Belcher told Sylvester that 'it is only the parsons and the pacifists who want peace at any price, and the others say that before we talk peace we must smash Hitler'.[67] Sylvester then telephoned through Belcher's message to Bron-y-de. 'I have put this over the wire, and am awaiting the reactions from Churt!' he wrote.[68]

Lloyd George rose to the challenge with all his accustomed brilliance. On arriving at Caernarvon, he explained to his worried constituency workers 'the importance of making clear our war aims'.[69] He drew on his experience of the Great War. The first thing he had done on becoming Prime Minister in 1916 was to come to Caernarvon to spell out Britain's war aims. 'We had to make it absolutely clear for the benefit of our own population, and for the neutrals as well, what we were fighting for.'[70] On that occasion Germany had played into Britain's hands by refusing to state her own war aims. His policy of explicitness, in bold contrast with Germany's prevarication, had helped to bring America onto the Allied side. Now it was the other way round. Hitler had stated that he had achieved his war aims, that there was no need for the war to continue and that he was ready to attend a peace conference; and he had set a clear agenda for discussion. 'It was a very clever move on his part', Lloyd George observed.[71] Once again, Hitler had wrongfooted Chamberlain. Misunderstanding the realities as ever, Chamberlain had utterly failed to match the occasion. He had put himself in the wrong by ruling out negotiation. 'It is no use', said Lloyd George, 'slamming doors in the face of a man, when it is really *his* game to do so. Hitler is now able to say: "I talk peace, and what did they do? They simply say: You are a liar, a thief and a cheat; and we will not answer you".'[72] Chamberlain had handed Hitler a huge propaganda victory. Hitler's peace offer was a public statement addressed to world opinion. That opinion was important. 'Russia and Italy would make all the difference in the world. And there is America outside, too.'[73]

Contrary to Sylvester's expectations, the speech in the Pavilion at Caernarvon on 21 October was a triumph. Lloyd George showed himself at his superlative best – on Sylvester's admission, 'an outstanding success'.[74] The Pavilion was crammed to capacity, with an audience of around 8000. Hundreds stood in the aisles. Those seated rose to their feet and applauded as Lloyd George entered. His speech in the Commons, he declared, had been 'grossly, and, he feared, viciously misrepresented'.[75] Sylvester records how Lloyd George, departing widely from his notes, warmed to his theme, and, weaving his old magic on the mood of his listeners, captivated that enormous throng. He had them 'in his hands . . . You could have heard a pin drop. The only noise was the tumultuous applause which punctuated his discourse.'[76] 'I stood in the wings', he continued,

> and watched his play-acting to these masses of people. It was superb. One moment he was playing up to the blue-blooded Tories – and many were present – talking about our superb air force and about the greatest navy in the world; you could feel them puff with pride. Next he was playing up to the peacemongers, by advocating a conference and peace . . . Thus he carried everybody off their feet, and there was not even a single heckle or question. He had them so that he could make them laugh or cry at his will and pleasure.[77]

III

How fair was Sylvester? Were Lloyd George's hopes of peacemaking mere flights of fancy and wishful thinking? Were his sympathisers really to be put down as 'only the parsons and the pacifists' and his idea of a peace conference no more than, in Sylvester's words, 'pure concentrated bosh'? Even Sylvester accepted that Lloyd George's call attracted 'a strong minority' in the Commons.[78] Evidence now available points to a measure of support for peace considerably wider than is commonly supposed. It is no longer enough to marginalise this as the views of Tory extremists, Mosleyites and Communists.[79] True, as Paul Addison points out, 'Lloyd George found scarcely anyone of significance in public life to support him';[80] but his views produced behind-the-scenes echoes in the corridors of power. The Leo Amery diaries, published in 1988, indicate 'some approval' for peace moves in the Conservative 1922 Committee. They also report a discussion on 28 September 1939 between Amery and the veteran Foreign Office anti-appeaser, Robert Vansittart, who, according to Amery, 'was definitely pessimistic and inclined to think that we might have at any rate to toy with any offer of a conference put forward in order to gain time for our preparations'.[81]

David Carlton has also pointed to pressure on Downing Street from the Dominions. Smuts of South Africa, Menzies of Australia and Savage of New Zealand all called for a reappraisal of British policy in the light of Hitler's offer, and a willingness to consider revision of Versailles.[82] All the Dominions urged a reformulation of peace aims along the lines of national self-determination and a peace conference, its agenda to include redrawing the boundaries of Poland and Czechoslovakia. This was exactly what Lloyd George proposed. Like Lloyd George, the Dominions felt that Chamberlain's rejection of Hitler's peace offer 'went too far in the direction of "slamming the door" on further discussion'.[83] The Soviet ambassador, Ivan Maisky, provides another source of information. In his diary, and his despatches to the Soviet Foreign Minister, Molotov, published in 1992, he details individual discussions held in October 1939 with Leslie Burgin, the minister of supply, Walter Elliot, the minister of health, R.A. Butler, deputy foreign secretary, and with Horace Wilson, Chamberlain's special adviser, all of whom made it clear that in principle the government was prepared, in Butler's words, 'to make peace tomorrow', to make substantial colonial concessions to Germany and to settle for a Poland and Czechoslovakia confined to their ethnic boundaries; to accept, in other words, the reality of a 'Greater Germany' under Nazi rule.[84]

For Chamberlain, there were two obstacles to peacemaking: the reluctance of the major neutrals to take part and hold the ring at a conference – only the smaller states volunteered their good offices – and, above all, the person of Hitler. Horace Wilson told Maisky that Britain could deal with any other German, but not with him.[85] Lloyd George was less squeamish in his desire to seize the chance, fast vanishing, of an accommodation. Hitler's escape from an assassination attempt on 8 November suggested an opportunity to re-establish a line of personal communication, given the remarkably favourable impression which the two men had formed of each other three years before at Berchtesgaden. Lloyd George now thought to indicate by a friendly signal to Hitler that there were those in Britain who favoured a positive response to his offer. Sylvester wrote to his wife: 'Very privately, incredible though it seems, he actually talked of sending a cable to Hitler the other day congratulating him on his escape!!! He is still keen on peace; but it does not look very opportune.'[86]

It was true that the moment had passed for taking up Hitler's offer. Chamberlain had dismissed it out of hand on the grounds that Hitler could not be trusted. Yet Hitler's call for peace at this juncture may have been sincere.[87] He had neither wanted nor expected war with Britain. He was an admirer of the British Empire. He had settled his immediate scores with Poland. His offer may or may not have been genuine. If it was, then as Lloyd George argued, what was to be lost by taking it up? If it was not, there was, in his view, equal reason to put Hitler to the test. On 9 October, Lloyd George wrote to the Foreign Office. It might well be, he allowed, 'that Hitler's peace offer has no other purpose than simply that of a peace offensive to weaken us. That is why I would have a peace counter-offensive which would baffle him and strengthen us.'[88] Hitler would be exposed and isolated before world opinion, including German opinion, as the sole obstacle to peace, public enemy number one; and if that were so, Britain would re-enter the struggle confident in the knowledge that there was no alternative.[89] But the moment had come and gone. Public opinion seemed, for the present, resolved to see the thing through, or at any rate to sit out the 'phoney war'. The loss of the *Royal Oak* to a German submarine at Scapa Flow and a bellicose speech by Ribbentrop on 21 October stiffened British resistance. Lloyd George was marginalised in the press as eccentric and out of touch.

In his accounts of Lloyd George's activities in the autumn of 1939, Sylvester invariably placed them in a bad light. He never allowed that Lloyd George might in his way be considered a 'patriot' or might be inspired by other than personal considerations. 'What is the cause of all this?' he wrote on 29 November, returning to the same basic charge. 'It is simply that he hates so much those in power, and he is doing it out of pique. He wants them to fail', Sylvester insisted, 'and to hell to the country and what happens to it.'[90] In the circumstances of the time, however, were Lloyd George's hopes of peacemaking so very outré? Britain had manifestly failed in the object for which she had ostensibly gone to war, namely to save Poland. Britain might stave off defeat in the all-out war with Germany which was her only official policy. Prospects of victory were remote and uncertain. Yet Britain and France were both undefeated, indeed untried. While this was so, was it not common prudence – rather than to fling Hitler's olive branch back in his face – to investigate the possibilities, however slim, of a settlement before the horrors of total war were unleashed on the west? Was it cowardly or unworthy of Lloyd George to 'do all he can to stop the war before we are "bust" completely' or 'to try to stop this war before the Empire is smashed'?[91]

Lloyd George himself expressed no regrets, except at what he saw as the loss of a unique opportunity. 'Although many people will hardly believe it', he protested, 'I am only thinking of this grand old country of ours.'[92] His Caernarvon speech closed with this sober exhortation:

> Let us seize this, maybe the last opportunity for years, to confer, before the indescribable horror and calamity of a great war brings death and anguish to millions of households in many lands.[93]

IV

As 1940 opened, Lloyd George continued to speak out on the war, though not against it. On 28 February he warned the Commons of the appalling risk of Britain sliding into war with Russia on the side of Finland.[94] The speech was well received. He was once more in tune with a mounting disquiet and lack of confidence in the Chamberlain government. Behind his concentration on its shortcomings in the conduct of the war he continued to gauge his own chances of a return to power. Reading approving press comment on his Finland speech, he told Sylvester and Frances Stevenson: 'I have a great part to play in this war yet.'[95]

In April, as the Germans overran Denmark and Norway and the British expeditionary force in Norway was edged out, it became clear that Chamberlain's position as Prime Minister was approaching its crisis. There was talk of a ministry under Lloyd George. 'Ah', said Lloyd George to Sylvester, 'but it would have to be made perfectly clear that I could not bring about a decisive victory, as I did last time. We have made so many mistakes that we are not in nearly so good a position.'[96] A Lloyd George administration, in other words, was likely to negotiate a compromise peace.

On 7 May, Lloyd George lunched with Nancy Astor, Thomas Jones, Garvin and others. Lady Astor openly told him that they were vetting him as a possible successor to Chamberlain. What would be his attitude, they asked him, if he were invited to form a government? Lloyd George cited historical precedent. 'Clemenceau had waited until France was in the very gravest danger.'[97] The inference was clear, as Jones noted. Lloyd

George 'preferred to await his country's summons a little longer, but... he expected to receive it as the peril grew'.[98] Lloyd George convinced his listeners, in Jones's words, that

> he ought to be in the War Cabinet and that he would be far better off there than Neville, not only because of his resource and drive, but because he was built on a scale more commensurate with that of the enemy to be conquered. His conception of the struggle had nothing of the pettiness or complacency of Neville and his party entourage.[99]

Next day in the House of Commons, Lloyd George again proved his mettle. In the debate on the Norway campaign, he delivered one of the most powerful and effective speeches of his entire career, with a crushing attack on Chamberlain. It was his last and not his least contribution to history. He was passionate, he was vehement, he was direct. He aimed his shafts with accuracy, and they struck home. He reviewed Chamberlain's record with contempt. The 'guarantees' which Chamberlain had so lavishly and so recklessly distributed – to Czechoslovakia, to Poland, to Finland, to Norway – had all proved worthless: 'Our promissory notes are now rubbish on the market.'[100] Chamberlain at bay, in a moment of pride, distress and folly, had appealed to his 'friends in the House – and I have friends... to support us in the lobby tonight' with their votes. It was this lapse which had persuaded Lloyd George to enter the debate. It was not a question, he said, of the Prime Minister's friends. It was a far bigger issue. Chamberlain had appealed for 'sacrifice'. Lloyd George rolled the word on his tongue and almost spat it back at the Prime Minister. The nation was 'prepared for every sacrifice', he said, 'so long as it has leadership'. Then, in a famous peroration, he went for the kill. 'I say solemnly that the Prime Minister should give an example of sacrifice, because there is nothing which can contribute more to victory in this war than that he should sacrifice the seals of office.'[101] Chamberlain 'winced and wilted' under these blows.[102] Two days later he resigned and was succeeded by Churchill. The same morning, 10 May, Hitler launched his blitzkrieg across Holland and Belgium.

Instead of withdrawing from the political arena in dignified retirement to the backbenches or the House of Lords, however, Chamberlain, to Lloyd George's intense disgust, remained in office as Lord President of the Council and leader of the Conservative Party. He was as proud, unrepentant and tenacious of power as ever. His authority in Churchill's Cabinet was stronger, and Churchill's position far less secure, than would seem in retrospect.[103] The Conservative parliamentary majority was enormous; and Chamberlain's personal majority, in what had in effect been a vote of censure, was still substantial. Among many Conservative backbenchers the afterthought remained that Chamberlain, for whom they retained much goodwill, had been ousted by a disloyal caucus under Churchill, egged on by Lloyd George. Two-thirds of Chamberlain's ministers remained in the new administration; and Halifax, who after Chamberlain, had been most closely associated with Chamberlain's foreign policy, was still Foreign Secretary. Despite Churchill's inclusion in his Cabinet of the two Labour spokesmen, Attlee and Greenwood, it was Chamberlain, holding the balance between Halifax and Churchill, who held Churchill in check. He also retained his power of veto on Lloyd George's entry into the government. Lloyd George perceived this as soon as he learned the composition of the new Cabinet. He professed to be 'glad to be out of it. It would be like the old horse in the pantomime, with the front legs of a race horse and the hind legs of a mule.'[104]

This was sour grapes. Frances Stevenson noted that Lloyd George was 'very much upset when he realised that the War Cabinet was fixed'.[105] He had expected that, the main offices having been filled, Churchill would offer him responsibility for agriculture. He had himself pronounced medically fit by Lord Dawson in anticipation of a summons. None came. 'That suits me to the ground at the present moment', he told Sylvester on May 12. 'I would simply be there fretting and fuming, and having no real authority...Neville would have infinitely more authority than I would have, and he would oppose everything I proposed.' 'This is not the end by any means', he insisted.[106]

Chamberlain remained the immovable obstacle. On 13 May, when Churchill first entered the Commons as Prime Minister, it was Chamberlain, not Churchill, who was cheered by the Conservatives. Lloyd George was generous to Churchill in his words of welcome in the House, and Churchill was moved to tears; but in the lobby afterwards Lloyd George asked him 'if he could not fight Neville Chamberlain, how could he hope successfully to tackle Hitler?'[107]

Such were the words he used to Churchill; but to Frances Stevenson he told a different story, as the news became suddenly grave with the German breakthrough that day across the Meuse at Sedan and the rapid follow-up across France. One after another, the French armies were surrounded and scattered. The British Expeditionary Force began its retreat towards the Channel, with every likelihood of interception, rout and captivity. As disaster loomed in the air, the idea of ceasefire began to be whispered. Churchill himself, while adamant against surrender, warned Roosevelt that 'the weight may be more than we can bear'.[108]

Lloyd George was stunned by the speed and magnitude of Hitler's success. He was sombre and thoughtful. 'He talks about giving in without fighting', Frances Stevenson told Sylvester on 15 May, 'because he thinks we are beaten.'[109] The next day, Lloyd George lunched with Churchill at Admiralty House – Chamberlain was taking his time about moving out of Downing Street – and returned 'looking very grim'. 'Things are very bad', he told Sylvester. Afterwards 'he said he was glad to be out of this War Cabinet. He would definitely not serve with Neville Chamberlain.'[110] Four days later, as the Germans reached the Channel, he again distanced himself from the Cabinet, 'this gang', as he called it.[111] The next day he was again denouncing Chamberlain to Sylvester for having dragged Britain into war unprepared and without Russia. These enormities made him 'hesitate whether to go into anything in which Neville Chamberlain is concerned'. 'You cannot do anything unless you have supreme authority', he added significantly.[112]

On 28 May, at the height of the Dunkirk evacuation, Churchill at last offered Lloyd George a position in the Cabinet – subject to Chamberlain's approval! Lloyd George responded the next day in a letter of dignified refusal. He would not consider a conditional offer. He remained 'genuinely anxious to help to extricate my country from the most terrible disaster into which it has ever been plunged by the ineptitude of her rulers'. However, he added, 'several of the architects of this disaster are still leading members of your Government, and two of them are in the Cabinet'.[113] His original draft was still more outspoken. He named Chamberlain and Halifax as 'directly responsible for the terrible mess in which we have been landed'; and described Chamberlain, with understandable bitterness, as 'so indispensable to you that you cannot invite to your counsels a man who had the greatest and most successful experience in the conduct of the last war without first of all obtaining his doubtful assent'.[114] Churchill's reply candidly confirmed his political dependence on Chamberlain: 'I cannot complain in any way of what you say in your letter. The Government I have formed is founded upon the leaders of the three parties, and like you, I have no party of my own.'[115]

A week later, on 4 June, as the Germans raced towards Paris, Churchill at last summoned Lloyd George to Downing Street. This time he made him a firm offer. Churchill had appealed to Chamberlain's patriotism and the need for national unity, and Chamberlain had reluctantly consented. But now Lloyd George raised the stakes by refusing to serve as long as Chamberlain was in the Cabinet. As his car drew up to No. 10, he told Sylvester: 'I won't go in with Neville.'[116] When Churchill formally made him the offer, he asked for time to think it over. His thoughts, like everyone's, were on events across the Channel, now unfolding with terrifying speed towards their denouement. The Germans swept on unopposed, west through Normandy and Brittany, south to the Loire and the Rhone. The Maginot line was taken from the rear. On 14 June, they entered Paris. Dijon fell on 16 June, Lyons on the twentieth. The 84-year-old Marshal Pétain became Prime Minister and immediately requested an armistice. Hitler came to Compiègne to flaunt his colossal revenge in the same railway carriage in which Foch had dictated the armistice in 1918. The stage seemed set for the invasion of England. Nothing like this had been seen since Napoleon's army stood at Boulogne; and, viewed from that perspective, Hitler, said Lloyd George, was 'the greatest figure in Europe since Napoleon, and possibly greater than him'.[117] On 18 June, Churchill called on his countrymen to prepare for 'their finest hour'.

The days passed. Churchill's offer to Lloyd George went unanswered. Might not Lloyd George, Chamberlain remarked to Churchill, be 'waiting to be the Marshal Pétain of Britain?'[118] It was fair comment, save that Lloyd George held far better cards than the Marshal. Britain was down, but certainly not out. Lloyd George indeed continued to stand apart from the government. Not only did he continue to raise difficulties about Chamberlain, but he was increasingly dismissive of the Cabinet generally, which he contrasted with his own War Cabinet of World War I. Churchill apart, it was 'a cabinet which is not a cabinet at all', he told Sylvester, but 'a council of war of duds and mutts'. 'Winston has brains, but the others have none, for an emergency.'[119] The French catastrophe and its consequences for Britain were more and more shaping his thoughts. What now stood between him and the prosecution of his designs was Churchill himself. Sylvester recorded that Lloyd George was certain that 'Winston is bust'.[120] Sylvester and Frances Stevenson tried to persuade him that it was his duty in the supreme national emergency to join the Cabinet. Beaverbrook, Garvin, Thomas Jones, Boothby and Macmillan added their pleas. He was, Jones recorded, 'adamant against going in'.[121] He continued to harp on Churchill's dependence on Chamberlain, which, he said, would frustrate any contribution of his own. 'Whatever I put up would be suspect and would be opposed.'[122] Sylvester confirmed his growing alienation from the government: 'He keeps saying, "I am not going in with this gang. There will be a change".'[123]

These objections were largely disingenuous, a smokescreen to conceal the widening gap between Lloyd George and Churchill. Churchill's policy was resistance to the last. If Britain could hold out for three months, something might turn up in the shape of America's intervention. If not, it was better to go down fighting. Lloyd George certainly agreed with the necessity of outside help. 'My view', he told Jones, 'is that even if we ward off invasion in the next three months, we cannot beat the enemy without Russia and America.'[124] Of their intervention there was not the remotest prospect or probability. And after that? 'If this long island story of ours is to end at last', Churchill had told the Cabinet on 28 May, 'let it end only when each one of us lies choking in his own blood upon the ground.'[125] Such rodomontade, the expression of Churchill's sublime, swashbuckling valour, roused the spirit and cheered the heart. 'We shall never surrender', he told the Commons a week later.[126] But if Churchill radiated indomitable courage, Lloyd George had logic on his side. His realism was based on rational suppositions, not, like Churchill's, on faith and determination. If Britain was to avoid the fate of France and not become Hitler's vassal, she must sue for peace while still uninvaded and militarily undefeated.

On 19 July, a triumphant Hitler, totally victorious in east and west, absolute master of Continental Europe from the Bug to the Atlantic, made his second peace offer to Britain from the Reichstag. It was not undignified. It was not implausible. It suggested the kind of settlement with Britain which he had aimed at before the war, and which, as he said, had always been his first aim: Britain to accept Germany's Continental hegemony, Britain and the Empire to remain unmolested – 'an empire which it was never my intention to destroy or even to harm'.[127] Churchill declined to reply publicly to Hitler, 'not being', as he observed, 'on speaking terms with him'.[128] A few days later, through Halifax, he reaffirmed his war aims in ringing and defiant terms. Not merely would Britain 'never surrender'; she would settle for nothing less than victory. This was magnificent bravado from a country awaiting imminent invasion.

On 21 September, at the height of the 'Battle of Britain', Lloyd George discussed the situation with Maisky. The Russian ambassador noted that Lloyd George considered there to be no chance of peace as long as Churchill was bent on 'victory'.[129] Two days later, Frances Stevenson told Sylvester that Lloyd George was aiming at 'coming in on the peace settlement, that he will be able to make peace where Winston won't'.[130] On 3 October, Chamberlain, mortally ill, resigned from the Cabinet.

Sylvester asked Lloyd George if he would not now at last join Churchill. Lloyd George replied: 'I shall wait until Winston is bust.'[131]

V

In seeking to enlist Lloyd George, it is likely that Churchill did after all envisage an alternative to total victory other than total defeat. By bringing Lloyd George into the Cabinet, he no doubt intended to stiffen the nation's resolve – and Lloyd George's. But he also saw in Lloyd George the man who, if Britain were to go under, was best fitted to talk to Hitler.[132] Churchill himself would never negotiate with 'That Man'. Under pressure in the Cabinet, especially from Halifax, he had conceded that if Hitler offered the right terms, they should be considered. He made it clear, however, what small likelihood he saw of that.

But Churchill had certainly contemplated the possibility of peacemaking. On 21 May, in a letter to Roosevelt, he portrayed a situation in which 'members of the present administration were finished and others came in to parley amid the ruins'.[133] Three months later Hitler launched the Blitz on London. Churchill, true to form, surveyed from the rooftops the exhilarating spectacle of the capital under bombardment. He animated and personified a nation's determination to win through despite all odds. Less heroically, Lloyd George, ensconced below ground at Bron-y-de in a luxuriously furnished private air-raid shelter, listened to Lord Haw-Haw as well as to the BBC, in order, as he said to find the truth half-way between the two. If Churchill should go down exultant to death amid the ruins, Lloyd George was ready to resurface to do the parleying. The lion might succumb, the old fox was still capable of leadership.

Notes

Unless otherwise indicated the place of publication is London.

Abbreviations

AMAE   Archives du Ministère des Affaires Etrangères, Paris
BDFA   *British Documents on Foreign Affairs: Reports and Papers from the Foreign Office Confidential Print* (eds) Kenneth Bourne and Donald Cameron Watt, Part 2, Series 1. *The Paris Peace Conference of 1919* (ed.) Michael Dockrill, vol. 4, *British Empire Delegation Minutes* (1989)
BLP   Bonar Law Papers, House of Lords Record Office
Burnett, *Reparation*   Philip M. Burnett, *Reparation at the Paris Peace Conference*, vols 1–2 (New York, 1940)
CAB   Cabinet Papers, Public Record Office, Kew
FC   Fonds Clemenceau, Service historique de l'Armée de Terre, Vincennes
FO   Foreign Office Papers, Public Record Office, Kew
Frances Stevenson, *A Diary   Lloyd George. A Diary by Frances Stevenson*, (ed.) A.J.P. Taylor (1971)
HC   Parliamentary Debates, House of Commons
Jones, *A Diary*   Thomas Jones, *A Diary with Letters 1931–1950* (Oxford, 1954)
LGP   Lloyd George Papers, House of Lords Record Office
Lloyd George, *Peace Treaties*   David Lloyd George, *The Truth about the Peace Treaties*, vols 1–2 (1938).
LP   Lothian Papers, Scottish Record Office, Edinburgh
Mantoux, *Délibérations*   Paul Mantoux, *Les Délibérations du Conseil des Quatre. Notes de l'officier interprète*, vols 1–2 (Paris, 1955).
PRFRUS   *Papers Relating to the Foreign Relations of the United States. The Paris Peace Conference of 1919*, vols 1–13 (Washington, 1943–47)
PWW   *The Papers of Woodrow Wilson* (ed.) Arthur S. Link, vols 45, 56–60 (Princeton, 1984–9)
Riddell, *Intimate Diary   Lord Riddell's Intimate Diary of the Peace Conference and After* (1933)
Riddell Diaries   The Riddell Diaries 1908–1923 (ed.) J.M. McEwen (1986)
Smuts Papers   Selections from the Smuts Papers (eds) W.K. Hancock and J. Van der Poel, vol. 4 (Cambridge, 1966)
Sylvester, *The Real Lloyd George*   A.J. Sylvester, *The Real Lloyd George* (1947).
Sylvester, *Life with Lloyd George   Life with Lloyd George. The Diary of A.J. Sylvester 1931–45* (ed.) Colin Cross (1975)
The Treaty of Versailles. A Reassessment   The Treaty of Versailles. A Reassessment after 75 Years, (eds) Manfred F. Boemeke, Gerald D. Feldman and Elisabeth Glaser (Cambridge, 1998)

Preface

1. Ian Packer, *Lloyd George* (1998), p. 1. Cf. Thomas Jones, entry on Lloyd George in *The Dictionary of National Biography 1941–1954* (1959), p. 527.
2. Andrew Roberts, *Eminent Churchillians* (1994), p. 139.
3. First published as *Lloyd George, Woodrow Wilson and the Guilt of Germany: an Essay in the Pre-History of Appeasement* (Leicester University Press, 1984), then as *Guilt at Versailles: Lloyd George and the Pre-History of Appeasement* (1985) and in a German translation by Wilfred von Oven with an introduction by Hannsjoachim W. Koch, as *Die Drachensaat von Versailles. Die Schuld der 'Friedensmacher'* (Leoni am Starnbergersee: Druffel-Verlag, 1988).
4. In earlier drafts, Chapters 1, 2 and 6 appeared in the journal *Diplomacy & Statecraft* between 1995 and 1999, Chapter 3 in *The Life and Times of David Lloyd George* (ed.) Judith Loades (Bangor, 1991), and Chapter 4 in *Peace without Victory? The Paris Peace Conference of 1919* (eds) Michael Dockrill and John Fisher (2001).
5. Alan Sharp, 'Lloyd George and Foreign Policy, 1918–1922. The "And Yet" Factor', in *The Life and Times of David Lloyd George* (ed.) Judith Loades (Bangor, 1991), pp. 129–42.
6. Frances Stevenson, *A Diary* (1971), p. 261.
7. Erik Goldstein, 'Neville Chamberlain, the British Official Mind and the Munich Crisis', in *The Munich Crisis, 1938. Prelude to World War II* (eds) Igor Lukes and Erik Goldstein (1999), p. 276. See Kenneth O. Morgan, 'Lloyd George and Germany', *Historical Journal*, 39:3 (1996), 755–66.
8. Martin Pugh, *Lloyd George* (1988), p. 192.
9. 9 May 1940, in Sylvester, *Life with Lloyd George*, p. 265.
10. See Owen Lloyd George, *A Tale of Two Grandfathers* (2000).
11. According to A.T. Davies, Lloyd George was 'a singularly complex and not always a very consistent character, whose threads it was – and is – hard to unravel': *The Lloyd George I Knew. Some Side-Lights on a Great Character* (1948), p. 117. A.J. Sylvester agreed that 'his character is the most complex I have ever known': *Life with Lloyd George*, p. 91. See Thomas Jones, 'Lloyd George', in *The Dictionary of National Biography 1941–1954* (1959), p. 528, for confirmation by a third of Lloyd George's secretaries.

Introduction

1. Harold Nicolson, *The Observer*, 12 November 1961.
2. The Earl of Birkenhead, *Contemporary Personalities* (1924), p. 38.
3. Austen Chamberlain, *Down the Years* (1935), pp. 241–2.
4. David Lloyd George, *The Truth about Reparations and War Debts* (1932), p. 67.
5. Birkenhead, *Contemporary Personalities*, p. 39.
6. Quoted in J. Hugh Edwards, *Lloyd George. The Man and Statesman*, vol. 1, (n.d.), p. xii.
7. Harold Macmillan, *The Past Masters. Politics and Politicians 1906–1939* (1975), pp. 35–6.
8. *Lord Riddell's War Diary 1914–1918* (1933), p. 258.
9. Frances Stevenson, *A Diary*, p. 324.

10. Lloyd George, *War Memoirs*, p. 1371.
11. Raymond Poincaré, *Au service de la France. Neuf années de souvenirs*, vol. 11, *A la recherche de la paix, 1919* (Paris, 1974), p. 245.
12. Sylvester, *Life with Lloyd George*, p. 28.
13. Adolf Hitler, *Mein Kampf*, Unexpurgated edition, (n.d.), p. 412.
14. Riddell, *Intimate Diary*, p. 133.
15. Frances Stevenson, *A Diary*, p. 324.
16. J. Hugh Edwards, *Lloyd George*, p. xii.
17. Frances Stevenson, *A Diary*, p. 324.
18. Frances Stevenson, *The Years that are Past*, p. 261.
19. J. Hugh Edwards, *Lloyd George*, p. xii.
20. Thomas Jones, *Lloyd George*, p. 281.
21. Sylvester, *Life with Lloyd George*, p. 178.
22. Lloyd George, *War Memoirs*, vol. 1 (1938 edition), p. 811.
23. Frances Stevenson, *The Years that are Past*, p. 266. Cf. Thomas Jones, quoted in A. Lentin, *Guilt at Versailles, Lloyd George and the Pre-History of Appeasement* (1985), p. 120.
24. Jones, *A Diary*, p. 457.
25. Jones, *A Diary*, p. 464.
26. Frances Stevenson, *A Diary*, pp. 142–3.
27. Cecil H. King, *With Malice Towards None. A War Diary* (1970), p. 46.
28. John Maynard Keynes, *Essays in Biography* (1933), p. 36.
29. Lloyd George, *War Memoirs*, vol. 1, p. 861.
30. Frances Stevenson, *A Diary*, p. 143.
31. Sylvester, *Life with Lloyd George*, p. 244.
32. His desire to contribute to a postwar peace conference explains Lloyd George's controversial acceptance of a peerage in the 1945 New Year Honours shortly before his death in March. This was felt by his critics to be a denial of his radical antecedents and has been attributed to the ambition of Frances Stevenson, who became the Countess Lloyd George. (Sir Cuthbert Headlam, diary, 1 January 1945, in *Parliament and Politics in the Age of Churchill and Atlee. The Headlam Diaries 1935–1951* (ed.) Stuart Ball (Cambridge, 1999), p. 440.) Lloyd George had represented Caernarvon Boroughs uninterruptedly for over half a century. At the age of 81 and in failing health, he feared his inability to fight another campaign at the forthcoming general election, and was rightly advised that the seat might be lost in any event. Feeling the need of a parliamentary basis from which to amplify his views or perhaps even to justify his presence at a peace conference, he accepted a peerage as Earl Lloyd George of Dwyfor. A.J. Sylvester commented: 'Lloyd George's respect for the hereditary peerage, as such, was nil. It was a platform Lloyd George wanted, not a title.' Lloyd George did not live to take his seat. Olwen Carey Evans, *Lloyd George was my Father* (Llandysul, 1985), p. 170; Sylvester, *Life with Lloyd George*, pp. 330–8; Frances Stevenson, *The Days that are Past*, pp. 274–5; W.R.P. George, *The Times*, 1 April 1995.

Chapter 1

1. Beaverbrook, *Men and Power 1917–1918* (1956), p. 325.
2. Birkenhead, *Contemporary Personalities* (1924), p. 39.

3. Arthur Walworth, *Wilson and his Peacemakers. American Diplomacy at the Paris Peace Conference 1919*, (New York, 1986), p. 403.
4. PPW, vol. 59, p. 623.
5. Lentin, *Guilt at Versailles*, p. 107.
6. *The Political Diaries of C.P. Scott 1911–1928* (ed.) T. Wilson (1970), p. 357; *Smuts Papers*, p. 89.
7. Lentin, *Guilt at Versailles*, p. 119.
8. Kenneth O. Morgan, *Lloyd George* (1974), p. 132.
9. Alan Sharp, *The Versailles Settlement. Peacemaking in Paris, 1919* (1991), p. ix. Cf. George W. Egerton, 'The Lloyd George War Memoirs: a Study in the Politics of Memory', *Journal of Modern History*, 60 (1988), 55–94.
10. G.M. Young, *Stanley Baldwin* (1952), p. 41.
11. Lord Hardinge, *The Old Diplomacy. The Reminiscences of Lord Hardinge of Penshurst* (1947), p. 242.
12. J.L. Garvin, quoted in *The Political Diaries of C.P. Scott*, p. 371.
13. Jones, *A Diary*, pp. xxix–xxx.
14. Mantoux, *Délibérations*, vol. 1, pp. 85–108; *Riddell Diaries*, p. 263.
15. 114 HC Deb. 5s, col. 2938.
16. *Riddell Diaries*, p. 257.
17. Harold Spender, *The Prime Minister* (1920), p. 308.
18. Riddell, *Intimate Diary*, p. 101.
19. Archbishop Randall Davidson, diary, 15 September 1918, Lambeth Palace Library, Davidson Papers, Box 13.
20. Quoted in Erik Goldstein, *Winning the Peace. British Diplomatic Strategy, Peace Planning, and the Paris Peace Conference 1916–1920* (Oxford, 1991), p. 284.
21. Paul Cambon, *Correspondance 1870–1924*, vol. 3 (Paris, 1946), p. 337.
22. Austen Chamberlain, *Down the Years* (1935), p. 242.
23. *The Diary of Beatrice Webb* (eds) N. and J. MacKenzie, vol. 3 (1984), p. 333.
24. Lord Hardinge to Sir H. Butler, 23 April 1919, Cambridge University Library, Hardinge Papers 40/172. Cf. his *The Old Diplomacy*, p. 229. Sybil Crowe and Edward Corp show that Hardinge's charge was much exaggerated: *Our Ablest Public Servant. Sir Eyre Crowe 1864–1925* (Braunton, Devon, 1993), pp. 329–30, 374–5.
25. E.J. Dillon, *The Peace Conference* (1919), p. 54; Charles Seymour, *Geography, Justice and Politics at the Peace Conference of 1919* (New York, 1951), p. 9.
26. Riddell, *Intimate Diary*, p. 80.
27. Lloyd George, *Peace Treaties*, vol. 1 (1938) , p. 404.
28. Frances Stevenson, *A Diary*, p. 177.
29. Louis Loucheur, *Carnets Secrets 1908–1932* (ed.) J. de Launey (Brussels, 1962), p. 72.
30. Frances Stevenson, *A Diary*, p. 177.
31. Maurice Hankey, diary, 20 April 1919, Churchill College, Cambridge, Hankey Papers HNKY 1/6/46.
32. Roy F. Harrod, *The Life of John Maynard Keynes* (1953), pp. 280–1.
33. Lloyd George, *Peace Treaties*, vol. 1, p. 297.
34. Riddell, *Intimate Diary*, pp. 29–30; John Maynard Keynes, *Two Memoirs* (1949), pp. 56–62; C.P. Vincent, *The Politics of Hunger. The Allied Blockade of Germany 1915–1919* (Athens, Ohio, 1985), pp. 111–13; Jacques Raphaël-Leygues,

Georges Leygues. Le 'père' de la marine. (Ses carnets secrets de 1914–1920) (Paris, 1983), p. 215.

35. Riddell, *Intimate Diary*, p. 24.
36. *Riddell Diaries*, p. 263.
37. Frances Stevenson, *A Diary*, p. 178.
38. op.cit., p. 171.
39. Walworth, *Wilson and his Peacemakers*, p. 211.
40. Lentin, *Guilt at Versailles*, p. 121.
41. Lord Hardinge to Sir R. Graham, 12 February 1920, Hardinge Papers 42/147.
42. Paul Cambon to Stéphen Pichon, 14 June 1919, AMAE, Série A, No. 306/25.
43. Lentin, *Guilt at Versailles*, p. 122.
44. Riddell, *Intimate Diary*, p. 36.
45. 114 HC Deb. 5s, col. 2942.
46. See Lorna S. Jaffe, *The Decision to Disarm Germany. British Foreign Policy towards Postwar German Disarmament* (1985).
47. BDFA, p. l09.
48. BDFA, p. 94.
49. Harold Nicolson, *Peacemaking 1919* (1933), p. 359.
50. Lentin, *Guilt at Versailles*, p. 99.
51. Inga Floto, *Colonel House in Paris. A Study of American Policy at the Peace Conference* (Aarhus, 1973), p. 314.
52. Lloyd George, *Peace Treaties*, vol. 1, p. 405.
53. ibid.
54. op. cit. p. 406.
55. op. cit., p. 409.
56. ibid.
57. op.cit., p. 406.
58. Mantoux, *Délibérations*, vol. 1, p. 48.
59. Camille Barrère to Stéphen Pichon, 6 June 1919, AMAE Série Z. Europe 1918–1929, vol. 44, Grande Bretagne/54.
60. Lloyd George, *Peace Treaties*, vol. 2, p. 859.
61. Alan Sharp, 'Lloyd George and Foreign Policy 1918–1922. The "And Yet" factor', in *The Life and Times of David Lloyd George* (ed.) Judith Loades (Bangor, 1991), p. 129.
62. Lentin, *Guilt at Versailles*, p. 93.
63. BDFA, p. 93.
64. 117 HC Deb. 5s, col. 1127; 'Outline of Peace Terms', 23 March 1919, House of Lords Record Office, LGP, F/147/3/2. See J.F. Willis, *Prologue to Nuremberg: the Politics and Diplomacy of Punishing War Criminals of the First World War* (1982). Lloyd George rallied an initially sceptical Imperial War Cabinet, 5 November 1918, Public Record Office, CAB 23/42/4-7.
65. Sir Henry Wilson, *Life and Diaries* (ed.) C.E. Calwell, vol. 1 (1927), p. 149.
66. 114 HC Deb. 5s, col. 2950.
67. loc. cit., col. 1213; Lloyd George to Randall Davidson, 30 May 1919, Davidson War Box, 27.
68. BDFA, p. 108.
69. Frances Stevenson, *A Diary*, p. 183.
70. Robert Cecil, diary, 31 May 1919. Cf. 24 May 1919, British Library, Add Mss 51131/161.

71. Lloyd George, *Peace Treaties*, vol. 1, p. 406.
72. Lentin, *Guilt at Versailles*, p. 51.
73. 114 HC Deb. 5s, col. 2953.
74. A. MacKintosh, *From Gladstone to Lloyd George. Parliament in Peace and War* (1921), p. 309.
75. Lentin, *Guilt at Versailles*, p. 80.
76. Olwen Carey Evans, *Lloyd George was My Father* (Llandysul, 1985), p. 104.
77. Frances Stevenson, *A Diary*, p. 180.
78. 'British Empire Interests', 23 March 1919, LGP, F/147/3/2.
79. ibid.
80. ibid.; P. Kerr to Lloyd George, 2 March 1919, Scottish Record Office, LP, GD40/17/1238.
81. Lentin, *Guilt at Versailles*, p. 112; British Empire Delegation Minutes, 1 June 1919, CAB 23/44/12.
82. See A. Lentin, 'Philip Kerr e "l'aggressione della Germania"', in *Lord Lothian. Una Vita per la Pace* (ed.) G. Guderzo (Florence, 1986), pp. 63–7.
83. Imperial War Cabinet Minutes, 6 November 1918, CAB 23/44/12; Lloyd George, *Peace Treaties*, vol. 1, p. 490.
84. Imperial War Cabinet Minutes, 19 February 1919, CAB 23/9/73.
85. Mantoux, *Délibérations*, vol. 1, p. 83.
86. Lentin, *Guilt at Versailles*, p. 55.
87. Lloyd George, *Peace Treaties*, vol. 1, p. 46l.
88. Lentin, *Guilt at Versailles*, pp. 57–80.
89. *Smuts Papers*, p. 89.
90. Lord Derby to A.J. Balfour, 18 March 1919, British Library Add Mss 49744/26l.
91. Lentin, *Guilt at Versailles*, p. 48.
92. Mantoux, *Délibérations*, vol. 1, p. 61.
93. Thomas Lamont, 'Reparations', in *What Really Happened at Paris. The Story of the Peace Conference 1918–1919* (eds) Edward M. House and Charles Seymour (New York, 1921), pp. 267–8.
94. Lentin, *Guilt at Versailles*, p. 43.
95. 114 HC Deb. 5s, col. 2948.
96. George N. Barnes, *From Workshop to War Cabinet* (1924), p. 26l.
97. Lentin, *Guilt at Versailles*, p. 67.
98. Marc Trachtenberg, *Reparation in World Politics. France and European Economic Diplomacy 1916–1923* (New York, 1980) pp. 63–6; Sally Marks, 'Smoke and Mirrors: in Smoke- Filled Rooms and the Galerie des Glaces', in *The Treaty of Versailles. A Reassessment*, p. 344.
99. Lentin, *Guilt at Versailles*, p. 62.
100. Nicolson, *Peacemaking*, p. 350.
101. Lentin, *Guilt at Versailles*, p. 108. However, Harold Temperley, in his standard *History of the Peace Conference of Paris*, vol. 2 (1920), p. 45, held that 'there is no doubt that the Allies were justified in exacting this confession of a moral obligation'.
102. G. Grahame to P. Kerr, 3 April 1919, LP, GD40/17/1368; R. Bridgeman, memorandum, 14 June 1919, LP, GD40/17/1357/2.
103. F.S. Northedge, *The Troubled Giant. Britain among the Great Powers 1916–1939* (1966), p. 105.

104. Georges Clemenceau, *Grandeurs et Misères d'une Victoire* (Paris, 1930), p. 99.
105. Frances Stevenson, *A Diary*, p. 197.
106. Beatrice Webb, *Diaries, 1912–1924* (ed.) M. Cole (1952), p. 111.
107. Lentin, *Guilt at Versailles*, p. 122.
108. Riddell, *Intimate Diary*, p. 57.
109. Inga Floto, *Colonel House in Paris*, p. 314.
110. Lentin, *Guilt at Versailles*, pp. 120–1; John Hemery, 'The Emergence of Treasury Influence in British Foreign Policy 1914–1921' (unpublished doctoral dissertation, University of Cambridge, 1988), pp. 424–5.
111. Beaverbrook, *The Decline and Fall of Lloyd George* (1963), p. 307.
112. Basil Liddell Hart, *Memoirs*, vol. 1 (1965), p. 359.
113. Thomas Jones, in *The Dictionary of National Biography 1941–54* (1959), p. 528.
114. Thomas Lamont to Sir William Wiseman, 19 March 1919, LGP, F/213/5/6.
115. Harold Nicolson, *Curzon. The Last Phase* (1934), p. 223.
116. *The Times*, 17 April 1919.
117. Lentin, *Guilt at Versailles*, p. 123.
118. *Memoirs of a Conservative. J.C.C. Davidson's Memoirs and Papers, 1910–37* (ed.) Robert Rhodes James (1969), pp. 91–2.
119. Randall Davidson, diary, 6 July 1919. Davidson Papers, 13; Beaverbrook, *Men and Power 1917–1918* (1956), pp. 306–9, 387–92.

Chapter 2

1. Sir James Headlam-Morley, *A Memoir of the Paris Peace Conference 1919* (ed.) Agnes Headlam-Morley (1972), p. 180.
2. ibid.
3. J.W. Scobell Armstrong, *Yesterday* (1955), p. 123.
4. Ann Wedderburn-Maxwell, *A Privileged Child* (Bournemouth, 1985), p. 3.
5. R.S. Sayers, *The Bank of England 1891–1944*, vol. 1 (Cambridge, 1976), p. 101. Cf. Robert Boothby, *Recollections of a Rebel* (1978), p. 22.
6. Cunliffe to Sumner, 13 July 1919, FO 608/310.
7. Harold Nicolson, *Peacemaking 1919* (1933), p. 350.
8. Norman Davis referred to 'The Heavenly Twins' on 25 March 1919. Keynes, memo, LP, GD40/17/1303. So did Thomas Lamont, addressing the American commissioners on 3 June 1919, PRFRUS, vol. 11, p. 200. *The News of the World*, 11 January 1920, publicised the nickname. A letter to his wife of 25 June 1919 suggests that Cunliffe was aware of the nickname.
9. A.J. Sylvester, 'Notes on Peace Conference', National Library of Wales, Aberystwyth, A.J. Sylvester Papers, Box 10/1/18.
10. *Yorkshire Post*, 7 January 1920.
11. Lloyd George, *The Truth about Reparations and War Debts* (1932), p. 17. Cf. his *Is It Peace?* (1923), p. 41.
12. John Maynard Keynes, *Collected Writings*, vol. 16 (1971), p. 469.
13. John Maynard Keynes, *The Economic Consequences of the Peace* (1919; 1920 edition), p. 129.
14. King's College, Cambridge, Keynes Papers EC/7/2/2. On the omission of Cunliffe and Sumner from *The Economic Consequences of the Peace*, see letter

to Keynes from Austen Chamberlain, Chancellor of the Exchequer, 22 December 1919, and Keynes's reply, Birmingham University Library, Austen Chamberlain Papers, AC 35/1/9. Keynes's decision was influenced by his mother, who had read the typescript of *The Economic Consequences of the Peace* and considered his references to Sumner to be libellous. Keynes Papers EC/1/9.

15. Alan Sharp, *The Versailles Settlement. Peacemaking in Paris, 1919* (1991), p. 98.
16. Cunliffe's reputation as Governor of the Bank of England was dealt a further blow by Beaverbrook in 'Nabobs and Tyrants', in *Men and Power 1917–1918* (1956), pp. 91–112. Cf. Andrew Boyle, *Montagu Norman. A Biography* (1967). For recent criticism of Cunliffe and Sumner on traditional lines, see A. Lentin, *Guilt at Versailles*; Bruce Kent, *The Spoils of War. The Politics, Economics and Diplomacy of Reparations 1918–1932* (Oxford, 1989), pp. 66–80. On Sumner generally, see A. Lentin, 'Lord Sumner 1859–1934: Acerbic Master of Law and Language', *The Law Society's Gazette*, 27 June 1984, pp. 1852–4 and forthcoming entry in *The New Dictionary of National Biography*. John Hemery is the first to argue a positive role for Cunliffe and Sumner, in his unpublished doctoral dissertation 'The Emergence of Treasury Influence in British Foreign Policy 1914–1921' (Cambridge University, 1988). There is a brief entry on Cunliffe by A. Lentin in *The Dictionary of National Biography. Missing Persons* (ed.) C.S. Nicholls (Oxford, 1993), pp. 164–5. Cf. Cunliffe's obituary in *The Times*, 7 January 1920. There are personal glimpses of Cunliffe by his daughter, Ann Wedderburn-Maxwell, in *A Privileged Child*.
17. *Memoirs of a Conservative. J.C.C. Davidson's Memoirs and Papers*, pp. 61–2.
18. Frances Stevenson, *The Years that are Past*, p. 102.
19. Cunliffe, letter to his wife, 20 June 1919, Cunliffe Papers (in the possession of the present Lord Cunliffe). On Cunliffe's humour, see Lloyd George, *War Memoirs*, vol. 1 (1938), pp. 68–9. *The Sheffield Telegraph*, 7 January 1920, cites a wartime visit of King George V and Queen Mary to the Bank of England, Cunliffe acting as guide. 'Rarely have the King and Queen looked so genuinely amused as they were then by his dry humour. He was bubbling over with fun.' For an example of his temper at the Peace Conference, see Sylvester, *The Real Lloyd George*, p. 38.
20. Cunliffe's inarticulateness may be exaggerated. Addressing, as chairman, the Second Subcommittee of the Reparations Commission at the Peace Conference on 21 February 1919, he spoke for 55 minutes. Cunliffe, letter to his wife, 21 February 1919.
21. 'A screen, more than ordinarily close, of British reserve.' *Bankers Magazine*, February 1920, p. 242.
22. Montagu Norman to Sir John Clapham, 1 September 1944, Bank of England archives, G15/31.
23. Thomas Lamont, in PPW, vol. 60, p. 494.
24. Lloyd George, *War Memoirs*, vol. 1 (1938), p. 68.
25. *The Times*, 7 January 1920.
26. Ann Wedderburn Maxwell, *A Privileged Child*, p. 3.
27. *Lord Riddell's War Diary 1914–1918* (1933), p. 2.
28. Bentley Gilbert describes the handling of the financial crisis in August 1914 as 'one of Lloyd George's greater wartime achievements'. *David Lloyd George. A Political Life. The Organiser of Victory 1912–1916* (1992), p. 116, pp. 113–16.

Cf. Lloyd George, *War Memoirs*, vol. 1 (1938), pp. 40, 68–9; *Peace Treaties*, vol. 1 (1938), p. 459. According to Cunliffe, he and Lloyd George had faced the crisis of August 1914 'like lions'. Sayers, *Bank of England*, vol. 1, p. 74. Even Keynes paid tribute to Cunliffe's courage in 1914, 'War and the Financial System, August 1914', *Economic Journal*, 24 (September 1914), pp. 460–86.

29. Cunliffe was a member of the Balfour mission to the United States in 1917. The American Secretary of the Treasury, McAdoo, recorded that he 'came to know Cunliffe well, and I was much pleased by his way of doing things. He was calm, unperturbed, clear-headed, and thoroughly at home in everything pertaining to finance. I like men who know their business. Lord Cunliffe knew his.' *Crowded Years. The Reminiscences of William G. McAdoo* (Boston, MA, 1932), p. 394. Among British officials, however, Cunliffe's insouciance in preferring a private fishing expedition to a tour of the Federal Gold Reserve, raised some eyebrows.

30. Beaverbrook, *Men and Power*, pp. 94–5. Cf. his *Politicians and the War 1914–1916* (1960), pp. 146–8.

31. Beaverbrook, *Men and Power*, p. 103.

32. Bonar Law to Lloyd George, 17 July 1917, BLP, Box 65, folder 3/19; Beaverbrook, *Men and Power*, p. 103, 104. Cf. Kathleen Burk, 'The Treasury: from Impotence to Power', in *War and the State. The Transformation of British Government, 1914–1919* (ed.) Kathleen Burk (1982), pp. 84–107.

33. 'I have seldom seen Bonar Law so incensed.' Beaverbrook, *Men and Power*, p. 105.

34. Bonar Law to Cunliffe, 17 July 1917, BLP, Box 65, folder 3/19.

35. Bonar Law to Lloyd George, 9 July 1917, BLP, Box 65, folder 3/20.

36. Beaverbrook, *Men and Power*, pp. 110–11; Robert Blake, *The Unknown Prime Minister. The Life and Times of Andrew Bonar Law 1858–1923* (1955), pp. 61–2, 351–4. Blake's view that Cunliffe resigned from the governorship was criticised by Beaverbrook, who, in a letter to *The Times*, 10 October 1955, observed that Cunliffe 'did not resign. He was dismissed.' Cf. Robert Blake, article in *Evening Standard*, 12 October 1955; J.C. Davidson, *Memoirs of a Conservative*, pp. 61–2; A.J.P. Taylor, *Beaverbrook* (1972), pp. 625–6. Accounts of the controversy and copies of relevant documents are in the Bank of England archives G15/31. *The Financier*, 7 January 1920, attributed Cunliffe's resignation to ill health brought on by overwork.

37. *First Interim Report of the Committee on Currency and Foreign Exchanges after the War*, Command Paper 9182, London (1918). The committee was reconvened in July 1919 and its recommendations were accepted by Austen Chamberlain as Chancellor of the Exchequer in December. K. Hutchison, *The Decline and Fall of British Capitalism* (1966), p. 193.

38. On the Hughes Committee, see Robert E. Bunselmeyer, *The Cost of the War 1914–1919. British Economic War Aims and the Origins of Reparations* (1975), pp. 94–104; A. Lentin, *Guilt at Versailles*, pp. 19–21; Imperial War Cabinet Committee on Indemnity Report, Proceedings and Memoranda, CAB 27/43. According to L.F. Fitzhardinge, Cunliffe was chosen by Hughes in consultation with Bonar Law, *The Little Digger 1914–1952. William Morris Hughes. A Political Biography*, vol. 2 (1979), p. 380. According to John Hemery (p. 435), Lord Reading recommended Cunliffe's appointment.

39. Lentin, *Guilt at Versailles*, p. 21; Keynes, *The Economic Consequences of the Peace* (1919), p. 129. I follow the American use of billion, meaning a thousand million.

40. Minutes of meeting of Dominion Prime Ministers, 11 April 1919, LGP, F/28/3/26. Cf. Imperial War Cabinet Committee on Indemnity Report, Proceedings and Memoranda 1918 Public Record Office, CAB 27/43, meeting of 29 November 1918. It was rumoured that Cunliffe, who admitted that 'he had been pressed to arrive at it between a Saturday and a Monday', found inspiration during Sunday morning service in church. L.F. Fitzhardinge, *The Little Digger*, vol. 2, p. 381. Sylvester, *Life with Lloyd George*, p. 75.

41. Lentin, *Guilt at Versailles*, p. 21.

42. Imperial War Cabinet Committee on Indemnity. Report, meeting of 29 November 1918, CAB 27/43; Lentin, *Guilt at Versailles*, pp. 19–24.

43. Sumner had recently associated himself with the 'Diehard' wing of the Conservative party headed by Lord Salisbury, who, in 1922, was to urge Bonar Law to appoint him as Lord Chancellor. I think it likely that Salisbury was also instrumental in recommending Sumner to Bonar Law as a candidate for the reparations delegation in 1919.

44. The Hughes Committee submitted to Lloyd George the names of Hughes and Cunliffe as British delegates on reparations at the Peace Conference on 13 December 1918. Bunselmeyer, *The Cost of the War*, p. 104. Cf. Hughes to Hankey, 9 January 1919, House of Lords Record Office, J.C. Davidson Papers; Hankey to Hughes, 9 January 1919, LGP, F/23/4/27.

45. For the minutes of the Second Subcommittee, see Burnett, *Reparation*, vol. 2, pp. 594–770. Fuller minutes are given in *La Paix de Versailles. La Commission de Réparations des Dommages*, vol. 2 (Paris, 1932), pp. 703–943.

46. Lamont was a partner in J.P. Morgan & Co., America's principal private lenders to Britain during the war. He had met Cunliffe at his home, Headley Court, in 1917, apparently 'considered him an able friend', and expected from him a friendly and cooperative attitude at the Peace Conference. Edward M. Lamont, *The Ambassador from Wall Street. The Story of Thomas W. Lamont, J.P. Morgan's Chief Executive* (Lanham, Maryland, 1994), pp. 95, 108.

47. Thomas Lamont, 'Reparations', in *What Really Happened at Paris* (eds) Edward M. House and Charles Seymour (New York, 1921), p. 277.

48. Cunliffe, letter to his wife, 21 February 1919.

49. Lamont, 'Reparations', loc. cit., p. 259.

50. Stephen Schuker, 'Origins of American Stabilization Policy in Europe: the Financial Dimension, 1918–1924', in *Confrontation and Cooperation. Germany and the United States in the Era of World War I, 1900–1924* (ed.) Hans-Jürgen Schröder (Oxford, 1993), pp. 377–407.

51. Cunliffe, letter to his wife, 21 February 1919.

52. Trachtenberg, *Reparation in World Politics*, p. 59. Colonel House, after hearing a report from Lamont, observed, 'I thought the British were as crazy as the French but they seem only half as crazy, which still leaves a good heavy margin of lunacy', diary, 21 February, 1919, in Burnett, *Reparation*, vol. 1, p. 600.

53. Cunliffe, letter to his wife, 1 March 1919.

54. Lamont, 'Reparations', loc. cit., p. 277.

55. Kerr to Lloyd George, 28 February 1919, LP, GD40/17/1235; Kerr to Lloyd George, 1 March 1919, LGP, F/89/2/56; Cunliffe to Lloyd George, 2 March 1919, LGP, F/89/2/37.

56. Norman Davis confirmed that Cunliffe finally consented to name £8 billion in the Second Subcommittee report, provided that the Americans agreed to this figure. Lamont and Davis refused to go above £6 billion. Norman Davis, 'Peace Conference Notes', 5 July 1919, in Burnett, *Reparation*, vol. 1, p. 50.

57. House, diary, 27 February 1919, in *The Intimate Papers of Colonel House* (ed.) Charles Seymour, vol. 4 (1928), p. 355.

58. Lentin, *Guilt at Versailles*, pp. 36–7.

59. 'Notes of meeting of Council of Four', 26 March 1919, PWW, vol. 56, p. 292.

60. Lamont to Burnett, 25 June 1934, in Burnett, *Reparation*, vol. 1, p. 50. According to Lamont, Cunliffe was the chief obstacle to agreement. 'I have been having a difficult time with your friend, Cunliffe, and do not consider it altogether my fault.' Lamont to Edward Grenfell, March 1919, in Edward M. Lamont, *The Ambassador from Wall Street*, p. 109.

61. Cunliffe to Lloyd George, 2 March 1919, LGP, F/89/2/37.

62. Cunliffe's first instinct was to return to London 'for an interview with the P.M', but deferred this on learning of Lloyd George's imminent return to Paris. Cunliffe, letter to his wife, 1 March 1919.

63. Louis Loucheur, *Carnets secrets*, p. 71.

64. Lentin, *Guilt at Versailles*, p. 48.

65. Edwin Montagu, memorandum, 4 April 1919, Trinity College, Cambridge, Montagu Papers AS-I-12-18.

66. Edward M. Lamont, *The Ambassador from Wall Street*, p. 113. The reference is to Acts, xxvii: 28: 'Then Agrippa said unto Paul, Almost thou persuadest me to be a Christian.'

67. 26 March 1919, PWW, vol. 56, p. 292. On the same day, Sumner was holding out for £11 billion. Hemery, 'The Emergence of Treasury Influence', p. 223.

68. Norman Davis, memo to Wilson, 25 March 1919, Burnett, *Reparation*, vol. 2, pp. 711–12. Keynes, memo, 25 March 1919, LP, GD40/17/1303.

69. Keynes, memo, 25 March 1919, LP, GD40/17/1303.

70. Cunliffe, letter to his wife, 4 March 1919.

71. First interim report of 2nd Subcommittee, 8 April 1919, Burnett, *Reparation*, vol. 2, p. 748; Minutes of meeting of 2nd Subcommittee, 17 February 1919, pp. 596–7. On 8 April, Cunliffe wrote to his wife: 'I had the report approved by the P. M.' According to Sir John Bradbury, Permanent Secretary to the Treasury, Cunliffe, asked to explain the extent of the levy on German gold reserves, replied: 'Because it's twice as much as they've got.' Kenneth O. Morgan, *Consensus and Disunity. The Lloyd George Coalition Government 1918–1922* (Oxford, 1979), p. 140.

72. Burnett, *Reparation*, vol. 2, pp. 935–6, 941.

73. Cunliffe, letter to his wife, 8 April 1919. Cunliffe added that as chairman of the plenary committee meeting, Hughes, in opposing the report of the Second Subcommittee, 'registered his vote against it while deciding that Sumner and myself had no vote'. The ploy was unsuccessful. 'All voted with one accord that the Report as it stood should be forwarded to the big "4" without delay' and 'left Hughes to slink off.'

74. Lentin, *Guilt at Versailles*, p. 77; Douglas Newton, *British Policy and the Weimar Republic, 1918–1919* (Oxford, 1997), pp. 355–7, 395.
75. L.S. Amery, *My Political Life*, vol. 2 (1953), p. 179.
76. Lentin, *Guilt at Versailles*, p. 52.
77. Cunliffe, letter to his wife, 11 April 1919.
78. Cunliffe, letter to his wife, 10 April 1919. Cunliffe wrote to his wife on 12 April that 'the P. M. and all the other P. M.'s lost their tempers with Hughes at breakfast yesterday'.
79. Cunliffe, letter to his wife, 11 April 1919.
80. Minutes of meeting of Dominion Prime Ministers, 11 April 1919, LGP, F/28/3/26. For Hughes's intransigence and Lloyd George's attempts to appease him, see Lentin, *Guilt at Versailles*, p. 77; Hughes to Lloyd George, 11 April and Lloyd George to Hughes, 14 April 1919, LGP, F/28/3/26 and F/28/3/27; Maurice Hankey to his wife, 12 April, Hankey Papers, HNKY 3/25.
81. LGP, F/28/3/26.
82. Lentin, *Guilt at Versailles*, pp. 94–5.
83. Frances Stevenson, *The Years that are Past*, p. 156.
84. Cunliffe, memorandum to Lloyd George, 1 June 1919, LP, GD40/17/62/11-12.
85. Nicolson, *Peacemaking 1919*, p. 359.
86. Thomas Jones, *Whitehall Diary* (ed.) Keith Middlemas, vol. 1 (Oxford, 1969), p. 88.
87. Lloyd George, *Peace Treaties*, vol. 1, p. 461.
88. Minutes of meeting of British Empire delegation, 15 March 1919, quoted in Hemery, p. 210.
89. For a traditional interpretation of Lloyd George's reparations strategy, see Chapter 1, Section V and Lentin, *Guilt at Versailles*, *passim*.
90. PWW, vol. 60, p. 47. 'Lloyd George appointed these men [Cunliffe and Sumner] when he had great flights [i.e. flights of fancy] in regard to this matter and now he cannot control them.' Colonel House, diary, 24 March 1919, in Arthur Walworth, *Wilson and his Peacemakers*, p. 177. For the views on Cunliffe and Sumner later expressed by Lloyd George, see *The Truth about Reparations and War Debts* (1932), pp. 17–18; *Peace Treaties*, vol. 1, pp. 473–4. For the view of Lloyd George expressed by the American delegates, see Lamont, 'Reparations', loc. cit. For recent studies, see Erik Goldstein, 'Britain: the Home Front', in *The Treaty of Versailles. A Reassessment*, pp. 147–66. For a more critical view, see A. Lentin, 'The Peacemakers and their Home Fronts: a Comment', in *The Treaty of Versailles. A Reassessment*, pp. 222–7.
91. Lloyd George, *Peace Treaties*, vol.1, p. 474.
92. Norman Davis, memo to Woodrow Wilson, 25 March 1919, PWW, vol. 56, p. 270; Edward M. Lamont, *The Ambassador from Wall Street*, p. 111.
93. Colonel House, diary, 6 March 1919, in Inga Floto, *Colonel House in Paris*, p. 152; and diary, 24 March 1919 in PWW, vol. 56, p. 208.
94. Inga Floto, *Colonel House in Paris*, p. 152.
95. Cunliffe, letter to his wife, 24 June 1919.
96. 'Protests at these low figures', Loucheur, diary, 14 March 1919, *Carnets secrets*, p. 71.
97. At a Cabinet meeting on 14 April 1919, Lloyd George reported that current discussions on the apportionment of reparations totalling £7.3 billion would

give £2.2 billion to Britain and £5.1 billion to France. Bonar Law remarked: 'What will our lunatics at home say to this?' Thomas Jones, *Whitehall Diary*, vol. 1, p. 84.

98. Charles Seymour, quoting James Shotwell, in *Letters from the Paris Peace Conference* (ed.) Harold B. Whiteman (Yale, 1965), pp. 275–6.

99. House, diary, 6 March 1919, in Floto, p. 152.

100. 'I'm rather depressed at the prospect of many more months of this work, and I think I shall have a fresh [?indecipherable] quarrel with the P. M. and go home in a temper.' Cunliffe to his wife, 20 April 1919.

101. On 19 February 1919 the War Cabinet resolved to order Cunliffe, Sumner and Hughes 'to return to London immediately to discuss the matter', CAB/23/9/73. On the same day Curzon telegraphed this summons to Paris. Cunliffe, however, was authorised to remain in Paris by Balfour on the grounds that 'I cannot be spared...It would be a pity to miss a week when I am just getting my subcommittee to the point, and Balfour agrees.' Cunliffe, letter to his wife, 22 February 1919.

102. Cunliffe, letter to his wife, 2 April 1919.

103. ibid.

104. Cunliffe, letter to his wife, 3 April 1919. On 5 May, Cunliffe wrote to Sumner: 'I got into trouble with the P. M. for being absent', FO 608/310.

105. Cunliffe, letter to his wife, 11 April 1919.

106. Perhaps Lloyd George also wanted to keep Cunliffe away from London at the time when the parliamentary agitation over reparations was at its peak. It is true that in a letter to his wife on 1 March 1919 Cunliffe threatened to denounce 'Keynes and the Board of Trade and certain of the Treasury' in the House of Lords; but in the context, this suggests letting off steam rather than a serious threat. Unlike Hughes, Cunliffe remained conspicuously loyal to Lloyd George.

107. Cunliffe, letter to his wife, 20 April 1919. Cunliffe twice underlined the word 'ordered'. Cunliffe and Sumner were appointed to advise on reparations from Austria and Bulgaria to balance the appointment of Smuts and Keynes. For Cunliffe and the Austrian treaty, see Keynes, *The Economic Consequences of the Peace*, p. 233; Sir Francis Oppenheimer, *Stranger Within. Autobiographical Pages* (1960), pp. 386, 395; Sybil Crowe and Edward Corp, *Our Ablest Public Servant. Sir Eyre Crowe* (1993), pp. 346–7. On Cunliffe and the Bulgarian treaty, see Cunliffe, letter to his wife, 24 June 1919.

108. Cunliffe, letter to his wife, 18 April 1919. Admitting that 'of course it's a great compliment', Cunliffe added that if Lloyd George imagined that he would be willing 'to take on the job . . . he is making a mistake'. Cunliffe, letter to his wife, 19 April 1919.

109. Mantoux, *Délibérations*, vol. 1, p. 226.

110. Speech at Newcastle-upon-Tyne, 29 November 1918, Lentin, *Guilt at Versailles*, p. 21; Alan Sharp, 'Lloyd George and Foreign Policy, 1918–1922. The "And Yet" Factor', in *The Life and Times of David Lloyd George* (ed.) Judith Loades (Bangor, 1991), pp. 135–8.

111. Keynes to Austen Chamberlain, 28 December 1919, Austen Chamberlain Papers, AC35/1/10.

112. Edward M. Lamont, *The Ambassador from Wall Street*, p. 109.

113. Balfour to Philip Kerr, 7 July 1919, British Library, Balfour Papers, Add Mss 45750/78. Montagu complained bitterly at Lloyd George's failure to back up the £6 billion recommendations of the unofficial reparations subcommittee. S.D. Waley, *Edwin Montagu* (1964), p. 213. Cf. Bernard Baruch, quoted in Trachtenberg, *Reparation in World Politics*, p. 360.

114. BDFA, p. 111.

115. Lloyd George, *Peace Treaties*, vol. 1, p. 463.

116. 'British Empire interests' and 'Outline of Peace Terms', 23 March 1919, LGP, F/147/3/2. Both documents were drafted after discussion at Fontainebleau the day before between Lloyd George, Cunliffe and Sumner. See Douglas Newton, *British Policy and the Weimar Republic*, p. 370. On the geopolitical implications of reparations, cf. Stephen Schuker, 'The End of Versailles', in *The Origins of the Second World War Reconsidered* (ed.) Gordon Martel (1986), p. 58.

117. 'British Empire interests' and 'Outline of Peace Terms'.

118. ibid.

119. In the Fontainebleau Memorandum Lloyd George proposed the apportionment of reparations at 30 per cent for Britain and 50 per cent for France. France refused to accept these percentages. Final agreement was not reached until June 1920. The ratio was 52 per cent for France and 22 per cent for Britain. Alan Sharp, *The Versailles Settlement*, pp. 88–9.

120. Committee on Indemnity proceedings, 2 December 1918, CAB 27/43; Cunliffe, letter to his wife, 21 February 1919. Cf. Sumner: 'It was unheard of that a debtor who owed the full amount now, and was being given time, should get his discharge at the end of 30 years by the simple process of not paying in full in the meantime.' Memorandum, 2 April 1919, FO 608/287.

121. BDFA, p. 111.

122. ibid.

123. Committee on Indemnity proceedings, 2 December 1918, CAB/27/43. The point was more elegantly made in the 'Reply of the Allied and Associated Powers' to the German counter-proposals, 16 June 1919: 'Somebody must suffer for the consequences of the war. Is it to be Germany, or only the peoples she has wronged?' PRFRUS, vol. 13, p. 49.

124. Smuts to Lloyd George, 26 March 1919, LGP, F/45/9/29. Cf. *Smuts Papers*, pp. 215–16; George Barnes to Lloyd George, 2–3 June 1919, LGP, F/4/3/17, 19, 21; Lentin, *Guilt at Versailles*, p. 96.

125. BDFA, p. 112.

126. BDFA, p. 104. Furthermore, the German counter-offer was interest free and conditional on territorial concessions by the Allies.

127. BDFA, p. 96. Cunliffe had made the same point in a letter to his wife, 20 April 1919. In *The Economic Consequences of the Peace*, Keynes himself gave a critical analysis of the German counter-offer, which he described as 'somewhat obscure, and also rather disingenuous'. *Economic Consequences*, p. 204. Cf. Sally Marks, 'Smoke and Mirrors: in Smoke-Filled Rooms and the Galerie des Glaces', in *The Treaty of Versailles. A Reassessment*, pp. 354–5; Elisabeth Glaser, 'The Making of the Economic Peace', loc. cit., p. 396; Niall Ferguson, 'The Balance of Payments Question: Versailles and After', loc. cit., pp. 407–8.

128. BDFA, p. 104.

129. ibid. The bill for reconstruction of the French war zone eventually reached some £30 billion. Denise Artaud, 'Reparations and War Debts. The Restoration of French Financial Power, 1919–1929', in *French Foreign and Defence Policy, 1918–1940. The Decline and Fall of a Great Power* (ed.) Robert Boyce (1998), p. 90.

130. Lloyd George to George Barnes, 2 June 1919, LGP, F/4/3/20. Cf. Lloyd George to Smuts, 3 June 1919, *Smuts Papers*, p. 218.

131. Bernard Baruch, in an account published in 1921, candidly admitted: 'No-one knew how much Germany could pay. No-one yet knows how much Germany can pay.' *The Making of the Reparation and Economic Sections of the Treaty* (1921), p. 46.

132. Minutes of meeting of British Empire delegation, 15 March 1919, quoted in Hemery, p. 210.

133. BDFA, p. 111.

134. ibid.

135. Riddell, *Intimate Diary*, p. 3; Lloyd George, *Peace Treaties*, vol. 1, pp. 453–4, 465–6. Cf. Norman Davis, 'Peace Conference Notes', 5 July 1919, quoted by Gerald D. Feldman, 'A Comment', in *The Treaty of Versailles. A Reassessment*, p. 445.

136. Etienne Mantoux, *The Carthaginian Peace or the Economic Consequences of Mr Keynes* (1946; 1965 edition, Pittsburgh), pp. 129–32.

137. Sumner, memorandum, 18 March 1919, in PWW, vol. 56, pp. 70–1; Sally Marks, 'Smoke and Mirrors', in *The Treaty of Versailles. A Reassessment*, p. 338.

138. Bruce Kent, *The Spoils of War*, p. 36.

139. Nicolson, *Peacemaking 1919*, pp. 90–1.

140. Lamont to Burnett, 25 June 1934, in Walworth, *Wilson and his Peacemakers*, p. 403. Of Cunliffe as Governor of the Bank of England, Montagu Norman commented 'clear case of megalomania' and 'a dangerous and insane colleague', diary, 27 February and 21 March 1918, in Andrew Boyle, *Montagu Norman*, pp. 122–3.

141. Keynes to Austen Chamberlain, 28 December 1919, Austen Chamberlain Papers AC35/1/10.

142. Lloyd George, *Peace Treaties*, vol. 1, p. 474.

143. Etienne Mantoux, *The Carthaginian Peace or The Economic Consequences of Mr Keynes*; Sally Marks, 'Reparations Reconsidered; a Reminder', *Central European History*, 2 (1969), 356–65, and 'The Myths of Reparations', *Central European History*, 11 (1978), 231–55; Charles S. Maier, *Recasting Bourgeois Europe: Stabilization in France, Germany and Italy in the Decade after World War I* (Princeton, 1975), pp. 249–53; Marc Trachtenberg, *Reparation in World Politics*, pp. 66–8, 72–84; Stephen A. Schuker, 'American "Reparations" to Germany, 1919–33; Implications for the Third-World Debt Crisis', *Princeton Studies in International Finance*, 61 (1988), 92–7; Donald E. Moggridge, *Maynard Keynes: an Economist's Biography* (1992), pp. 342–5. For a contrary view, see Niall Ferguson, 'The Balance of Payments Question: Versailles and After', in *The Treaty of Versailles. A Reassessment*, p. 425; Gerald D. Feldman, loc.cit., pp. 445–6. The figure set for reparations in 1921 by the permanent Reparations Commission was £6.6 billion.

144. Cunliffe, memorandum to Lloyd George, 1 June 1919, LP, GD40/17/62/14.

145. ibid.
146. Lentin, *Guilt at Versailles*, p. 113.
147. Donald. E. Moggridge, *Maynard Keynes*, p. 246. Vansittart commented that Keynes's intellect revealed to him (Keynes) 'its magnitude compared with those of . . . Lords Cunliffe and Sumner', *The Mist Procession* (1958), p. 223.
148. Cunliffe, letter to his wife, 2 April 1919.
149. Cunliffe, letter to his wife, 3 April 1919.
150. Riddell, *Intimate Diary*, p. 47.
151. *La Conférence de la Paix*, vol. 2, p. 735.
152. Cunliffe, letter to his wife, 8 April 1919.
153. See Stephen Schuker, 'Origins of American Stabilization Policy in Europe: the Financial Dimension, 1918–1924', loc.cit., pp. 385–6. After the American rejection of Keynes's proposals, Cunliffe produced his own scheme. See Cunliffe to Sir Brian Cockayne, 18 May 1919, Bank of England archives G30/4/138-147.
154. Cunliffe, letter to his wife, 8 April 1919. The issue of the German merchant fleet was eventually resolved by agreement between Lloyd George and Wilson on 8 May 1919. Germany transferred the bulk of its merchant shipping to Britain: Burnett, *Reparation*, vol. 1, pp. 112–19; vol. 2, pp. 724–6, 730–4; Seth P. Tillman, *Anglo-American Relations at the Paris Peace Conference of 1919* (Princeton, 1961), pp. 170–1.
155. Cunliffe, letter to his wife, 25 June, 1919.
156. *Field*, 17 January 1920.
157. Cunliffe, letter to his wife, 2 April 1919. The letter continues: 'but I daresay I am as much of a one [financier] as some of the rest'. According to Vansittart, Cunliffe 'had the humour to profess himself as ignorant of finance as Lloyd George', *The Mist Procession*, p. 223.
158. Lloyd George, *War Memoirs*, vol 1, p. 62.
159. Geoffrey Madan, *Geoffrey Madan's Notebook* (Oxford, 1984), p. 87.
160. André Tardieu, *The Truth about the Treaty* (1921) pp. 328–9.
161. op. cit., p. 303.
162. Minutes of Second Subcommittee, 21 February 1919, *La Conférence de la Paix*, vol. 2, p. 736.
163. Robert Cecil, diary, 27 February 1919, British Library Add Mss 51131.
164. Meeting of Dominion Prime Ministers, 11 April 1919, LGP, F/28/3/26.
165. Riddell, *Intimate Diary*, p. 47.
166. ibid.
167. *Lord Riddell's War Diary 1914–1918* (1933), p. 370.
168. Lloyd George, *War Memoirs*, vol. 1, p. 69.
169. Lloyd George, *Peace Treaties*, vol. 1, p. 446.
170. Cunliffe, memorandum to Lloyd George, 1 June 1919, LP, GD40/17/62/11-12.
171. Burnett, *Reparation*, vol. 2, p. 622. For a fuller version, see *La Conférence de la Paix*, vol. 2, pp. 735–6. Trachtenberg criticises Cunliffe's invocation of Germany's 'credit', *Reparation in World Politics*, pp. 57–8. But see Etienne Mantoux, *The Carthaginian Peace*, pp. 116–17.
172. Burnett, *Reparation*, vol. 2, p. 622.
173. Cunliffe to Sumner, 13 July 1919, FO 608/310. Reparations as a guarantee of German good behaviour weighed with Cunliffe consistently since the

Hughes Committee; Bunselmeyer, p. 103. Cunliffe did not exclude the possibility, remote, it is true, that Germany's good behaviour might relieve her of part of her reparations debt; *La Conférence de la Paix*, vol. 2, p. 736. Lloyd George too saw heavy reparations as a guarantee against German rearmament; minutes of War Cabinet meeting March 4 1919, quoted in Trachtenberg, p. 48.

174. BDFA, p. 92.
175. 114 HC Deb. 52, col. 1219–20.
176. Alan Sharp, 'Lloyd George and Foreign Policy, 1918–1922. The "And Yet" Factor', loc. cit., p. 140; *The Versailles Settlement, 1919*, pp. 98–9.
177. BDFA, p. 111. For the moral aspects of British peacemaking, see 'Reply of the Allied and Associated Powers to the Observations of the German Delegation on the Conditions of Peace', in PRFRUS, vol. 13, pp. 44–9; Lentin, *Guilt at Versailles*, passim; Trevor Wilson, *The Myriad Faces of War. Britain and the Great War, 1914–1918* (1986), pp. 831–2, 836–41; and David Dubinskii, 'British Liberals and Radicals and the Treatment of Germany, 1914–1920', unpublished PhD dissertation (Cambridge, 1992), pp. 174–216.
178. *The Times*, 7 and 8 January 1920. 'His name, which was so familiar in political, financial and Fleet Street circles, has now been forgotten. It would seem to be lost and gone forever.' Beaverbrook, *Men and Power*, pp. 99, 100.
179. March 1920, Keynes Papers, EC/7/2/18-19. Keynes wrote, and then deleted from the proofs of *The Economic Consequences of the Peace:* 'If any expert committee reported that Germany could pay this sum [£120 billion p. a.], they lied.' Keynes Papers, EC10/14-15.
180. March 1920, Keynes Papers, EC/7/2/18-19. The immediate public impact of *The Economic Consequences of the Peace* is doubtless reflected in an obituary notice on Cunliffe by the City editor of the *Daily Express*, 7 January 1920: 'It has still to be decided . . . whether the work accomplished at Versailles was as successful as the achievements in Threadneedle Street.' According to Andrew McFadyean, Secretary to the permanent British Reparation Commission in Paris, 'There cannot have been many books which effected so swift and complete a reversal in public opinion. It certainly governed all British thought in the Reparations Commission.' Sir Andrew McFadyean, *Recollected in Tranquillity* (1964), p. 71.
181. Cunliffe, letter to his wife, 24 June 1919.
182. Robert Boothby, *Recollections of a Rebel* (1978), p. 23. Boothby relates the incident to the winter of 1918/19, i.e. before the Peace Conference; but late 1919 must surely be meant.

Chapter 3

1. Riddell, *Intimate Diary*, p. 100.
2. William R. Keylor (ed.), *The Legacy of the Great War. Peacemaking, 1919* (New York, 1998), p. 11.
3. André Tardieu, *La Paix* (Paris, 1921), p. 237.

4. 'Notes of a meeting held at President Wilson's house', 28 June 1919, BLP, Box 38. See 'Traité entre la France et la Grande Bretagne', 28 June 1919, AMAE, Série Y. Internationale 1918–1940, vol. 409/1-4.
5. E. Beau de Loménie, *Le débat de ratification du traité de Versailles à la Chambre des Députés et dans la presse en 1919* (Paris, 1945), p. 60.
6. Georges Clemenceau, *Grandeurs et Misères d'une Victoire*, pp. 208, 210, 162.
7. P.M.H. Bell, *France and Britain 1900–1940: Entente and Estrangement* (1996), p. 122. See A. Lentin, 'The Treaty that Never Was: Lloyd George and the Abortive Anglo-French Alliance of 1919', in *The Life and Times of David Lloyd George* (ed.) Judith Loades (Bangor, 1991), pp. 115–28; '"*Une aberration inexplicable*"? Clemenceau and the Abortive Anglo-French Guarantee Treaty of 1919', *Diplomacy and Statecraft*, 8 (1997), 31–49; 'Lloyd George, Clemenceau and the Elusive Anglo-French Guarantee Treaty, 1919. "A disastrous episode"?' *Anglo-French Relations in the Twentieth Century* (eds) Alan Sharp and Glyn Stone (2000), pp. 104–19.
8. Lloyd E. Ambrosius, *Woodrow Wilson and the American Diplomatic Tradition. The Treaty Fight in Perspective* (Cambridge, 1987), p. 214. The American treaty was not even submitted to the Senate. William R. Keylor, 'The Rise and Demise of the Franco-American Guarantee Pact, 1919–1921', *Proceedings of the Annual Meeting of the Western Society for French History*, vol. 15 (1988), 367–77.
9. Lord Hardinge, *The Old Diplomacy*, p. 242.
10. LP, GD40/17/1174/1.
11. Paul Cambon to Stéphen Pichon, 2 April 1919, Service Historique de l'Armée de Terre, Vincennes, FC, 6N73.
12. Maurice Barrès, quoted in Lentin, '"*Une aberration inexplicable*"?', loc.cit., p. 40.
13. Foch, memorandum of 31 March 1919, FC, 6N74.
14. House, diary, 22 February 1919, in *The Intimate Papers of Colonel House*, vol. 4, p. 344.
15. Robert Cecil, diary, 18 March 1919, British Library, Add Mss 51131.
16. 'Conversation entre M. Lloyd George et le Maréchal Foch', 1 December 1918, FC, GN73.
17. Georges Clemenceau, *Grandeurs et Misères d'une Victoire*, p. 200.
18. 'Conversation entre M.Lloyd George et le Maréchal Foch', 1 December 1918, FC, GN73.
19. 29 December 1918. *Journal Officiel de la République Française. Chambre des Députés, Débats parlementaires, 1918* (Paris, 1918), pp. 3732–3.
20. Philip Kerr, 'Notes of an interview between M.Clemenceau, Colonel House and myself', 7 March 1919, LP, GD40/17/1173.
21. Tardieu, 'Deuxième conversation', FC, 6N73.
22. LP, GD40/17/1174/1.
23. Poincaré, diary, 14 March 1919. R. Poincaré, *Au service de la France*, vol. 11, *A la recherche de la paix 1919* (Paris, 1974), p. 245.
24. Georges Leygues, diary, 12 March 1919, in Jacques Raphaël-Leygues, *Georges Leygues*, p. 216.
25. 'Un coup de théâtre' was Poincaré's expression, *Le Temps*, 12 September 1921.
26. Lord Hankey, *The Supreme Control at the Paris Peace Conference 1919* (1963), p. 144.

27. For the Rhineland crisis and its resolution at the Peace Conference, see LP, GD40/17/1173 and 1174; Tardieu, *La Paix*, pp. 162–241; Clemenceau, *Grandeurs et Misères*, pp. 198–212; Mermeix (Gabriel Terrail), *Le Combat des Trois. Notes et documents sur la Conférence de la Paix* (Paris, 1922), pp. 191–200; Harold I. Nelson, *Land and Power. British and Allied Policy on Germany's Frontiers 1916–19* (Toronto, 1963), pp. 216–48; Walter A. McDougall, *France's Rhineland Diplomacy, 1914–1924: the Last Bid for a Balance of Power in Europe* (Princeton, NJ, 1978), pp. 3–96; Robert McCrum, 'French Rhineland Policy at the Paris Peace Conference, 1919', *Historical Journal*, 21:3 (1978), 623–48; David Stevenson, *French War Aims against Germany* (Oxford, 1982), pp. 156–8, 165–75, 188; Alan Sharp, *The Versailles Settlement. Peacemaking in Paris, 1919* (1991), pp. 106–13; Stephen A. Schuker, 'The Rhineland Question: West European Security at the Paris Peace Conference of 1919', in *The Treaty of Versailles. A Reassessment*, pp. 275–312 .

28. Lord Hardinge suggests that neither Balfour nor 'any other member of the Cabinet' was aware of the treaty's existence until 6 May: *Old Diplomacy*, pp. 241–2. It certainly seems that the Cabinet was not informed beforehand of Lloyd George's offer to Clemenceau (Lloyd George to Bonar Law, 31 March 1919, LGP, F/37/3/40). A draft agreement was first submitted for Balfour's approval on 22 April ('Papers respecting Negotiations for an Anglo-French Pact', Cmd. 2169, *House of Commons Sessional Papers* (1924), p. 287). Lloyd George did not notify the British Empire delegation until 5 May (BDFA, p. 65). On 6 May he told Clemenceau that 'he had already informed the Imperial War Cabinet' (PRFRUS, vol. 5, p. 475). On 5 May, Lloyd George requested Balfour to draft a further text for signature by both of them (LGP, F51/1/22), which Lloyd George handed to Clemenceau the next day. This is no doubt the occasion witnessed by Hardinge and of which he notes (in a remark attributed to Philip Kerr, p. 241) 'Lloyd George had only sent the paper to Mr Balfour to put the phraseology into proper shape.'

29. Clemenceau, *Grandeurs et Misères*, p. 163.

30. 'Une éclatante innovation', Tardieu, *La Paix*, p. 225.

31. Harold Nicolson, *The Congress of Vienna. A Study in Allied Unity, 1812–1822* (1946), p. 51.

32. Clemenceau, *Grandeurs et Misères*, p. 163.

33. Louis Loucheur, to whom Clemenceau revealed Lloyd George's offer on the evening of 14 March, noted in his diary: 'Il paraissait impossible de refuser une pareille offre.' *Carnets Secrets*, p. 72.

34. Lloyd George, *Is it Peace?* (1922), p. 8.

35. Loucheur, *Carnets Secrets*, p. 72. Lloyd George had mentioned the Channel tunnel to both House and Clemenceau on 12 March and repeated his undertaking to Foch on 31 March. *The Intimate Papers of Colonel House*, vol. 4, p. 360; Mantoux, *Délibérations*, vol. 1, p. 95. Stephen A. Schuker, 'The Rhineland Question', loc. cit., p. 295. Both Harold Nelson and Stephen Schuker are sceptical about Lloyd George's representations. For Schuker (p. 296), Lloyd George was 'blowing smoke'; Nelson comments: 'the ebullient Welshman surely jested!' These are reasonable, perhaps likely verdicts; but Lloyd George was not fantasising. He included the Channel tunnel as a corollary to the guarantee to France in a policy statement on 23 March (LGP, F/147/3/2/2). The tunnel was under active consideration by the British Cabinet. See

A. Sharp, 'Britain and the Channel Tunnel 1919–1920', *Australian Journal of Politics and History*, 25 (1979), 210–15.

36. Mantoux, *Déliberations*, vol. 1, p. 48

37. Mantoux, *Délibérations*, vol. 1, p. 51.

38. Lloyd George, *Peace Treaties*, vol. 1, pp. 411, 413–14.

39. Mantoux, *Délibérations*, vol. 1, p. 73.

40. 'Prime Minister's Reply to M. Clemenceau', 2 April 1919, LGP, F/147/2.

41. 'Papers Respecting Negotiations for an Anglo-French Pact', loc. cit., p. 287; Tardieu to Pichon, 22 April 1919, AMAE, Papiers d'agents, Pichon, vol. 7/53-9.

42. Mantoux, *Délibérations*, vol. 1, p. 352.

43. LGP, F/51/1/22; LP, GD40/17/62. PRFRUS, vol. 5, pp. 474–5, 494; vol. 3, p. 379.

44. Mantoux, *Délibérations*, vol. 2, p. 140.

45. Mantoux, *Délibérations*, vol. 1, p. 51.

46. 'Papers Respecting Negotiations for an Anglo-French Pact', loc. cit., p. 287; LGP, F/51/1/22; Balfour Papers, British Library, Add Mss 49750/16.

47. BDFA, p. 65. A 15-year term was also mentioned to Lloyd George by Sir Henry Wilson on 27 April. Riddell, *Intimate Diary*, p. 61.

48. Harold I. Nelson, *Land and Power: British and Allied Policy on Germany's Frontiers 1916–1919* (1963), p. 246.

49. BDFA, p. 66.

50. Balfour Papers, British Library, Add Mss 49750/18; LGP, F/30/3/40. Cf. Lloyd George to Dominion Prime Ministers, 10 May 1919, LGP, F/5/3/56. The final draft of the treaty stated that the treaty would not bind any of the Dominions 'unless and until it is approved by the Parliament of the Dominion concerned'.

51. PRFRUS, vol. 6, p. 735.

52. 'Minutes of a Meeting of the British Empire Delegation', 5 May 1919, BDFA, p. 66.

53. LGP, F/5/5/14/2.

54. Clemenceau, *Grandeurs et Misères*, pp. 206–7.

55. Henri Mordacq, *Le Ministère Clemenceau: Journal d'un Témoin*, vol. 3 (Paris, 1930), p. 293.

56. LGP, F/30/3/40.

57. Wilson to Henry White, 17 April 1919, PWW, vol. 57, p. 432; Mantoux, *Délibérations*, vol. 1, pp. 319; PRFRUS, vol. 5, p. 457. Schuker, 'The Rhineland Question', p. 304. All three Commissioners to the American delegation at Paris opposed the American guarantee. PRFRUS, vol. 11, p. 133.

58. House, diary, 12 March 1919, *The Intimate Papers of Colonel House*, vol. 4, p. 360.

59. 'Minutes of a meeting of the British Empire Delegation', 5 May 1919, BDFA, p. 65. Nelson (*Land and Power*, p. 245) argues that 'Lloyd George's reference to the Senate clearly explains the British reservation that the guarantee would only come into force for Great Britain when the United States had also ratified it.' It does nothing of the sort, though it may suggest a *mental* reservation on Lloyd George's part.

60. Clemenceau, *Grandeurs et Misères*, p. 163.

61. op. cit., p. 207.

62. Mantoux, *Délibérations*, vol. 2, p. 140.
63. LGP, F/51/1/22.
64. David Hunter Miller, diary, 5 May 1919, *My Diary at the Conference of Paris*, vol. 1 (New York, 1924), p. 294.
65. PRFRUS, vol. 6, p. 735; Hankey, *The Supreme Control*, p. 186.
66. PRFRUS, vol. 6, p. 736.
67. The French version, produced after the meeting, for signature in the final draft, reads: 'Le présent traité n'entrera en vigueur qu'au moment où ce dernier sera ratifié.'
68. David S. Newhall, *Clemenceau: a Life at War* (Lampeter, 1991), p. 483.
69. Riddell, *Intimate Diary*, p. 20.
70. Lloyd George, *Peace Treaties*, vol. 2, p. 433.
71. Clemenceau and Tardieu both denied having been deceived by Lloyd George. Tardieu told Bonsall, 'We knew that such a pledge required parliamentary sanction in both countries, and while I fear we were left "holding the bag".... we were not hoodwinked.' Stephen Bonsall, *Suitors and Suppliants. The Little Nations at Versailles* (Port Washington, NY, 1964), pp. 216–17. This does not address the question whether the Frenchmen were aware of the link between the British and American treaties introduced in the final draft. Tardieu, however, appears to hint at subterfuge. Arguing that Lloyd George foresaw the rejection of the American treaty, Tardieu adds: 'he saw to it that in this event Britain would be free to act or stand aside as she desired' (p. 217). How did he 'see to it' unless by the insertion of the word 'only'?
72. Bonsall, *Suitors and Suppliants*, p. 217.
73. Mantoux, *Délibérations*, vol. 1, p. 93. Cf. Lloyd George to Botha, 26 June 1919, LGP, F/5/5/14/2.
74. Walter A. McDougall, *France's Rhineland Diplomacy 1914–1924* (Princeton, 1978), p. 60.
75. 123 HC Deb. 5s, col. 762.
76. Clemenceau, *Grandeurs et Misères*, p. 99.
77. 'Minutes of a Meeting of the British Empire Delegation', 1 June 1919, BDFA, p. 113.
78. 117 HC, Deb. 5s, cols. 1123–4.
79. Riddell, diary, 1 March 1919, *Riddell Diaries*, p. 258; Lloyd George to Bonar Law, 31 March 1919, LGP, F/30/3/40.
80. BDFA, p. 65.
81. Nelson, *Land and Power*, p. 246.
82. David S. Newhall, *Clemenceau* (Lampeter, 1991), p. 441; Clemenceau, *Grandeurs et Misères*, pp. 162–3. I have argued elsewhere that in choosing between the Rhineland and the British guarantee, Clemenceau chose wisely. This is not to deny the extent of his deception by Lloyd George. See Lentin ' "Une aberration inexplicable"?', loc.cit., pp. 31–49; and 'Lloyd George, Clemenceau and the Elusive Anglo-French Guarantee Treaty', loc.cit.
83. Birkenhead, *Contemporary Personalities* (1924), p. 35.
84. See minutes of British Empire delegation of 5 May, 1 June, 10 June 1919, BDFA, pp. 66, 99–103, 112–15, 121, 124; Botha to Lloyd George, 6 May, 15 May 1919, Lloyd George to Botha, 10 May 1919, *Smuts Papers*, pp. 150–1, 155, 158–9; Lloyd George to Botha, 26 June 1919, LGP, F/5/5/14.

85. Mantoux, *Délibérations*, vol. 1, p. 73; Lloyd George to Botha, 26 June 1919, LGP, F/5/5/14/2. Lord Derby, British Ambassador in Paris, assured a French journalist that 'we had given our word, and though we were sorry that America was not a participant in the agreement, our word stood and would stand'. Derby, diary, 27 November 1919, in Lentin, ' "Une aberration inexplicable" ', p. 43.

86. David R.Watson, *Georges Clemenceau: a Political Biography* (1974), p. 347.

87. On 12 March, two days before Wilson's return, Lloyd George asked Colonel House whether America would join Britain in the guarantee. House said he did not know. *The Intimate Papers of Colonel House*, vol. 4, p. 360.

88. Lloyd George, *Peace Treaties*, vol. 1, p. 403.

89. LGP, F/147/3/2/2.

90. Sylvester, *The Real Lloyd George*, p. 244.

91. Quoted in L.S. Amery, *My Political Life*, vol. 2 (1953), pp. 98–9.

92. Riddell, *Intimate Diary*, p. 45.

93. Walter A. McDougall, *France's Rhineland Diplomacy*, p. 70.

94. Winston S. Churchill, *The Gathering Storm* (1967 edition), p. 6.

95. Mantoux, *Délibérations*, vol. 2, pp. 270–1.

96. *Journal Officiel. Chambre des Députés. Débats parlementaires, 1919* (Paris, 1919), p. 1619.

97. 'Notes of Anglo-French Conversation at Downing Street, December 13 1919', FC, 6N72/20.

98. *Riddell Diaries*, p. 301.

99. Reporting on a discussion with Lord Derby, the French diplomat, Camille Barrère noted: 'Lord Derby m'a demandé alors de lui dire franchement la cause du mécontentement français...Je lui ai fait remarquer tout d'abord que l'origine du malaise de l'opinion française remontait à la Conférence de Paix et au traitement de la question des frontières. L'opinion française avait attribué à l'opposition anglaise le refus d'attribuer à la France la frontière historique qui seule pouvait assurer sa sécurité et la mettre à l'abri du retour d'une terrible aventure.' Barrère to Millerand, 5 April 1920, AMAE, Série Z, Europe 1918–1940, vol. 44, Grande Bretagne, p. 201.

100. Sir George Graham to Philip Kerr, 3 April 1920, LP, GD40/17/1368.

101. Riddell, *Intimate Diary*, p. 188

102. *Riddell Diaries*, p. 315.

103. *Riddell Diaries*, p. 317.

104. ibid.

105. Riddell, *Intimate Diary*, p. 188.

106. Jusserand to Quai d'Orsay, 16 April 1920, AMAE, Série Z, Europe 1918–1940, vol. 44, Grande Bretagne, p. 252.

107. Riddell, *Intimate Diary*, p. 188.

108. *Clemenceau. The Events of his Life. As told by himself to his Former Secretary Jean Martet*, (tr.) M. Waldman (1930), p. 21.

Chapter 4

1. See William R. Keylor, 'Versailles and International Diplomacy', in *The Treaty of Versailles. A Reassessment*, pp. 469–505.

2. BDFA, pp. 98–9.
3. '*Une paix trop douce pour ce qu'elle a de dur.*' Jacques Bainville, *Les conséquences politiques de la paix* (Paris, 1919; 1995 edition), p. 35.
4. *Smuts Papers*, p. 223.
5. Fisher to Gilbert Murray, 11 June 1919, Bodleian Library, Oxford, Fisher Papers, 7.
6. Keynes, *Collected Writings*, vol. 16, p. 469.
7. *The Political Diaries of C.P. Scott 1911–1928*, p. 375.
8. *Smuts Papers*, p. 223.
9. *Smuts Papers*, p. 280.
10. Violet Bonham-Carter, *Champion Redoutable. The Diaries and Letters of Violet Bonham-Carter 1914–1945* (ed.) Mark Pottle (1998), p. 107.
11. *The Times*, 7 February 1920.
12. Lentin, *Guilt at Versailles*, pp. 141–3. Soon after publication, Keynes's verdict became 'conventional wisdom' in the Foreign Office, the Treasury, the Bank of England, the City, the Round Table and the Royal Institute of International Affairs network. Scott Newton, *Profits of Peace. The Political Economy of Anglo-German Appeasement* (Oxford, 1996), p. 73.
13. Elisabeth Glaser, 'The Making of the Economic Peace', in *The Treaty of Versailles. A Reassessment*, p. 381.
14. Gordon Martel, 'From *Round Table* to *New Europe*: Some Intellectual Origins of the Institute of International Affairs', in *Chatham House and British Foreign Policy 1919–1945* (ed.) Andrea Bosco and Cornelia Navari (1994), p. 33.
15. Quoted by Gordon Martel, 'A Comment', in *The Treaty of Versailles. A Reassessment*, p. 631.
16. James S. Barnes, *Half a Life* (1933), p. 298.
17. *Smuts Papers*, p. 87.
18. *Smuts Papers*, p. 144.
19. Nicolson, *Peacemaking 1919*, p. 353. See Michael Dockrill, 'The Foreign Office and the "Proposed Institute of International Affairs 1919"', in *Chatham House and British Foreign Policy, 1914–45*, pp. 73–4.
20. Nicolson, op. cit., p. 359.
21. James Headlam-Morley, *A Memoir of the Paris Peace Conference*, p. 161.
22. Lord Vansittart, *The Mist Procession* (1958), p. 220.
23. *Smuts Papers*, p. 87.
24. Lloyd George to Archbishop Davidson, 30 May 1919, Randall Davidson War Box 27.
25. Alma Luckau, *The German Delegation at the Paris Peace Conference* (New York, 1941), pp. 414, 418.
26. *Smuts Papers*, p. 256.
27. *Smuts Papers*, p. 270.
28. *Smuts Papers*, pp. 271–2.
29. Riddell, *Intimate Diary*, p. 268; Jan Christian Smuts, *Jan Christian Smuts* (1952), p. 224.
30. *Smuts Papers*, p. 162.
31. *Smuts Papers*, p. 195.
32. Nicolson, *Peacemaking 1919*, pp. 280–1.
33. *Smuts Papers*, p. 83.
34. Headlam-Morley, *A Memoir*, p. 103.

35. op. cit., p. 104.
36. Lentin, *Guilt at Versailles*, p. 94.
37. Fisher, diary, 31 May 1919, Fisher Papers.
38. *Smuts Papers*, p. 212.
39. S.D. Waley, *Edwin Montagu* (1964), p. 211.
40. ibid.
41. Gordon Martel, 'From *Round Table* to *New Europe*', loc. cit., p. 33.
42. Jules Cambon, 'La Paix', *Revue de Paris*, Nov.–Dec. 1937, pp. 27, 31.
43. Etienne Mantoux, *The Carthaginian Peace* (1952), p. 17.
44. Michael Fry, 'British Revisionism', in *The Treaty of Versailles. A Reassessment*, p. 568.
45. Keynes to Norman Davis, 5 June 1919, Keynes Papers, PT/1.
46. Milner, diary, 1 June 1919, Bodleian Library, Oxford, Milner Papers.
47. Michael Fry, 'British Revisionism', loc. cit., p. 565.
48. S.D. Waley, *Edwin Montagu*, p. 212.
49. BDFA, p. 106.
50. Nigel Nicolson, *Portrait of a Marriage* (1973), p. 143.
51. R.H. Beadon, *Some Memories of the Peace Conference* (1933), p. 44.
52. Milner Papers.
53. Dominic Hibberd, *The First World War* (1990), p. 187.
54. *Smuts Papers*, p. 252.
55. Headlam-Morley, *A Memoir*, p. 118.
56. Agnes Headlam-Morley, in Headlam-Morley, *A Memoir*, p. xxx.
57. Edward Hallett Carr, *From Napoleon to Stalin and Other Essays* (1980), p. 166. On Carr himself, see Jonathan Haslam, *The Vices of Integrity. E.H. Carr, 1892–1982* (1999), pp. 24–33.
58. On Headlam-Morley, see Arnold Toynbee, *Acquaintances* (1967), pp. 161–8; E.H. Carr, *From Napoleon to Stalin and Other Essays* (1980), pp. 165–9; Alan Sharp, 'James Headlam-Morley: Creating International History', *Diplomacy and Statecraft*, 9:3 (November 1998), 266–83. And see his 'Some Relevant Historians – the Political Intelligence Department of the Foreign Office', *Australian Journal of Politics and History*, 34:3 (1989), 359–68.
59. Nicolson, *Peacemaking 1919*, p. 364
60. loc. cit., p. 311.
61. *Smuts Papers*, p. 171.
62. Lloyd George to Randal Davidson, 30 May 1919, Davidson War Boxes, 27.
63. *Smuts Papers*, pp. 83–7; Mantoux, *Délibérations*, vol. 1, pp. 46, 48.
64. BDFA, p. 109.
65. *Smuts Papers*, p. 218. For Smuts's reply to Lloyd George see *Smuts Papers*, pp. 219–21. Lloyd George omitted Smuts from the list of colleagues to whom he expressed gratitude on presenting the Treaty of Versailles in the House of Commons.
66. BDFA, pp. 98–9.
67. Headlam-Morley, *A Memoir*, p. 43.
68. op.cit., p. 103.
69. Headlam-Morley to G. Saunders, 8 March 1919, in K.M. Wilson, *George Saunders on Germany 1919–1920* (Leeds, 1987), p. 17.
70. Headlam-Morley, *A Memoir*, p. 95.
71. Headlam-Morley to Saunders, 12 June 1919, in Wilson, *George Saunders*, p. 42.

72. Headlam-Morley, *A Memoir*, p. 74.
73. op. cit., p. 168.
74. op. cit., p. 179.
75. BDFA, p. 108.
76. *Smuts Papers*, p. 85.
77. BDFA, p. 98.
78. Quoted in Robert Cecil, diary, 20 May 1919, Cecil Papers, British Library, Add Mss 51131.
79. Headlam-Morley, *A Memoir*, p. 162.
80. Headlam-Morley to Saunders, 8 March 1919, in Wilson, *George Saunders*, p. 17.
81. Keynes to Sir John Bradbury, 4 May 1919, Keynes Papers PT/1.
82. *Smuts Papers*, p. 149.
83. Abraham to Kerr, 3 June 1919, LP GD40/17/62/19.
84. PRFRUS, vol. 11, p. 222.
85. BDFA, p. 97.
86. BDFA, p. 102.
87. *Smuts Papers*, p. 216.
88. *Smuts Papers*, p. 217.
89. *Riddell Diaries*, p. 265.
90. BDFA, p. 108.
91. ibid.
92. BDFA, p. 107.
93. Headlam-Morley, *A Memoir*, p. 164.
94. Keynes, 'Dr Melchior: a Defeated Enemy', *Two Memoirs* (1949), p. 50.
95. BDFA, p. 114.
96. BDFA, p. 99.
97. Austen Chamberlain to his sister Hilda, 9 June 1919, in *The Austen Chamberlain Diary Letters. The Correspondence of Sir Austen Chamberlain with his Sisters Hilda and Ida, 1916–1937* (ed.) R.C. Self (Cambridge, 1995), p. 116.
98. Smuts, statement, 18 July 1919, *Smuts Papers*, p. 272.
99. Douglas Newton, *British Policy and the Weimar Republic, 1918–1919* (Oxford, 1997), p. 339.
100. Headlam-Morley, *A Memoir*, p. 22.
101. op. cit., p. xxxvi.
102. Cecil, diary, 20 May 1919, British Library, Add Mss 51131.
103. Headlam-Morley, *A Memoir*, p. 170.
104. *Smuts Papers*, p. 189.
105. C.P. Vincent, *The Politics of Hunger. The Allied Blockade of Germany, 1915–1919* (Athens, Ohio, 1985), p. 103.
106. Douglas Newton, *British Policy*, p. 362.
107. op. cit., p. 381.
108. Cecil to Lloyd George, 14 May 1919, LGP, F/6/6/45.
109. Headlam-Morley, A *Memoir*, p. 162.
110. *Smuts Papers*, p. 118.
111. Nicolson, *Peacemaking 1919*, p. 269.
112. loc. cit., p. 294.
113. Headlam-Morley, *A Memoir*, p. 84.
114. Nicolson, *Peacemaking 1919*, pp. 361–2.

115. Beadon, *Some Memories of the Peace Conference*, p. 172.
116. op. cit., p. 175.
117. *Smuts Papers*, p. 255.
118. Sir Esme Howard, *Theatre of Life* (1936), p. 389; B. J. C. McKercher, *Esme Howard. A Diplomatic Biography* (Cambridge, 1989), pp. 198–9.
119. Nicolson, *Peacemaking 1919*, p. 370.
120. *Smuts Papers*, p. 271.
121. Jan Christian Smuts, *Jan Christian Smuts*, p. 227.
122. *Smuts Papers*, p. 188
123. *Smuts Papers*, p. 87.
124. Lentin, *Guilt at Versailles*, p. 29.
125. A dinner was held at the Hotel Majestic on 15 March 1919 for the Balliol men in the British delegation. Nicolson noted that 'at least 60% of the Civil Staff were at Balliol. We feel proud.' *Peacemaking 1919*, p. 284.
126. Carr, *From Napoleon to Stalin*, p. 166.
127. Cecil, diary, 22 May 1919, British Library, Add Mss 51131; Randall Davidson, diary, 8 December 1918, Davidson Papers, Lambeth Palace Library; George Bell, diary, 7 December 1918, Bell Papers, Lambeth Palace. See Cornelia Navari, 'Chatham House and the Broad Church View of British Foreign Policy', in *Chatham House and British Foreign Policy 1919–1945*, pp. 345–9.
128. *Smuts Papers*, p. 188.
129. *Smuts Papers*, p. 270.
130. *Smuts Papers*, p. 256. The reference is to John, 4: 21–23.
131. *Smuts Papers*, p. 257
132. *Smuts Papers*, p. 286.
133. 117 HC 114 Deb. 5s, col. 1219.
134. Headlam-Morley, A *Memoir*, p. 52
135. *Smuts Papers*, p. 176.
136. *Smuts Papers*, p. 213.
137. *Smuts Papers*, p. 158.
138. *Smuts Papers*, p. 248.
139. *Smuts Papers*, p. 251.
140. *Smuts Papers*, p. 157.
141. *Smuts Papers*, p. 223.
142. James S. Barnes, *Half a Life*, p. 299.
143. *Smuts Papers*, p. 225.
144. Headlam-Morley, *A Memoir*, p. 104.
145. Abraham to Kerr, 3 June 1919, LP, GD40/17/61/19.
146. ibid.
147. Headlam-Morley, *A Memoir*, p. 162.
148. *A Memoir*, pp. 161–2.
149. 114 HC Deb. 5s, col. 2956.
150. Quoted by Martel, 'A Comment', in *The Treaty of Versailles. A Reassessment*, p. 631.
151. Jan Christian Smuts, *Jan Christian Smuts*, p. 224.
152. Lentin, *Guilt at Versailles*, p. 97.
153. Bruce Arnold, *Orpen. Mirror to an Age* (1981), pp. 361–2.

Chapter 5

1. Winston S. Churchill, *The Second World War*, Book 1, *The Gathering Storm* (9th edition, Geneva, 1967), pp. 224–5.
2. Winston S. Churchill, *Great Contemporaries* (1935; 1948 edition), p. 203.
3. E.H. Haraszti, *The Invaders. Hitler Occupies the Rhineland* (Budapest, 1983), p. 149.
4. Sylvester, *Life with Lloyd George*, p. 12.
5. Thomas Jones, *A Diary*, p. 147.
6. Sylvester, *Life with Lloyd George*, p. 145.
7. The cloak-and-dagger background to the projected meeting between Baldwin and Hitler in 1936 deserves mention. Ribbentrop first approached Thomas Jones in April. On 11 May, Jones accepted Ribbentrop's invitation to visit him in Berlin, where he flew on 15 May as Baldwin's secret emissary. On 16 May Ribbentrop pressed on him Hitler's ardent wish to meet Baldwin. On 17 May, Jones met Hitler himself at Munich, where Hitler pressed for a meeting with Baldwin. Jones reported to Baldwin on 20 May. Baldwin was all ears, commenting 'This is like an Oppenheimer story.' Details of a visit were aired between Baldwin and Jones and Jones and Ribbentrop. Would Hitler fly to Chequers? Baldwin had never flown and disliked the sea. Ribbentrop said that Hitler could sail to close to the Kent coast. On 8 June Baldwin said he preferred a formal meeting in Berlin, accompanied by Eden. On 16 June, Ribbentrop pressed Jones for a decision, otherwise 'Hitler would think we were playing with him and delaying the reply to his invitation for some sinister reason... Eden strongly objected to the proposed meeting and the matter was dropped.' Thomas Jones, *A Diary*, pp. 186, 194–202, 205, 207–8, 214, 218, 224.
8. Sylvester, *Life with Lloyd George*, p. 145.
9. Jones, *A Diary*, p. 236.
10. Jones, *A Diary*, p. 271.
11. Sylvester, *Life with Lloyd George*, p. 153.
12. Jones, *A Diary*, p. 271.
13. Sylvester, *The Real Lloyd George*, p. 197.
14. Sylvester, *Life with Lloyd George*, p. 146.
15. Sylvester, *The Real Lloyd George*, p. 197.
16. Sylvester, *Life with Lloyd George*, p. 147. Eduard Beneš, President of Czechoslovakia. Lloyd George formed an unfavourable impression of him as Czech Foreign Minister at the Paris Peace Conference, where Lloyd George believed that Beneš had deceived him about the size of the German minority in Czechoslovakia.
17. Sylvester, *Life with Lloyd George*, p. 148.
18. Sylvester, *The Real Lloyd George*, p. 200.
19. Sylvester, *The Real Lloyd George*, p. 200.
20. Sylvester, *Life with Lloyd George*, p. 147.
21. Jones, *A Diary*, pp. 247–8.
22. Sylvester, *Life with Lloyd George*, p. 148.
23. Sylvester, *The Real Lloyd George*, p. 201.
24. Jones, *A Diary*, p. 248.

25. Jones, *A Diary*, p. 252.
26. Sylvester, *The Real Lloyd George*, p. 204.
27. Jones, *A Diary*, p. 245.
28. Sylvester, *The Real Lloyd George*, p. 205.
29. T.P. Conwell-Evans, 'Notes of a conversation between Lloyd George and Hitler at Berchtesgaden, 4 September 1936', appendix to Martin Gilbert, *The Roots of Appeasement* (1966), p. 198.
30. Sylvester, *The Real Lloyd George*, p. 205.
31. Conwell-Evans, loc. cit., p. 200.
32. Sylvester, *The Real Lloyd George*, p. 206.
33. Conwell-Evans, p. 201.
34. Conwell-Evans, pp. 201–2; Sylvester, *The Real Lloyd George*, p. 205.
35. Sylvester, *The Real Lloyd George*, p. 206.
36. Sylvester, *The Real Lloyd George*, p. 205.
37. Conwell-Evans, p. 199.
38. Conwell-Evans, p. 202.
39. Conwell-Evans, p. 205.
40. Thomas Jones, *Lloyd George* (1951), p. 246.
41. Sylvester, *Life with Lloyd George*, p. 148.
42. Sylvester, *The Real Lloyd George*, p. 204.
43. Sylvester, *Life with Lloyd George*, p. 148.
44. Sylvester, *The Real Lloyd George*, p. 210.
45. Sylvester, *Life with Lloyd George*, p. 149. See *Documents on German Foreign Policy 1918–1945*, Series C, vol. 5 (1966), p. 946.
46. Sylvester, *The Real Lloyd George*, p. 211.
47. Jones, *A Diary*, p. 248.
48. Conwell-Evans, p. 209.
49. Sylvester, *Life with Lloyd George*, p. 150.
50. Sylvester, *The Real Lloyd George*, p. 213.
51. Sylvester, *The Real Lloyd George*, p. 214.
52. ibid.
53. Sylvester, *The Real Lloyd George*, pp. 214–15; Conwell-Evans, p. 211.
54. Conwell-Evans, p. 208.
55. Jones, *A Diary*, pp. 251–2.
56. Conwell-Evans, p. 208.
57. Ian Kershaw, *Hitler 1889–1936: Hubris* (1998), p. 591.
58. Riddell, *Intimate Diary*, p. 176.
59. Sylvester, *The Real Lloyd George*, p. 212.
60. Jones, *A Diary*, p. 252.
61. Jones, p. 252.
62. Jones, p. 249.
63. Jones, p. 250.
64. Jones, *A Diary*, p. 273.
65. Conwell-Evans, p. 197. Hitler was also attracted by Lloyd George's voice. Gerwin Strobl, *The Germanic Isle. Nazi Perceptions of Britain* (Cambridge, 2000), p. 113.
66. Hitler, *Mein Kampf*, Unexpurgated edition (n.d.), p. 412.
67. Jones, *A Diary*, p. 274.
68. Paul Schmidt, *Hitler's Interpreter* (1951), p. 57.

69. The Hossbach memorandum, 5 November 1937, *Nazism 1919–1945*, vol. 3, *Foreign Policy, War and Racial Extermination* (ed.) J. Noakes and G.Pridham (Exeter, 1988), p. 683. See G.T. Waddington, '*Haßgegner*: German Views of Great Britain in the Later 1930s', *History*, 81 (1996), 22–39. In 1937, Ribbentrop invited Churchill to discuss the same proposals as he had outlined to Lloyd George: 'an Anglo-German entente or even alliance' in return for 'a free hand in the East of Europe' for a German *Lebensraum*, to include Poland, White Russia and the Ukraine. Churchill said that he was sure the British government would not agree. Ribbentrop replied, 'In that case, war is inevitable.' Churchill, *The Gathering Storm*, pp. 200–1.

70. Jones, *A Diary*, p. 245. See Andreas Hillgruber, 'England's Place in Hitler's Plans for World Domination', *Journal of Contemporary History*, 9:1 (1974), 8–9, 13, and Gerwin Strobl, *The Germanic Isle*, p. 75.

71. Conwell Evans, p. 198. Hitler's admiration for the British Empire was stimulated by repeated viewings at the Berghof of the film, *The Bengal Lancers*, Strobl, *The Germanic Isle*, p. 75.

72. Jones, *A Diary*, p. 247.

73. Sylvester, *The Real Lloyd George*, p. 205.

74. Sylvester, *The Real Lloyd George*, p. 200.

75. ibid.

76. Peter Rowland, *Lloyd George* (1975), p. 736.

77. ibid.

78. ibid.

79. Sylvester, *The Real Lloyd George*, p. 214.

80. Rowland, *Lloyd George*, p. 736; Sylvester, *Life with Lloyd George*, p. 151.

81. Sylvester, *The Real Lloyd George*, p. 200.

82. Rowland, *Lloyd George*, p. 736. According to Frances Stevenson, Lloyd George's copy of *Mein Kampf* was an expurgated edition which omitted all reference to his ambitions on Russia. *The Years that are Past*, p. 230.

83. Sylvester, *The Real Lloyd George*, p. 203.

84. Sylvester, *The Real Lloyd George*, p. 214.

85. *Akten zur Deutschen Auswärtigen Politik 1918–1945*, series D, vol. 8 (Frankfurt-am-Main, 1961), p. 233. See *Hitler's Table-Talk 1941–1944* (ed.) Hugh Trevor-Roper (1953; Oxford, 1988 edition), pp. 657.

86. Sylvester, *The Real Lloyd George*, p. 213.

87. *Hitler's Table-Talk*, pp. 259–60.

88. Frances Stevenson, *The Years that are Past*, p. 257.

89. Lloyd George to Conwell Evans, 17 December 1937, Rowland, *Lloyd George*, p. 745.

90. R.A.C. Parker, *Churchill and Appeasement* (2000), p. 195.

91. Sylvester, *Life with Lloyd George*, p. 275. Frances Stevenson claims that Lloyd George planned the window 'long before he ever went to Berchtesgaden'. *The Years that are Past*, p. 268.

Chapter 6

1. Lord Moran, *Winston Churchill. The Struggle for Survival 1940–1965* (1966), pp. 325–6.

2. A.J. Sylvester, *The Real Lloyd George* (1947), p. ix.
3. A.J. Sylvester Papers, Box No. 34/5, Letters of 20, 27 September, 3–6, 9, 11, 13, 17–18, 23, 25 October, 10, 18, 21–22, 29 November 1939.
4. Sylvester, letters to his wife, 4 and 11 October 1939.
5. Sylvester, letter to his wife, 5 October 1939.
6. Sylvester, letter to his wife, 29 November 1939.
7. Sylvester, letters to his wife, 13 and 6 October 1939.
8. Lloyd George, *War Memoirs*, vol. 1 (1938), pp. 642, 811. See *The Neville Chamberlain Diary Letters*, vol. 1 (Aldershot, 2000), pp. 65–70.
9. *The Austen Chamberlain Diary Letters. The Correspondence of Sir Austen Chamberlain with his Sisters Hilda and Ida, 1916–1937* (ed.) R.C. Self (Cambridge, 1995), pp. 473, 476.
10. Address to Council of Action rally, Manchester, 23 October 1936, Peter Rowland, *Lloyd George* (1975), p. 738.
11. Sylvester, *Life with Lloyd George*, p. 235.
12. R.A.C. Parker, *Chamberlain and Appeasement. British Policy and the Coming of the Second World War* (1993), p. 214.
13. Jones, *A Diary*, p. 457.
14. 325 HC Deb. 5s, cols. 1591, 1599.
15. 332 HC Deb. 5s, col. 261.
16. 342 HC Deb. 5s, col. 2551.
17. Speech at Llandudno, 19 January 1939, Peter Rowland, *Lloyd George*, p. 754.
18. Sylvester, *Life with Lloyd George*, p. 225.
19. 345 HC Deb. 5s, col. 2509.
20. 345 HC Deb. 5s, col. 2510.
21. 347 HC Deb. 5s, col. 71.
22. 347 HC Deb. 5s, col. 73.
23. 351 HC Deb. 5s, col. 299.
24. Lloyd George, *Peace Treaties*, vol. 1, p. 406.
25. Sylvester, letter to his wife, 27 September 1939.
26. loc. cit.
27. Paul Addison, 'Lloyd George and Compromise Peace in the Second World War', in *Lloyd George: Twelve Essays* (ed.) A.J.P. Taylor (1971), p. 367.
28. Sylvester, letter to his wife, 20 September 1939.
29. Sylvester, letter to his wife, 27 September 1939. Cf. Robert Boothby, *I Fight to Live* (1947), pp. 195–6.
30. Sylvester, letter to his wife, 20 September 1939.
31. Sylvester, letter to his wife, 27 September 1939.
32. Sylvester, letter to his wife, 20 September 1939.
33. Sylvester, *Life with Lloyd George*, p. 237; Harold Nicolson, *Diaries and Letters 1939–1945* (ed.) Nigel Nicolson (1967), p. 35.
34. Sylvester, *Life with Lloyd George*, p. 237.
35. 351 HC Deb. 5s, cols. 1871–2.
36. Ivan Maisky, telegram to Molotov, 3 October 1939, in *Dokumenty Vneshnei Politiki. 1939 god* [*Documents on Foreign Policy. The Year 1939*], book 2, (Moscow, 1992), p. 153.
37. 351 HC Deb. 5s, col. 1879.
38. Sylvester, letter to his wife, 5 October 1939.
39. Sylvester, letter to his wife, 3 October 1939.

40. Sylvester, letter to his wife, 4 October 1939.
41. ibid.
42. Sylvester, letter to his wife, 3 October 1939.
43. Sylvester, letter to his wife, 4 October 1939.
44. Sylvester, letter to his wife, 5 October 1939.
45. Sylvester, letter to his wife, 4 October 1939.
46. ibid.
47. Sylvester, letter to his wife, 5 October 1939.
48. Sylvester, letter to his wife, 6 October 1939. Lloyd George received 2700 letters in October 1939. Of 2450 letters received by Chamberlain in three days after Lloyd George's speech, over three-quarters favoured peace. G.N. Esnouf, 'British Government War Aims and Attitudes towards a Negotiated Peace, September 1939 to July 1940' (unpublished doctoral dissertation, King's College, London, 1988), p. 49; Christopher Hill, *Cabinet Decisions on Foreign Policy. The British Experience October 1938–June 1941* (Cambridge, 1991), p. 295.
49. Sylvester, letter to his wife, 5 October 1939.
50. ibid.
51. ibid.
52. Hitler, *My New Order* (ed.) Raoul de Roussy de Sales (New York, 1973), p. 744.
53. Sylvester, letter to his wife, 6 October 1939.
54. Sylvester, letter to his wife, 11 October 1939.
55. ibid
56. Sylvester, letter to his wife, 9 October 1939.
57. Peter Rowland, *Lloyd George* (1975), p. 756.
58. Sylvester, letter to his wife, 13 October 1939.
59. ibid. Maisky agreed that Lloyd George was 'for peace, for a peace conference now, and not after a war'. (Diary, 14 October 1939, *Dokumenty*, p. 188). Lloyd George discussed the prospects for peace with Maisky in his railway compartment at Euston before leaving for Caernarvon. Sylvester, *Life with Lloyd George*, p. 240; Maisky, telegram to Molotov, 20 October 1939, *Dokumenty*, pp. 204–5.
60. Sylvester, letter to his wife, 17 October 1939.
61. ibid.
62. ibid.
63. Sylvester, *Life with Lloyd George*, p. 239.
64. Sylvester, letter to his wife, 17 October 1939.
65. Sylvester, letter to his wife, 18 October 1939.
66. ibid.
67. ibid.
68. ibid.
69. Sylvester, *Life with Lloyd George*, p. 240.
70. Sylvester, *Life with Lloyd George*, p. 241.
71. ibid. On 2 October Hitler told Ciano that he did not expect his offer to be accepted and that he was making it 'only to place the enemy in the wrong'. *Documents on German Foreign Policy 1918–1945*, Series D, vol. 8 (1954), p. 189.
72. Sylvester, *Life with Lloyd George*, p. 241.
73. ibid.
74. Sylvester, letter to his wife, 23 October 1939.

75. *The Times*, 23 October 1939.
76. Sylvester, *Life with Lloyd George*, p. 242.
77. ibid.
78. Sylvester, letter to his wife, 5 October 1939.
79. Angus Calder, *The People's War* (1969; 1993 edition), p. 58.
80. Addison, loc. cit., p. 368.
81. Leo Amery, diary 4 October and 28 September 1939, in *The Empire at Bay. The Leo Amery Diaries 1929–1945* (eds) J. Barnes and D. Nicholson (1988), p. 573.
82. David Carlton, *Anthony Eden. A Biography* (1981), pp. 153–6.
83. Anthony Eden, quoted by David Carlton, loc. cit., p. 154.
84. Chamberlain himself may not have been so far removed from Lloyd George's thinking. After Lloyd George's speech of 3 October, Sylvester wrote: 'Winston was angry with his speech. Neville was not' (letter to his wife, 4 October 1939). The next day he wrote: 'So complex is the present situation that he [Lloyd George] thinks Neville and Sam Hoare are not unfavourable to him. Perhaps he is right.' To some extent, it appears that he was right. According to David Carlton (p. 154), Chamberlain and Halifax were privately inclining towards Lloyd George's position. In *Cabinet Decisions on Foreign Policy. The British Experience October 1938–June 1941* (Cambridge, 1991), Christopher Hill examines the varying reactions of members of Chamberlain's Cabinet. Chamberlain himself insisted that his speech of 12 October 'left the door open' (p. 126). Halifax was keen to spell out 'aims at any peace conference' and to involve neutrals (p. 141). Cf. Maisky, telegrams to Molotov, 17, 20, 27 and 30 October 1939, in *Dokumenty*, pp. 196, 204–5, 208, 234–5. On 16 November Maisky reported a discussion with Beaverbrook, who favoured 'the immediate summoning of a peace conference without preconditions' (loc.cit., p. 310). Cf. Schulenberg to Ribbentrop, 20 October, *Documents on German Foreign Policy 1918–1945*, Series D, vol. 8 (1954), p. 325.
85. Maisky, loc. cit., p. 234. Cf. Hill, op. cit., p. 116.
86. Sylvester, letter to his wife, 10 November 1939.
87. Strobl, *The Germanic Isle*, pp. 202–7; Hill, *Cabinet Decisions on Foreign Policy*, pp. 107, 297–8. In conversation with Ciano on 2 October 1939, Hitler 'remarked that Germany was not in fact interested in forcing a war in the west if such a war could be avoided'. He mentioned 'important European problems' arising from the defeat of Poland, 'which could not be solved unilaterally, but only in a generally calm atmosphere by means of a conference or by general agreement'. (*Documents on German Foreign Policy*, Series D, vol. 8 (1954), pp. 187, 189.) For more critical verdicts, see Alan Bullock, *Hitler. A Study in Tyranny* (1952; 1962 edition), pp. 563–4; J. Noakes and G. Pridam (eds), *Nazism 1919–1945*, vol. 3, *Foreign Policy, War and Racial Extermination* (Exeter, 1988), pp. 758–9; Gerhard L. Weinberg, *A World at Arms. A Global History of World War II* (Cambridge, 1994), pp. 93–4, and 'Hitler and England, 1933–1945: Pretense and Reality', in *Germany, Hitler and World War II. Essays in Modern German History* (Cambridge, 1995), pp. 85–94.
88. Nicholas Bethell, *The War that Hitler Won. September 1939* (1972), p. 184.
89. Addison, loc. cit., p. 369; Rowland, *Lloyd George*, p. 766; Sylvester, *Life with Lloyd George*, p. 241. In his discussion with Maisky at Euston on 19 October, Lloyd George admitted that the chances of a peace conference were slim, and urged Russia to force the issue by mediating between the

belligerents (Maisky, telegram to Molotov, 20 October 1939, in *Dokumenty*, pp. 204–5).

90. Sylvester, letter to his wife, 29 November 1939.
91. Sylvester, letters to his wife, 4 and 5 October 1939.
92. Rowland, *Lloyd George*, p. 779.
93. *The Times*, 23 October 1939.
94. The decisions to risk war with Russia by assisting Finland, 'defy rational analysis'. A.J.P. Taylor, *English History 1914–1945* (Oxford, 1965), p. 469.
95. Sylvester, *Life with Lloyd George*, p. 251.
96. Sylvester, *Life with Lloyd George*, p. 256.
97. Jones, *A Diary*, p. 457.
98. ibid.
99. ibid.
100. 360 HC Deb. 5s, col. 1281.
101. 360 HC Deb. 5s, col. 1283.
102. Frances Stevenson, *The Years that are Past*, p. 261.
103. Graham Stewart, *Burying Caesar. Churchill, Chamberlain and the Battle for the Tory Party* (1999; 2000 edition), pp. 414–24.
104. Sylvester, *Life with Lloyd George*, p. 260.
105. Sylvester, *Life with Lloyd George*, p. 261.
106. ibid.
107. Sylvester, *Life with Lloyd George*, p. 262.
108. John Lukacs, *Five Days in London. May 1940* (1999), p. 73
109. Sylvester, *Life with Lloyd George*, p. 262.
110. ibid.
111. Sylvester, *The Real Lloyd George*, p. 265.
112. Sylvester, *Life with Lloyd George*, p. 263.
113. Sylvester, *Life with Lloyd George*, p. 265.
114. ibid.
115. Sylvester, *Life with Lloyd George*, p. 266.
116. Sylvester, *Life with Lloyd George*, p. 267.
117. Cecil H. King, *With Malice towards None. A War Diary* (1970), p. 46.
118. John Charmley, *Churchill: the End of Glory* (1993), p. 417.
119. Sylvester, *Life with Lloyd George*, p. 268.
120. Sylvester, *Life with Lloyd George*, p. 269.
121. Jones, *A Diary*, p. 464.
122. ibid.
123. Sylvester, *The Real Lloyd George*, p. 272.
124. Jones, *A Diary*, p. 464.
125. Hugh Dalton, *The Fateful Years. Memoirs 1931–1945* (1957), pp. 335–6.
126. 361 HC Deb. 5s, col. 796.
127. Hitler, *My New Order*, p. 837. See Andreas Hillgruber, 'England's Place in Hitler's Plans for World Domination', loc. cit., p. 16.
128. John Lukacs, *The Duel: Hitler vs. Churchill: 10 May–31 July 1940* (Oxford, 1992), p. 194.
129. Maisky to Molotov, 21 September 1940, *Dokumenty Vneshnei Politiki. 1940– 22 iiuniia 1941* [*Documents on Foreign Policy. 1940–22 June 1941*] (Moscow, 1995), p. 622.
130. Sylvester, *Life with Lloyd George*, p. 279.

131. Sylvester, *Life with Lloyd George*, p. 281
132. Bernd Martin, 'Churchill and Hitler, 1940: Peace or War?', in *Winston Churchill. Studies in Statesmanship* (ed.) R.A.C. Parker (1995), p. 93.
133. Lukacs, *Five Days in London*, p. 73. In November 1940, when it was clear that Britain would not go under, Churchill offered Lloyd George the post of ambassador at Washington, left vacant by the death of Lord Lothian (Philip Kerr). No doubt his intention was to place Lloyd George out of harm's way. When Lloyd George refused, Churchill offered the position to Lord Halifax, who reluctantly accepted.

Bibliography

Manuscript Collections (A)

Public Record Office, Kew
British Empire Delegation Minutes, 1919
Foreign Office (Paris Peace Conference) Papers, 1919
Imperial War Cabinet Minutes, 1918–19
Imperial War Cabinet Committee on Indemnity. Report, Proceedings and
  Memoranda, 1918

Archives du Ministère des Affaires Etrangères, Paris
Papiers d'Agents, Pichon
Série A
Série Y. Internationale 1918–1940
Série Z. Europe 1918–1940

Service Historique de l'Armée de Terre, Vincennes
Fonds Clemenceau

Manuscript Collections (B)

Balfour Papers, British Library
George Bell Papers, Lambeth Palace Library
Bonar Law Papers, House of Lords Record Office
Robert Cecil Papers, British Library
Austen Chamberlain Papers, University of Birmingham
Cunliffe Papers, in the possession of the present Lord Cunliffe
J.C. Davidson Papers, House of Lords Record Office
Randall Davidson Papers, Lambeth Palace Library
H.A.L. Fisher Papers, Bodleian Library
Hankey Papers, Churchill College, Cambridge
Hardinge Papers, Cambridge University Library
Keynes Papers, King's College, Cambridge
Lloyd George Papers, House of Lords Record Office
Lothian Papers, Scottish Record Office, Edinburgh
Milner Papers, Bodleian Library
Montagu Papers, Trinity College, Cambridge
Montagu Norman Papers, Bank of England Archives
A.J. Sylvester Papers, National Library of Wales, Aberystwyth

Published Documentary Collections

(Unless otherwise indicated, the place of publication is London)

Akten zur Deutschen Auswärtigen Politik 1918–1945, Series D, vol. 8 (Frankfurt-am-Main, 1961).

British Documents on Foreign Affairs, (eds) K. Bourne and D.C. Watt, Part 2, Series 1. *The Paris Peace Conference of 1919*, vol. 4 (Bethesda, Maryland, 1989).

Philip M. Burnett, *Reparation at the Paris Peace Conference*, vols 1–2 (New York, 1940).

Documents on British Foreign Policy 1919–1939, 1st series, vol. 20 (1976).

Documents on German Foreign Policy, Series C, vol. 5 (1966); Series D, vol. 8 (1954).

Dokumenty Vneshnei Politiki. 1939 god [Documents on Foreign Policy. The Year 1939], book 2 (Moscow, 1992).

Dokumenty Vneshnei Politiki. 1940–22 iiuniia 1941 [Documents on Foreign Policy. 1940–22 June 1941] book 1 (Moscow, 1995).

First Interim Report of the Committee on Currency and Foreign Exchanges after the War, Command Paper (1918).

Journal Officiel de la République Française. Chambre des Débats. Débats parlèmentaires (Paris 1918, 1919).

La Paix de Versaille. La Commission de Réparations des Dommages, vol. 2 (Paris, 1932).

Paul J. Mantoux, *Les Délibérations du Conseil des Quatre: Notes de l'Officier Interprète*, vols 1–2, (Paris, 1955).

Nazism 1919–1945, vol. 3, *Foreign Policy, War and Racial Extermination* (eds) J. Noakes and G. Pridham (Exeter, 1988).

Papers Relating to the Foreign Relations of the United States. The Paris Peace Conference, 1919, vols 3, 5, 6, 11, 13 (Washington, 1943, 1945–47).

'Papers Respecting Negotiations for an Anglo-French Pact', Command Paper 2169. House of Commons Sessional Papers (1924).

Parliamentary Debates, House of Commons (Hansard) 5th series, 1919–40.

The Papers of Woodrow Wilson, (ed.) A.S. Link, vols 56, 59–60 (Princeton, 1987–89).

Diaries, Memoirs and Contemporary Sources

Leo S. Amery, *My Political Life*, vol. 2 (1953), p. 179.

—— *The Empire at Bay. The Leo Amery Diaries 1929–1945* (eds) J. Barnes and D. Nicholson (1988).

Jacques Bainville, *Les conséquences politiques de la paix* (Paris, 1919; 1995 edition).

George N. Barnes, *From Workshop to War Cabinet* (1924).

James S. Barnes, *Half a Life* (1933).

R.H. Beadon, *Some Memories of the Peace Conference* (1933).

Earl of Birkenhead, *Contemporary Personalities* (1924).

Violet Bonham-Carter, *Champion Redoutable. The Diaries and Letters of Violet Bonham-Carter 1914–1945* (ed.) Mark Pottle (1998).

Robert Boothby, *I Fight to Live* (1947).

—— *Recollections of a Rebel* (1978).

Paul Cambon, *Correspondance 1870–1924*, vol. 3 (Paris, 1946).

Olwen Carey Evans, *Lloyd George was My Father* (Llandysul, 1985)

Austen Chamberlain, *Down the Years* (1935).

—— *The Austen Chamberlain Diary Letters. The Correspondence of Sir Austen Chamberlain with his Sisters Hilda and Ida, 1916–1937* (ed.) R.C. Self (Cambridge, 1995).

Neville Chamberlain, *The Neville Chamberlain Diary Letters*, vol. 1, (Aldershot, 2000).

Georges Clemenceau, *Grandeurs et Misères d'une Victoire* (Paris, 1930).

—— *Clemenceau. The Events of his Life. As told by himself to his Former Secretary Jean Martet*, (tr.) M. Waldman (1930).

Hugh Dalton, *The Fateful Years. Memoirs 1931–1945* (1957).

Lord Davidson, *Memoirs of a Conservative. J.C.C. Davidson's Memoirs and Papers 1910–37* (ed.) Robert Rhodes James (1969).

A.T. Davies, *The Lloyd George I Knew. Some Side-Lights on a Great Character* (1948).

E. J. Dillon, *The Peace Conference* (1919).

William George, *My Brother and I* (1958).

Joseph Goebbels, *The Goebbels Diaries 1939–1941* (ed.) Fred Taylor (1982).

Lord Hardinge, *The Old Diplomacy. The Reminiscences of Lord Hardinge of Penshurst* (1947).

Sir Cuthbert Headlam, *Parliament and Politics in the Age of Churchill and Attlee. The Headlam Diaries 1935–1951* (ed.) Stuart Ball (Cambridge, 1999).

James Headlam-Morley, *A Memoir of the Paris Peace Conference 1919* (ed.) Agnes Headlam-Morley (1972).

Adolf Hitler, *Mein Kampf*, Unexpurgated edition (n.d.).

—— *Hitler's Table-Talk 1941–1944* (ed.) Hugh Trevor-Roper (1953; Oxford, 1988 edition).

—— *My New Order* (ed.) Raoul de Roussy de Sales (New York, 1973).

Edward M. House, *The Intimate Papers of Colonel House* (ed.) Charles Seymour, vol. 4 (1928).

Sir Esme Howard, *Theatre of Life* (1936).

Thomas Jones, *Whitehall Diary* (ed.) Keith Middlemas, vol. 1 (Oxford, 1969).

John Maynard Keynes, *The Economic Consequences of the Peace* (1919; 1920 edition).

—— *Two Memoirs* (1949).

—— *Essays in Biography* (1933).

—— *Collected Writings*, vol. 16 (1971).

Cecil H. King, *With Malice Towards None. A War Diary* (1970).

Basil Liddel Hart, *Memoirs*, vol. 1 (1965).

David Lloyd George, *Is It Peace?* (1923).

—— *The Truth about Reparations and War Debts* (1932).

—— *War Memoirs*, vol. 1 (2 vols, 1938).

—— *The Truth about the Peace Treaties*, vol. 1 (1938).

Owen Lloyd George, *A Tale of Two Grandfathers* (2000).

Louis Loucheur, *Carnets Secrets 1908–1932* (ed.) J. de Launay (Brussels, 1962).

A. MacKintosh, *From Gladstone to Lloyd George. Parliament in Peace and War* (1921).

Geoffrey Madan, *Geoffrey Madan's Notebook* (Oxford, 1984).

W.G. McAdoo, *Crowded Years. The Reminiscences of William G. McAdoo* (Boston, MA, 1932).

Andrew McFadyean, *Recollected in Tranquillity* (1964).

Mermeix (Gabriel Terrail), *Le Combat des Trois. Notes et documents sur la conférence de la paix* (Paris, 1922).

David Hunter Miller, *My Diary at the Conference of Paris*, vol. 1 (New York, 1924).

Henri Mordacq, *Le Ministère Clemenceau. Journal d'un Témoin*, vol. 3 (Paris, 1930).

Harold Nicolson, *Peacemaking 1919* (1933).

—— *Diaries and Letters 1939–1945* (ed.) Nigel Nicolson (1967).

Francis Oppenheimer, *Stranger Within. Autobiographical Pages* (1960).
Raymond Poincaré, *Au service de la France. Neuf années de souvenirs*, vol. 11, *A la recherche de la paix, 1919* (Paris, 1974).
E.T. Raymond, *Mr Lloyd George. A Biography* (1922).
Lord Riddell, *Lord Riddell's War Diary 1914–1918* (1933).
—— *Lord Riddell's Intimate Diary of the Peace Conference and After* (1933).
—— *The Riddell Diaries 1908–1923* (ed.) J.M. McEwen (1986).
Paul Schmidt, *Hitler's Interpreter* (1951).
J.W. Scobell Armstrong, *Yesterday* (1955).
C.P. Scott, *The Political Diaries of C.P. Scott 1911–1928* (ed.) Trevor Wilson (1970).
Charles Seymour, *Letters from the Paris Peace Conference* (ed.) Harold B. Whiteman (Yale, 1965).
Jan Christian Smuts, *Selections from the Smuts Papers* (ed.) W.K. Hancock and J. Van Der Poel, vol. 4, (Cambridge, 1966).
Harold Spender, *The Prime Minister* (1920).
Frances Lloyd George (Stevenson), *The Years that are Past* (1967).
—— *Lloyd George. A Diary by Frances Stevenson* (ed.) A.J.P. Taylor (1971).
A.J. Sylvester, *Life with Lloyd George. The Diary of A.J. Sylvester 1931–45* (ed.) C. Cross (1975).
André Tardieu, *La Paix* (Paris, 1921).
—— *The Truth about the Treaty* (1921).
Arnold Toynbee, *Acquaintances* (1967).
Lord Vansittart, *The Mist Procession* (1958).
Beatrice Webb, *Diaries 1912–1924* (ed.) M. Cole (1952).
—— *The Diary of Beatrice Webb* (eds) N. and J. MacKenzie, vol. 3 (1984).
Ann Wedderburn-Maxwell, *A Privileged Child* (Bournemouth, 1985).
Sir Henry Wilson, *Life and Diaries* (ed.) C. E. Calwell, vol. 1 (1927).
Bankers Magazine, 1920.
Daily Express, 1920.
Economic Journal, 1914.
Evening Standard, 1955.
Field, 1920.
Financier, 1920.
Manchester Guardian, 1919.
Observer, 1919, 1961.
News of the World, 1920.
Le Temps, 1921.
Times, 1919, 1920, 1939, 1955, 1995.
Sheffield Telegraph, 1920.
Yorkshire Post, 1920.

Secondary Studies

Books

Lloyd E. Ambrosius, *Woodrow Wilson and the American Diplomatic Tradition. The Treaty Fight in Perspective* (Cambridge, 1987).
Bruce Arnold, *Orpen. Mirror to an Age* (1981).

Bernard M. Baruch, *The Making of the Reparation and Economic Sections of the Treaty* (1921).

E. Beau de Loménie, *Le Débat de ratification du traité de Versailles à la Chambre des Députés et dans la presse en 1919* (Paris, 1945).

Lord Beaverbrook, *Men and Power, 1917–1918* (1956).

—— *Politicians and the War 1914–1916* (1960).

—— *The Decline and Fall of Lloyd George* (1963).

P.M.H. Bell, *France and Britain 1900–1940: Entente and Estrangement* (1996).

Nicholas Bethell, *The War that Hitler Won. September 1939* (1972).

Robert Blake, *The Unknown Prime Minister. The Life and Times of Andrew Bonar Law 1858–1923* (1955).

Stephen Bonsall, *Suitors and Suppliants. The Little Nations at Versailles* (Port Washington, NY, 1964).

Andrew Boyle, *Montagu Norman. A Biography* (1967).

Alan Bullock, *Hitler. A Study in Tyranny* (1952; 1962 edition).

Robert E. Bunselmeyer, *The Cost of the War 1914–1919. British Economic War Aims and the Origins of Reparations* (Hamden, CT, 1975).

Angus Calder, *The People's War* (1969; 1993 edition).

David Carlton, *Anthony Eden. A Biography* (1981).

Edward Hallett Carr, *From Napoleon to Stalin and Other Essays* (1980).

John Charmley, *Churchill: the End of Glory* (1993).

Winston Spencer Churchill, *Great Contemporaries* (1935; 1948 edition).

—— *The Second World War*, Book 1, *The Gathering Storm* (1948; Geneva, 1967 edition).

Sybil Crowe and Edward Corp, *Our Ablest Public Servant. Sir Eyre Crowe 1864–1925* (Braunton, Devon, 1993).

J. Hugh Edwards, *Lloyd George. The Man and Statesman*, vol. 1 (n.d.).

L.F. Fitzhardinge, *The Little Digger 1914–1952. William Morris Hughes. A Political Biography*, vol. 2 (1979).

Inga Floto, *Colonel House in Paris. A Study of American Policy at the Paris Peace Conference 1919* (Aarhus, 1973).

Bentley Gilbert, *David Lloyd George. A Political Life. The Organiser of Victory 1912–1916* (1992).

Martin Gilbert, *The Roots of Appeasement* (1966).

Erik Goldstein, *Winning the Peace. British Diplomatic Strategy, Peace Planning, and the Paris Peace Conference 1916–1920* (Oxford, 1991).

Lord Hankey, *The Supreme Control at the Paris Peace Conference 1919* (1963).

E.H. Haraszti, *The Invaders. Hitler Occupies the Rhineland* (Budapest, 1983).

Roy F. Harrod, *The Life of John Maynard Keynes* (1953).

Jonathan Haslam, *The Vices of Integrity. E.H. Carr, 1892–1982* (1999).

Dominic Hibberd, *The First World War* (1990).

Christopher Hill, *Cabinet Decisions on Foreign Policy. The British Experience October 1938–June 1941* (Cambridge, 1991).

K. Hutchison, *The Decline and Fall of British Capitalism* (1966).

Lorna S. Jaffe, *The Decision to Disarm Germany. British Foreign Policy towards Postwar German Disarmament* (1985).

Bruce Kent, *The Spoils of War. The Politics, Economics and Diplomacy of Reparations 1918–1932* (Oxford, 1989).

Ian Kershaw, *The 'Hitler Myth'. Image and Reality in the Third Reich* (Oxford, 1987).

——*Hitler 1889–1936: Hubris* (1998).

William R. Keylor (ed.), *The Legacy of the Great War. Peacemaking, 1919* (New York, 1998).

Edward M. Lamont, *The Ambassador from Wall Street. The Story of Thomas W. Lamont, J.P. Morgan's Chief Executive* (Lanham, Maryland, 1994).

A. Lentin, *Guilt at Versailles. Lloyd George and the Pre-History of Appeasement* (1985). First published as *Lloyd George, Woodrow Wilson and the Guilt of Germany. An Essay in the Pre-History of Appeasement* (1984).

John Lukacs, *The Duel: Hitler vs. Churchill: 10 May–31 July 1940* (Oxford, 1992).

——*Five Days in London. May 1940* (1999).

Alma Luckau, *The German Delegation at the Paris Peace Conference* (New York, 1941).

Harold Macmillan, *The Past Masters. Politics and Politicians 1906–1939* (1975).

Charles S. Maier, *Recasting Bourgeois Europe: Stabilization in France, Germany and Italy in the Decade after World War I* (Princeton, NJ, 1975).

Etienne Mantoux, *The Carthaginian Peace or the Economic Consequences of Mr Keynes* (1946; 1964 edition, Pittsburgh).

Gordon Martell (ed.), *The Origins of the Second World War Reconsidered* (1986).

Walter A. McDougall, *France's Rhineland Diplomacy, 1914–1924. The Last Bid for a Balance of Power in Europe* (Princeton, NJ, 1978).

B.J.C. McKercher, *Esme Howard. A Diplomatic Biography* (Cambridge, 1989).

Donald E. Moggridge, *Maynard Keynes. An Economist's Biography* (1992).

Lord Moran, *Winston Churchill. The Struggle for Survival 1940–1965* (1966).

Kenneth O. Morgan, *Lloyd George* (1974).

——*Consensus and Disunity. The Lloyd George Coalition Government 1918–1922* (Oxford, 1979).

Harold I. Nelson, *Land and Power. British and Allied Policy on Germany's Frontiers 1916–19* (Toronto, 1963).

David S. Newhall, *Clemenceau: a Life at War* (Lampeter, 1991).

Douglas Newton, *British Policy and the Weimar Republic, 1918–1919* (Oxford, 1997).

Scott Newton, *Profits of Peace. The Political Economy of Anglo-German Appeasement* (Oxford, 1996).

Harold Nicolson, *Curzon. The Last Phase* (1934).

——*The Congress of Vienna. A Study in Allied Unity, 1812–1822* (1946).

Nigel Nicolson, *Portrait of a Marriage* (1973).

F.S. Northedge, *The Troubled Giant. Britain among the Great Powers 1916–1939* (1966).

Ian Packer, *Lloyd George* (1998).

R.A.C. Parker, *Chamberlain and Appeasement. British Policy and the Coming of the Second World War* (1993).

——*Churchill and Appeasement* (2000).

Martin Pugh, *Lloyd George* (1988).

Jacques Raphaël-Leygues, *Georges Leygues. Le 'père' de la marines. (Ses carnets secrets de 1914–1920)* (Paris, 1983).

Andrew Roberts, *Eminent Churchillians* (1994).

Peter Rowland, *Lloyd George* (1975).

R.S. Sayers, *The Bank of England 1891–1944*, vol. 1 (Cambridge, 1976).

Charles Seymour, *Geography, Justice and Politics at the Peace Conference of 1919* (New York, 1951).

Alan Sharp, *The Versailles Settlement. Peacemaking in Paris, 1919* (1991).

Robert Skidelsky, *John Maynard Keynes*, vol. 1 (1983).

Jan Christian Smuts, *Jan Christian Smuts* (1952).

David Stevenson, *French War Aims against Germany* (Oxford, 1982).

Graham Stewart, *Burying Caesar. Churchill, Chamberlain and the Battle for the Tory Party* (1999; 2000 edition).

Gerwin Strobl, *The Germanic Isle. Nazi Perceptions of Britain* (Cambridge, 2000).

A.J. Sylvester, *The Real Lloyd George* (1947).

A.J.P. Taylor, *English History 1914–1945* (Oxford, 1965).

—— *Beaverbrook* (1972).

Harold W.V. Temperley (ed.), *A History of the Peace Conference of Paris*, vol. 2 (1920).

Seth P. Tillman, *Anglo-American Relations at the Paris Peace Conference of 1919* (Princeton, 1961).

Marc Trachtenberg, *Reparation in World Politics. France and European Economic Diplomacy 1916–1923* (New York, 1980).

C.P. Vincent, *The Politics of Hunger. The Allied Blockade of Germany 1915–1919* (Athens, Ohio, 1985).

S.D. Waley, *Edwin Montagu* (1964).

Arthur Walworth, *Wilson and his Peacemakers. American Diplomacy at the Paris Peace Conference 1919* (New York, 1986).

David R. Watson, *Georges Clemenceau: a Political Biography* (1974).

Gerhard L. Weinberg, *A World at Arms. A Global History of World War II* (Cambridge, 1994).

J.F. Willis, *Prologue to Nuremberg. The Politics and Diplomacy of Punishing War Criminals of the First World War* (1982).

K.M. Wilson, *George Saunders on Germany 1919–1920* (Leeds, 1987).

Trevor Wilson, *The Myriad Faces of War. Britain and the Great War, 1914–1918* (1986).

L.A.R. Yates, *United States and French Security 1917–1921* (New York, 1957).

G.M. Young, *Stanley Baldwin* (1932).

Articles

Paul Addison, 'Lloyd George and Compromise Peace in the Second World War', in *Lloyd George: Twelve Essays* (ed.) A.J.P. Taylor (1971), pp. 361–84.

Denise Artaud, 'Reparations and War Debts. The Restoration of French Financial Power, 1919–1929', in *French Foreign and Defence Policy 1918–1940. The Decline and Fall of a Great Power* (ed.) Robert Boyce (1998), pp. 89–106.

Kathleen Burk, 'The Treasury: from Impotence to Power', in *War and the State. The Transformation of British Government, 1914–1919* (ed.) Kathleen Burk (1982), pp. 84–107.

Jules Cambon, 'La Paix', *Revue de Paris* (November–December 1937), pp. 5–38.

Michael Dockrill, 'The Foreign Office and the "Proposed Institute of International Affairs 1919" ', in *Chatham House and British Foreign Policy 1919–45* (eds) Antonia Bosco and Cornelia Navari (1994), pp. 73–86.

George W. Egerton, 'The Lloyd George War Memoirs: a Study in the Politics of Memory', *Journal of Modern History*, 60 (1988), 55–94.

Gerald B. Feldman, 'A Comment', in *The Treaty of Versailles. A Reassessment*, pp. 441–7.

Niall Ferguson, 'The Balance of Payments Question: Versailles and After', in *The Treaty of Versailles. A Reassessment*, pp. 401–40.

Michael Fry, 'British Revisionism', in *The Treaty of Versailles. A Reassessment*, pp. 565–614.

Elisabeth Glaser, 'The Making of the Economic Peace', in *The Treaty of Versailles. A Reassessment*, pp. 371–99.

Erik Goldstein, 'Neville Chamberlain, the British Official Mind and the Munich Crisis', in *The Munich Crisis, 1938. Prelude to World War II* (eds) Igor Lukes and Eric Goldstein (1999), pp. 276–92.

—— 'Britain: the Home Front', in *The Treaty of Versailles. A Reassessment*, pp. 147–66.

Andreas Hillgruber, 'England's Place in Hitler's Plans for World Domination', *Journal of Contemporary History*, 9:1 (1974), 5–22.

Thomas Jones, 'Lloyd George', in *The Dictionary of National Biography 1941–1954* (1959), pp. 515–29.

William R. Keylor, 'The Rise and Demise of the Franco-American Guarantee Pact, 1919–1921', *Proceedings of the Annual Meeting of the Western Society for French History*, vol. 15 (1988), pp. 367–77.

—— 'Versailles and International Diplomacy', in *The Treaty of Versailles. A Reassessment*, pp. 469–505.

John Maynard Keynes, 'War and the Financial System, August 1914', *Economic Journal*, 24 (September 1914), 460–86.

Thomas Lamont, 'Reparations', in *What Really Happened at Paris. The Story of the Peace Conference 1918–1919* (eds) Edward M. House and Charles Seymour (New York, 1921), pp. 259–90.

A. Lentin, 'Lord Summer 1859–1934: Acerbic Master of Law and Language', *The Law Society's Gazette*, 27 June 1984, 1852–54.

—— 'Philip Kerr e "l'aggressione della Germania"', in *Lord Lothian. Una vita per la Pace* (ed.) G. Guderzo (Florence, 1986), pp. 63–7.

—— 'The Treaty that Never Was: Lloyd George and the Abortive Anglo-French Alliance of 1919', in *The Life and Times of David Lloyd George* (ed.) Judith Loades (Bangor, 1991), pp. 115–28.

—— 'Cunliffe, Walter, first Baron Cunliffe (1855–1920)', in *The Dictionary of National Biography. Missing Persons* (ed.) C.S. Nicholls (Oxford, 1993), 164–5.

—— '"Une aberration inexplicable"? Clemenceau and the Abortive Anglo-French Guarantee Treaty of 1919', *Diplomacy and Statecraft*, 8 (1997), 31–49.

—— 'The Peacemakers and their Home Front: a Comment', in *The Treaty of Versailles. A Reassessment*, pp. 221–43.

—— 'Lord Cunliffe, Lloyd George, Reparations and Reputations at the Paris Peace Conference, 1919', *Diplomacy & Statecraft*, 10:1 (1999), 50–86.

—— 'Lloyd George, Clemenceau and the Elusive Anglo-French Guarantee Treaty, 1919. "A disastrous episode"?', in *Anglo-French Relations in the Twentieth Century* (eds) Alan Sharp and Glyn Stone (2000), pp. 104–19.

—— 'John Andrew Hamilton, Lord Summer (1859–1934)', in *The New Dictionary of National Biography* (forthcoming).

Sally Marks, 'Reparations Reconsidered: a Reminder', *Central European History*, 2 (1969), 356–65.
—— 'The Myths of Reparations', *Central European History*, 11 (1978), 231–55.
—— 'Smoke and Mirrors: in Smoke-Filled Rooms and the Galerie des Glaces', in *The Treaty of Versailles: A Reassessment*, pp. 337–70.
Gordon Martel, 'From *Round Table* to *New Europe*: some Intellectual Origins of the Institute of International Affairs', in *Chatham House and British Foreign Policy 1919–1945*, pp. 13–39.
—— 'A Comment', in *The Treaty of Versailles. A Reassessment*. pp. 615–36.
Bernd Martin, 'Churchill and Hitler, 1940: Peace or War?', in *Winston Churchill. Studies in Statesmanship* (ed.) R.A.C. Parker (1995), pp. 83–96.
R. McCrum, 'French Rhineland Policy at the Paris Peace Conference, 1919', *Historical Journal*, 21:3 (1978), 623–48.
Kenneth O. Morgan, 'Lloyd George and Germany', *Historical Journal*, 39:3 (1996), 755–66.
Cornelia Navari, 'Chatham House and the Broad Church View of British Foreign Policy', in *Chatham House and British Foreign Policy 1919–1945*, pp. 345–69.
Stephen A. Schuker, 'The End of Versailles', in *The Origins of the Second World War Reconsidered* (ed.) Gordon Martel (1986), pp. 49–72.
—— 'The Rhineland Question: West European Security at the Paris Peace Conference of 1919', in *The Treaty of Versailles. A Reassessment*, pp. 275–312.
—— 'American "Reparations" to Germany, 1919–33; Implications for the Third-World Debt Crisis', *Princeton Studies in International Finance*, 61 (1988), 92–7.
—— 'Origins of American Stabilization Policy in Europe: the Financial Dimension, 1918–1924', in *Confrontation and Cooperation. Germany and the United States in the Era of World War I, 1900–1924* (ed.) Hans-Jürgen Schröder (Oxford, 1993), pp. 377–407.
Alan Sharp, 'Britain and the Channel Tunnel 1919–1920', *Australian Journal of Politics and History*, vol. 25 (1979), 210–15.
—— 'Some Relevant Historians – the Political Intelligence Department of the Foreign Office', *Australian Journal of Politics and History*, 34:3 (1989), 359–68.
—— 'Lloyd George and Foreign Policy 1918–1922. The "And Yet" Factor', in *The Life and Times of David Lloyd George* (ed.) Judith Loades (Bangor, 1991), 129–42.
—— 'James Headlam Morley: Creating International History', *Diplomacy and Statecraft*, 9:3 (November 1998), 266–83.
G.T. Waddington, '*Haßgegner*: German Views of Great Britain in the Later 1930s', *History*, 81 (1996), 22–39.
Gerhard L. Weinberg, 'Hitler and England, 1933–1945: Pretense and Reality', in *Germany, Hitler and World War II. Essays in Modern German History* (Cambridge, 1995), pp. 85–94.

Unpublished Doctoral Theses

David Dubinskii, 'British Liberals and Radicals and the Treatment of Germany, 1914–1920', Cambridge University (1992).
G.N. Esnouf, 'British Government War Aims and Attitudes towards a Negotiated Peace, September 1939 to July 1940', King's College, London University (1988).
John Hemery, 'The Emergence of Treasury Influence in British Foreign Policy 1914–1921', Cambridge University (1988).

Index